STO

AN ADAMS BUSINESS ADVISOR

Other titles in
THE ADAMS BUSINESS ADVISORS

Accounting for the New Business by Christopher R. Malburg
The All-In-One Business Planning Guide by Christopher R. Malburg
Marketing Magic by Don Debelak
The Small Business Valuation Book by Lawrence W. Tuller
Winning the Entrepreneur's Game by David E. Rye

AN ADAMS BUSINESS ADVISOR

Entrepreneurial Growth Strategies

STRATEGIC PLANNING, RESTRUCTURING
ALTERNATIVES, MARKETING TACTICS,
FINANCING OPTIONS, ACQUISITIONS,
AND OTHER WAYS TO PROPEL THE
NEW VENTURE UPWARD

LAWRENCE W. TULLER

BOB ADAMS, INC.
Holbrook, Massachusetts

Published by Bob Adams, Inc.
260 Center Street, Holbrook, MA 02343

ISBN: 1-55850-354-4 (hardcover)
ISBN: 1-55850-353-6 (paperback)

Printed in the United States of America.

J   I   H   G   F   E   D   C   B   A (hardcover)
J   I   H   G   F   E   D   C   B   A (paperback)

Library of Congress Cataloging-in-Publication Data
Tuller, Lawrence W.
    Entrepreneurial growth strategies: strategic planning, restructuring alternatives, marketing tactics, financing
options, acquisitions, and other ways to propel the new venture upward / Lawrence W. Tuller.
        p.   cm.   — (An Adams business advisor)
    Includes bibliographical references and index.
    ISBN 1-55850-354-4 : $29.95 — ISBN 1-55850-353-6 (pbk.) : $10.95
    1. Strategic planning. 2. Corporate reorganizations. 3. Consolidation and merger of corporations.
4. Business enterprises—Finance. I. Title. II. Series.
    HD30.28.T8   1994
    658.4'012—dc20   94-8713
                                                                                        CIP

Cover design: Marshall Henrichs

This book is available at quantity discounts for bulk purchases.
For information, call 1-800-872-5627.

Other books by Lawrence W. Tuller:
The Small Business Valuation Book
Buying In: A Complete Guide to Acquiring a Business or Professional Practice
Cutting Edge Consultants
The McGraw Hill Handbook of Global Trade and Investment Financing
The Complete Book of Raising Capital

Table of Contents

PART 3
STRATEGIES FOR BUYING A BUSINESS
OR PRODUCT LINE

Preface

Competition gets keener. Customers complain. Banks tighten the noose. Federal and state agencies interfere in business decisions. Employees demand higher wages. Suppliers want shorter terms. Taxes go up. Why worry about long-term growth strategies when it takes everything you've got to stay afloat in today's highly charged business environment? The answer is simple: because competitors are doing it.

As the years go by, the dynamism of the market pushes prices, costs, and customer demand in continuously changing directions. Markets that we controlled yesterday are lost to foreign competitors. Our products or services, once cherished by loyal customers, suddenly become obsolete. Operating costs keep rising while our prices get beaten down. Employees demand ever-higher wages and benefits without corresponding improvements in productivity. The result? Shrinking markets, declining sales, and squeezed profits, all translating into less cash—not only less cash to run our businesses but, more important, less cash to draw out for our personal needs.

To counteract these market forces, those businesses that lead the pack rely on long-term strategic planning to chart a course through the competitive labyrinth. By focusing on the achievement of long-term goals, they enhance their ability to control markets (and hence prices) and reduce expenses, thereby steadily improving their profitability and return on investment.

Flexibility is the key to achieving and then sustaining market control. Product (or service) lines, customer bases, and resources must change as market demand dictates. To stay abreast of these conditions, we must maintain a high degree of flexibility in our marketing, financing, and new product or service introductions.

Strategies to increase market share, reduce expenses, and achieve operating flexibility are not the exclusive domain of mature, long-standing companies. They apply equally to new businesses. In many respects, start-up businesses benefit more from focused marketing, impact advertising, and financial resilience than more established ones. Nor are growth strategies restricted to manufacturing, distribution, or retail companies. Well-conceived long-term strategies are important to the growth patterns and profitability of service businesses and professional practices as well.

This book contains recommendations for implementing more than 200 specific growth strategies, ranging from cost-effective publicity gimmicks to niche marketing, from recapitalizing debt obligations to issuing public stock, from motivating sales personnel to controlling cash expenditures, and from enhancing customer service to purging unprofitable product lines.

Few businesses are so unique that their growth strategies must be specially designed. However, first-stage start-up businesses, professional service businesses (including consulting), and overleveraged companies are three types that do call for special treatment. Selling, advertising, and financing strategies for first-stage start-ups must be viewed from a different perspective and in a different time frame from those relating to mature businesses. Attracting new business to professional service firms cannot be achieved using the same strategies that work for manufacturing, distribution, or retail companies. And business owners plagued with excessive bank debt know full well that their chances for long-term growth depend on current survival, which in turn rests on the implementation of hard-nosed, short-term recovery strategies. Growth strategies applicable to these special cases are revealed in Part 2.

Some businesses need a jump-start to overcome slow-growth inertia. The most viable way to open new markets, introduce new products, and capture new technology in short order is to buy a going business or major product line. The chapters in Part 3 will lead you through the search, valuation, financing, and transition phases of buying profitable domestic businesses, foreign businesses, and financially distressed businesses. Proven strategic ploys will show you how to accomplish the latter with virtually no cash down.

Unfortunately, the complexity and breadth of material related to importing and exporting precludes the inclusion of these important growth strategies. However, my forthcoming book in *The Adams Business Advisors* series is dedicated entirely to foreign trade as a long-term growth strategy. Readers will find ample descriptions and ideas for sourcing offshore materials and components, for getting started in exporting, and for expanding export markets currently being served.

You won't find management theory in this book. All suggestions and ideas have been tested in practice—many in the thirteen companies I have started from scratch, in the four businesses I have purchased, and during my more than fifteen years as a management consultant. Those recommendations that I have not personally used were successfully put into practice by other consultants and entrepreneurs.

Strategic planning is not an easy game to learn or to play. It requires the active participation of business owners and employees alike, and a good bit of creative give and take by everyone. To make growth strategies work in practice, a substantial amount of both resources and time must be committed. Many roadblocks will deter the implementation of what appear on paper to be sensible strategies. Ways must be found to get around these roadblocks, to get over them, or to push them aside. A close friend and business associate used an apt term to describe these obstacles: he called them "gitovers." To design and implement long-term growth strategies, you need to "gitover" recalcitrant banks, "gitover" doubting employees, "gitover" fierce competition, "gitover" demanding customers, and "gitover" stubborn suppliers, while never losing sight of the overriding long-term objective, profitable growth.

Hopefully, the ideas in this book will make your task a bit easier. Obviously, they are not all applicable to all companies. Pick and choose those that seem the most appropriate and then massage them to fit your needs. Even if this book opens only one door, crystallizes only one idea, highlights only one growth strategy that fits your business, it should be worth its price. Godspeed!

— Lawrence W. Tuller
Berwyn, Pennsylvania

Part 1

Basic Growth Strategies

Chapter 1

Keys to Growth

It is probably fair to say that no two business owners or managers regard growth in the same light. Take competitive price cutting, for instance. Strategies that rely on price cutting to increase sales (on the theory that higher volumes offset lower unit margins) assume that certain market segments will always demand the lowest-priced goods. These strategies have been well tested by such retailing giants as Sears and Montgomery Ward, who in their earlier days based their reputations on low-priced merchandise. More recently, Wal-Mart, Kmart, and many lesser-known discount stores have demonstrated the continued effectiveness of this approach for carving out market shares.

Foreign competitors also recognize low-price niche markets. During the 1950s and 1960s, imports from Japan were priced lower than American-made goods. Now, China, India, and certain Latin American nations have replaced Japan as suppliers of low-end merchandise. In the hospitality industry, the original Days Inns and Howard Johnson Motor Lodges captured market shares by offering the lowest-priced rooms of any nationwide chain.

However, price cutting is a short-term strategy. In an affluent society like the United States, consumers as a group tend to upgrade their buying habits relatively quickly as their incomes or expectations rise. While there will always be markets for the lowest-priced goods, the images of inferior quality and lack of after-sale customer service that typically accompany low prices will, over time, drive an increasingly affluent customer base to higher-priced competitors offering better quality and service. This is exactly what happened in the retail and hospitality industries. It also happened to Japanese imports. And it seems inevitable that it will eventually happen to Chinese imports.

Another favorite growth strategy is to emphasize return on investment. Although a limited number of boutique retailers have been eminently successful with this tactic, it is mainly popular with companies engaged in manufacturing or transportation. Most manufacturing businesses require relatively high-priced machinery to produce their products. High-cost equipment is a prerequisite for transportation companies (taxi fleets, trucking firms, barge lines, air transport companies, or ocean shipping lines). Since these companies need a sustainable revenue base and reasonable margins to cover the high cost of acquiring and maintaining these substantial assets, price cutting can be a disastrous strategy. Instead of price cutting, companies with return on investment objectives must focus on quality products, prompt delivery, and reliable customer service.

A third growth strategy fits banks, insurance agencies, real estate agencies, tax preparers, subcontract manufacturers, landscapers, certain classes of contractors, and other businesses that sell nonproprietary products. Without product differentiation, the only way these businesses can increase sales and profits is to focus market demand on something other than the product being sold—perhaps rapid delivery, extraordinary customer service, creative packaging, or guaranteed workmanship. Advertising and sales promotions proclaiming "satisfaction guaranteed," "courteous and helpful employees," "prime location," and so on, highlight competitive differences.

Growth strategies for personal service businesses take a slightly different tack. Professional practices, repair services, certain health care businesses, and so on, rely primarily on the reputation of the business owner or employees, or in some cases the name of the firm, to generate new business. The preferred approach to increasing market share is to enhance the public image of the business owner or company. Price, delivery, and after-sale service may be important ingredients, but none matches the impact of an outstanding reputation for high-quality personal service.

Successful long-term growth strategies combine the elements of pricing, delivery, quality, service, and reputation. They depend on the creation of a solid business base founded on the four keys to growth:

- Flexibility
- Planning
- Control
- Capital

FLEXIBILITY

Of the four keys, flexibility is probably the most difficult to achieve, yet the most crucial for sustained growth. The whole idea behind adding as much flexibility as possible is to permit rapid changes in strategies and implementation tactics as markets, competition, resources, and government regulations dictate. Take, for instance, the Rorake Motor Lodge. This was the only facility immediately adjacent to a small Midwestern airport. It provided accommodations for pilots and crews of private aircraft using the field. Then United Airlines announced the addition of this airport to its route schedule. Within a year, a Holiday Inn was built next door.

The owners of Rorake had intentionally remained flexible, keeping debt to a minimum, amenities sparse but comfortable, and a friendly atmosphere, with employees who knew many of the regular guests by name. By the time the Holiday Inn opened its doors, Rorake Motor Lodge boasted a new driving range, a par-three golf course, and a tray of fresh fruit in every room. Annual occupancy skyrocketed from 60 percent to 90 percent while the Holiday Inn struggled to stay open.

Flexibility comes in many forms, but most successful business owners would probably agree that the three most important are company structure, motivated employees, and cash liquidity.

Company Structure

At first glance, it might appear that something as basic as company structure should not enter into growth strategies. Yet, because it is so basic, many business owners disregard the benefits that can be derived from re-forming a company to fit long-term objectives. A good place to begin might be with the definition of "company structure."

The three legal company structures are proprietorship, partnership, and corporation. Within partnerships and corporations, several variations may be used. Partnerships may involve two or more partners with equal or unequal ownership interests. Partners may be *general partners*, with each sharing proportionately in the profits, losses, and liabilities of the business. One or more may be *limited partners*, with no responsibility for company liabilities and disproportionate share of profits and losses.

Some partnerships are called *joint ventures* or *strategic alliances* and are owned equally or unequally by two or more corporations, each donating specific resources to the business and reaping equal or proportionate profits. All partnerships have a limited life; that is, they cease to exist when a *general partner* withdraws or dies.

Corporations may be *closely held* businesses whose shares are owned by one or a limited number of shareholders. When ownership resides in a large number of shareholders who can buy and sell the corporation's shares in capital markets, the company is considered to be *publicly held*. Corporations may be domestic companies (that is, registered in one of the fifty states) or foreign companies (which means that they are domiciled in a country other than the United States).

Closely held corporations owned by family members or other private individuals (or qualified trusts) may elect under the IRS Code to be taxed as S corporations. In this case, the corporate form remains the legal entity, but profits and losses pass directly to shareholders for tax purposes. All corporations have an infinite life; that is, they continue to exist even if all shareholders die or withdraw.

The choice of company structure is related to the flexibility needed to achieve specific strategic objectives. For example, a company planning to expand through the acquisition of a going business or product line might find it convenient to use its common stock for part of the purchase price. The company could establish a market value for its shares by floating a public stock issue well in advance of the acquisition.

An alternative choice of structure might be more reasonable if the primary objective is to ensure continued growth of the business after an owner retires or dies. In that case, a partner—either a family member or an outsider—could be brought in to manage and eventually own the business. In addition, a S corporation could be used to minimize corporate and shareholder taxes.

Or strategic plans may call for the raising of a large amount of equity capital. Although issuing public shares is one way to achieve this objective, another might be to sell units in a limited partnership, either informally to friends and relatives or formally through a private placement.

Multiple business entities

Pragmatically, no single company structure can be fashioned to meet all contingencies. For this reason, structuring different segments or assets of a business into separate legal entities may provide the ultimate flexibility.

For instance, if a company owns a production plant, warehouse, storefront, or office building, such real estate could be sold to a general or limited partnership owned by the company's shareholders or the owner's relatives, then leased back to the operating company. Not only are significant tax savings possible, but the flexibility achieved by unburdening the company of expensive hard assets while increasing its cash reserves should enhance its ability to respond quickly to changing conditions.

Companies can effectively use multiple entities for four purposes:

1. To hold specific business assets

2. To conduct separate businesses

3. To conduct businesses in different locations

4. To raise capital

Obviously, a company's industry and size influence the applicability of each strategy. A small retail or service business serving a local market niche may never be concerned about satellite companies in different locations, either domestic or overseas. If a company doesn't own real estate or equipment or have excess cash to invest, it obviously cannot benefit from placing these assets in separate entities. A family business may never need outside capital.

On the other hand, conditions change. Tomorrow's expansion plans may dictate a fresh capital infusion or a business acquisition. Prudent estate planning may include bringing in a successor to run the company or planning for disposal of the business. Planning for a stream of income during your retirement years might suggest an independent investment program using a company's excess cash. Competition could force an export program or the sourcing of materials and components overseas. The dynamic nature of most businesses makes the need for flexible company structures virtually impossible to ignore.

Small and midsize companies have benefited by using multiple business entities for a variety of purposes. Obviously, a company's particular goals, market position, product offering, and personnel organization influence which, if any, of these strategies might be implemented; however, in most cases at least one or two should be helpful in achieving long-term objectives. The major benefits derived from multiple entities are to:

1. Obtain the full use of losses on personal returns

---

2. Retain certain assets when selling the business

3. Segregate personal from business assets

4. Relocate certain assets offshore

5. Include certain assets in your estate or exclude them from it

6. Reduce the total corporate tax bill

7. Conduct research and development activities

8. Obtain patents

9. Make business acquisitions

10. Develop investment programs

11. Manage retirement portfolios

12. Enhance estate planning

13. Reduce state taxes

14. Implement segregated management incentive programs

15. Develop offshore businesses

16. Raise equity capital

Motivated Employees

As business owners, we quickly recognize the value of motivated employees. However, few private businesses can afford the luxury of highly specialized employees dedicated to the accomplishment of single tasks or focused on narrow responsibilities. The very nature of closely held companies dictates that employees must wear many hats and pitch in wherever necessary to meet immediate needs. Although we tend to underestimate the breadth of employees' abilities, unless people are properly motivated they seldom show their true colors.

A case in point occurred a short time ago in a company that distributed, installed, and serviced residential heating and air conditioning systems. The entire payroll consisted of the business owner and six employees:

- One office manager–secretary–bookkeeper–receptionist
- One salesman
- Two service technicians
- Two equipment installers

When business slowed, the owner decided to run a sales promotion, offering a free water heater with every new heating/air conditioning system. Orders flooded in, and the two equipment installers were deluged with work. To motivate other employees to help out, the owner offered them a choice of two days' vacation, a $100 savings bond, or 2 percent of the selling price for each complete system installed on or ahead of schedule. Everyone pitched in while the owner covered the office and handled new orders. By the end of the six-month promotion, the company had doubled its sales volume.

Monetary rewards are not the only motivational technique. Many others, ranging from letters of commendation, to employee-of-the-month awards, to public announcements of promotions or tenure, to shares of company stock, have proven equally effective. Equity ownership seems to be a particularly effective stimulus to employee flexibility. When they have a stake in the success of a company's growth objectives, employees tend to be more willing to assume responsibilities and perform tasks outside of their specific job descriptions. This, in turn, creates an atmosphere in which employees can learn one another's skills, hone their problem-solving abilities, and come up with creative ideas for resolving bottlenecks in information flows and production schedules. These are all essential ingredients for achieving the flexibility needed to permit a company to move with the times.

Cash Liquidity

Regardless of the benefits derived from a strategically effective business structure and motivated employees, a company's flexibility to meet changing market conditions will be severely hampered if it does not have sufficient cash. Businesses that are short of operating cash and have reached their maximum line of credit will find it virtually impossible to make short- and long-term investments in those people skills, machinery and equipment, advertising campaigns, and product modifications demanded by new competition or changing market tastes.

Cash liquidity may be achieved through various means, depending on the business environment, a company's industry and size, the availability of credit, and the configuration of its customer base. Typical examples include:

- Turning excess or obsolete inventory into cash through Dutch auctions or fire sales
- Collecting overdue receivables by offering discounts
- Converting short-term loans to long-term debt
- Selling minority interests in the company to bring in fresh equity capital
- Selling unneeded vehicles or equipment
- Leasing out excess space
- Arranging sale/leaseback transactions
- Selling entire product lines
- Substituting employee stock ownership plans (ESOPs) for cash-draining employee benefit plans

The list of possibilities is indeed endless. The main idea behind building cash reserves is to achieve sufficient flexibility to take advantage of new market conditions as they arise. Nine times out of ten, companies saddled with excessive debt service and those that live hand-to-mouth and depend on current receipts to meet current or past-due obligations are unable to meet new demands from customers or exploit opportunities offered by suppliers. Liquidity is the name of the game, and without it, strategic opportunities are bound to be missed.

PLANNING

Planning is the second key to growth. Plans take many forms; sales plans, organization plans, budgets, financing plans, capital expenditure plans, and business plans all serve specific purposes. Ideally, companies should use each of these specialized plans as the occasion warrants. Unfortunately, few of us have the time or inclination to engage in extensive planning. We are too busy putting out fires, reacting to demands from customers, fencing with recalcitrant suppliers, smoothing the ruffled feathers of disgruntled employees, and massaging the egos of obstreperous bankers.

Nevertheless, ignoring the critical role that planning plays in growth strategies can be a fatal mistake. Without a roadmap, it's too easy to go off on tangents, wasting valuable time and money. Without a plan, we have nothing to measure progress against, and we cannot determine if we are meeting our long-term objectives. Without a beacon to point the way, we fail too often to see the forest for the trees and make errors in judgment based on the exigencies of the moment.

Laying out a roadmap that encompasses long-term strategies is known as *strategic planning*. Chapter 2 deals with the main ingredients of strategic planning, and several later chapters cover the types of long-term objectives that might be included in a strategic plan. Before embarking on that twisting road, however, it's important to sort out the various plans that can be used on a day-to-day basis to improve current market response times and flexibility.

A sales plan is generally a good place to begin. Weekly, monthly, or annual sales quotas are frequently used to provide a preliminary estimate of quantities to be purchased or products to be produced. Ideally, planned sales levels should be established at the lowest common denominator—that is, by salesperson, department (in the case of retail stores), product line, territory, facility location, or any other logical segment by which sales can be measured. To motivate employees, the achievement of sales goals should bring them immediate rewards—cash bonuses, vacation days, commendation certificates, and so on.

Organization plans can also prove helpful in determining how many employees, and what qualifications, are needed to meet sales plans or production schedules. Such plans form the basis for training programs, employee incentive plans, and cash forecasting. An organization chart, complete with job titles, brief descriptions of job responsibilities, and salaries, is a good place to begin. Time and again, companies have found that a formal organization chart helps structure a business into definable units and clarifies the role of each employee in making the overall company an efficient operating unit.

Capital expenditure plans should, by definition, be long-term. They need to be carefully matched with extended sales plans, perhaps for as long as five years. Capital expenditures for facilities and equipment, vehicles, and machinery required to meet sales forecasts should be estimated. Make-versus-buy or lease-versus-buy decisions can then be made far enough in advance to arrange financing, delivery, and installation in an orderly fashion.

Many companies find that the planning cycle cannot be completed without a detailed financing plan. This is especially true for businesses that require varying amounts of short-term working capital to support seasonal production and sales cycles. Extra capital might be needed to build inventory for an expected surge in market demand. Short-term borrowings might also be necessary to cover receivables dating programs. If production or purchasing cycles are long, extra financing is usually required to pay the bills before shipments are made. Such capital needs should be planned so that a company can make the most efficient use of internally generated cash and keep short-term debt to a minimum.

In some companies, business planning acts as a catalyst to assimilate these detailed sales, organization, capital, and financing plans into a coordinated blueprint for the entire company. Although full-fledged business plans updated annually certainly add a level of formality to a business operation by giving the planning process a life of its own, annual business plans often require too much administrative time to be cost-effective.

Take, for example, the case of micro businesses (by arbitrary definition, companies with annual sales of less than $1 million), which are too small to have the personnel, the time, or even the records to effectively compile a full business plan. Owners of these businesses are so close to day-to-day activities that annual business plans would most assuredly be overkill. Still, even micro businesses can benefit from the discipline of putting together sales and financing plans.

CONTROL

While the planning cycle tells you where you are going, effective controls help you get there. Two types of controls need to be developed:

1. Controls over the internal operations of a company (referred to as internal controls)

2. Controls over matters external to the company

Both types of controls help managers (or owners) master their own destinies. Just as planning lays out a strategic roadmap that points the way toward the achievement of long-term objectives, internal and external controls keep a company focused on its strategic plans and prevent it from straying too far afield.

Internal Control

Over the years, internal control has gained the undeserved reputation of a way to prevent employees from stealing. Such a reputation may be justified in companies located in deteriorated neighborhoods or that manufacture products using high-value components or materials (gold, silver, platinum, and so on) and, to a lesser extent, in businesses that deal primarily in cash or cash equivalents (such as banks and stock brokerages). By and large, however, the main purpose of internal control is to ensure that production, sales, customer service, accounting, and other functional departments operate as efficiently as possible and according to plan.

Internal controls come in various forms: financial controls, time controls, customer service controls, inventory controls, production controls, and so on. Regardless of type, however, effective controls are intended to accomplish one or all of three objectives:

1. To ensure efficient cash management
2. To monitor results against a predetermined policy or plan
3. To gather and report information

A common example of one form of internal control to enhance cash management is the assignment of responsibility for purchasing materials and supplies to one person and the responsibility for paying supplier invoices to another. Such a separation of duties ensures that only approved purchases are received and paid for. Weekly or monthly sales reports that list orders received by salesperson is an example of an internal control used for monitoring performance.

Financial systems and their concomitant reports are by far the most effective form of internal control for achieving long-term growth objectives. Formal financial statements—balance sheets, income statements, and cash flow schedules—prepared on a regular monthly basis provide the best indication of how a company has performed. Using these financial statements as a base, forecasted balance sheets, income statements, and cash flow schedules can be prepared to quantify the expected results of future strategic alternatives.

As a complement to financial statements, detailed cost systems accumulate the cost of producing and selling specific products or product lines, thereby enabling companies to set prices to yield the highest margin. Cost systems are also effective for monitoring market-directed changes in product or process design. Cost accounting systems need not be complex; simple ones work just as well for most private businesses. They entail the accumulation of payroll and material costs by operation or department, then summarizing these costs by business segment in internal reports. In those businesses that quote prices and build products to customer order, a cost system enables sales personnel to base selling prices and delivery schedules on quantifiable cost estimates.

In addition to financial statements and cost accounting reports, several other internal reports enhance internal control by providing historical and current sales, production, and financial information. The most common reports include the following.

In the Marketing Area:

- Customer orders received
- Order cancellations
- Shipments by customer and product line
- Customer order backlog
- Sales by territory or sales organization
- Industry statistics published by trade associations or other industry groups

- Historical pricing changes
- Sales discounts
- Customer returns

In the Production and Quality Control Departments:

- Actual labor hours by week or month
- Production units completed at each work station
- Scrap and product failure statistics
- Production schedules by day or by week
- Delivery promises kept
- Number of direct labor and support employees by function

In the Finance Area:

- Gross margin by product line
- Gross margin by customer
- Labor and material variance analyses (if a standard cost system is used)
- Comparisons of actual expenses to budget by cost center
- Annual cost center budgets
- Aged accounts receivable listing
- Aged accounts payable listing

External Control

Control over conditions external to the company is also important for maximizing long-term growth. Various strategies for controlling market share, including target advertising, cost-effective public relations campaigns, customized after-sale customer service, sales tactics and promotions, and the optimization of customer mix, are discussed in Chapters 4 and 5.

In addition, sustainable long-term growth depends on a company's ability to control relationships with financial institutions, investors, suppliers, and professional advisors (accountants, lawyers, insurance representatives, and so on). On the surface, one might assume that a single company would have little control in these areas. After all, how much influence can one company have on the lending policies of a major city bank, or the activities of auditors, or the pricing and delivery policies of large suppliers? Quite a bit if you make full use of the leverage available to any buyer.

Whether borrowing from a bank, contracting with an auditing firm, or seeking advice from legal counsel, you are the buyer. As a buyer, you have the right to demand terms and conditions that best suit the needs of the company. If one bank won't go along, apply for a loan from another, and another, and so on, until you finally get what you need. The same applies to professional advisors. As a buyer, you have the right to change lawyers or accountants if you are not getting the best service and price from your current firms.

Companies seldom hesitate to exercise buyer leverage when dealing with suppliers, but for some reason they tend to shy away from exercising the same control when dealing with financial institutions and professional advisors. However, to maximize growth possibilities, we must demand the same consideration from these suppliers as we do from suppliers of goods and materials.

CAPITAL

The fourth key to successful long-term growth strategies is the ability to attract and efficiently use capital. More than one small business (and large companies as well) has failed to achieve its sales goals or profit objectives because it lacked sufficient working capital to support increased inventory and receivables and/or the ability to attract adequate long-term capital for the acquisition of additional machinery, equipment, or facilities. It is certainly not uncommon for business owners steeped in technical knowledge or marketing acumen to be less sophisticated when it comes to raising capital. Nevertheless, the main reason for an inadequate capital base seems to be lack of attention to long-term capital strategies rather than a shortage of financial savvy.

Any business owner who has tried to negotiate increased lines of credit or long-term loans from a weak balance sheet knows how difficult this can be. Banks consider three factors as the primary determinants for extending credit:

- Amicable relationships with a company's principals
- Adequate loan collateral
- Sufficient cash flow for loan repayment

Long before you need a loan, it pays to court at least two banks, and preferably more. Having a relationship with one or two small banks and a couple of large ones can often provide leverage for playing one against another. Opening checking accounts in several banks (perhaps a payroll account in one and a regular account in another), investing in short-term bank securities (such as certificates of deposit) in different banks, starting a personal savings account or an individual retirement account—all establish relationships that can be leveraged when credit needs arise.

It's hard to plan for loan collateral. Receivables and inventory needed to secure short-term loans are what they are. There isn't much you can do to enhance the value of these assets other than being certain that all obsolete and slow-moving inventory has been segregated and that past-due receivables get collected or are excluded from the borrowing base.

A company can do something about its cash flow projections, however. Nothing kills a loan application faster than an ill-conceived cash flow projection, hastily assembled and without supporting documentation. Since banks know very little about their customers' businesses, they are mainly concerned with financial ratios calculated from the pro forma financial statements that support cash flow forecasts.

Here are the major ratios that banks use to measure the reliability of a company's cash flow forecast and its likelihood of meeting scheduled loan repayments.

1. Debt utilization ratios:

   - Total debt to equity
   - Long-term debt to equity
   - Total debt to total assets
   - Income before interest and taxes to interest expense
   - Income before fixed charges and taxes to fixed charges

2. Liquidity ratios:

   - Current assets to current liabilities
   - Cash plus cash equivalents minus inventory to current liabilities
   - Current assets to short-term debt
   - Fixed assets to long-term debt

3. Profitability ratios:

   - Gross profit to sales
   - Net income after taxes to sales
   - Net income after taxes to total assets
   - Net income after taxes to equity

4. Asset utilization ratios:

   - Sales to average receivables (turnover)
   - Cost of sales to average inventory (turnover)
   - Sales to fixed assets
   - Sales to total assets

It is virtually impossible to sustain favorable ratios across the board. But the more ratios that paint a picture of a healthy company and efficient management, the greater the probability of getting both the short-term credit and long-term loans necessary to support planned growth. For this reason, it makes sense to begin immediately, long before you need to borrow funds, to clean up your company's financial statements so that the most favorable ratios consistent with industry standards can be presented. This, more than any other step, will increase your leverage and hence your control over the willingness of lenders to grant loans.

Aside from having adequate access to debt capital, the long-term health of a company is directly related to the strength of its equity base. Those who have experienced the agonies of searching for new loans without an adequate equity base or who have been faced with unmanageable debt service payments when business cycles turn down should be well aware of the difficulty, if not the impossibility, of achieving long-term growth exclusively with leveraged capital. Yet, time and again we hesitate to give up part interest in our companies for equity contributions. Instead, we strive to meet unreasonable principal and interest payments by increasing sales, and usually fail.

A good case in point occurred with a medical equipment distributor during the last recession. The company employed twenty-one people and had seen sales climb at a 25 percent annual clip for the last few years, finally reaching a level of $7 million in 1990. The owner had started the company with minimum equity of $100,000, relying on short-term bank loans (which reached $800,000 in 1990) to fund the increased sales. The following year, the banking industry pulled in its horns and the company's lender called 25 percent of the loan to cover what it considered its undercollateralized position. Default followed, and by 1993 the distributor was but a fraction of its former size and on the verge of bankruptcy.

In this case, the chances of attracting equity investors to this lucrative, high-growth industry would have been excellent if the business owner had only tried. With an additional $200,000 of equity to replace the called bank loan, the company not only would have survived, but probably would have continued to enjoy its 25 percent annual growth rate. Much as it pains us to give up minority ownership interests, in the long term, this is a far better way to build financial flexibility and increase cash reserves than boosting a lender's profits.

LONG-TERM OBJECTIVES

While short-term goals are necessary for any business (if you don't take care of today's problems today, you won't be around long enough to exploit tomorrow's opportunities), most owners learn early in the game how to cope with the daily problems (and opportunities) that crop up. Few of us need or want ideas for producing or selling our products or services. Moreover, unless a company is already on the ropes, it seems presumptuous for consultants, professional advisors, or writers to tell business owners how to run their businesses. With very rare exceptions, business owners know far more about what works and what doesn't work in specific instances than any outsider.

Therefore, except for Chapter 7, the following chapters focus not on short-term management ideas, but on those long-term objectives that have proven time and again to be the cornerstones of strategic growth. Although many are as applicable to businesses that are just getting started as to mature companies, certain suggestions (such as those related to setting up offshore "twin plant" facilities) will obviously appeal primarily to well-established businesses. In contrast, businesses that are just getting started will find strategic suggestions related to market definition and public relations imaging more applicable.

Before proceeding, a few caveats are probably worth reviewing.

1. *Growth strategies* may focus on increased sales, improved profit margins, greater cash flow, or more effective asset deployment—or a combination thereof. Some businesses are extremely sensitive to changes in sales volume, and therefore benefit most from strategies for increasing sales steadily over the long term. Companies with a high fixed-cost

base—such as hotels or resorts, golf courses, apartment complexes, and most real estate-based companies—are prime examples of volume-sensitive businesses. At the other end of the spectrum, low-fixed-cost businesses, including most service-oriented companies, should focus on strategies that lead to more efficient asset deployment (mainly of non-balance sheet assets) and higher prices.

Between these extremes, strategies aimed at maximizing cash flow should balance the benefits of improved sales volume against those of higher unit margins. Personal service businesses, including professional practices, should focus on strategies to enhance their public reputation or goodwill.

2. *Industry or market limitations* can be overcome only with giant leaps forward, such as buying another business or tapping entirely new markets (perhaps foreign markets). Strategies aimed at increasing sales by achieving greater shares of current markets in stable or declining industries will at best result in modest growth: in many cases, maintaining current sales volumes and profit margins is the best that can be achieved. To break free of these restraints, companies must develop strategies that will add large groups of new products and/or customers in markets far afield from those currently being served.

The tapping of burgeoning foreign markets in developing countries might be just the ticket to jump-start a company languishing in mature domestic markets. The purchase of diverse product lines or the acquisition of an entire operating business could leapfrog a company into new markets and industries. Embarking on an R&D program, taking subcontract business, starting up facilities in new locations, or forming a joint venture with another company also offer possibilities for diversification.

3. *Tax considerations* play an important role in any strategic growth plan. Except for companies that operate at a loss, the payment of income taxes is normally the largest single expense of doing business. It makes sense, therefore, to develop tax minimization strategies as part of an overall strategic growth program. Family-owned businesses generally find S corporations to be a logical way to reduce tax burdens. Limited partnerships can also effectively reduce business taxes, although original tax-shelter benefits are no longer possible.

The use of multiple corporations or a combination of corporations, partnerships, trusts, and limited partnerships to hold specific assets can reduce tax liabilities in certain types of businesses. Companies with income arising from overseas transactions should seriously consider using tax-haven countries and foreign sales corporations (FSCs) as part of their strategic plans.

4. *Employing the same strategies as competitors* can only keep a company in a status quo condition. Reacting to the outbreak of price wars, to bom-

bardment advertising that saturates a given market, or to name-calling tactics does little to stimulate additional long-term business, although in the short term slight sales gains may be realized. To break out of the pack, unusual, perhaps higher-risk strategies must be tried. Examples might include spinning off business segments, focusing on narrower but higher-margin market niches, promoting environmentally safe products, or involving the company in socially conscious community activities.

5. *Major changes* to improve market position, acquire more efficient assets, recruit qualified personnel, design product line modifications, or develop new material sources cannot be achieved without a solid financial footing. The adage "it takes money to make money" holds true for most long-term growth strategies. Weakened balance sheets, overpowering debt service obligations, insufficient equity capital, and meager cash flows must be corrected before long-range strategies can be implemented.

This does not suggest rushing to the capital markets or banks for new financing, although either or both courses may eventually be needed. It does mean that all stops should be pulled out to strengthen internal cash reserves by cleaning up delinquent receivables, disposing of unneeded assets, implementing cash control procedures, and avoiding unnecessary expenditures for travel, entertainment, customer/supplier promotions, and other cash drains.

6. *Sustainable growth strategies* cannot be developed, implemented, or monitored without a well-conceived strategic plan. A strategic plan is the heart and soul of successful business growth, whether that growth is focused on sales, profit margins, cash flow, or asset deployment. Such a plan serves three main purposes:

- The discipline and analyses necessary to construct a strategic plan force business owners and key managers to come thoroughly to grips with every aspect of the business. This is just as important for a business that is just getting started as it is for a mature company.
- The roadmap provided by a strategic plan directs company resources in a meaningful, productive manner, without wasting employees' time or company money on start-stop tactics. It also points the way to appropriate market, product, organization, and financing plans.
- The essence of control is to track the results of policies and events against a predetermined estimate of expected outcomes. The monitoring of actual performance against a strategic plan gives companies a valuable tool for making new decisions about exploiting changes in market/product demand, sources of supply, and capital availability.

The following chapter takes a closer look at the major ingredients of strategic planning. It emphasizes the planning process itself, not specific plan content (which must be unique for each business). Some companies will accent asset development; others will attach more importance to market control; still others will find R&D, organization, or financial strategies more appropriate. Regardless of the company's specific needs, the benefits derived from the process of thinking through and constructing a strategic plan remain constant. It is the careful application of this process that will bring the best long-term results.

Chapter 2

Strategic Planning

Military leaders know that they cannot launch a major offensive until they have laid out a battle plan, marshaled resources (troops, materiel, equipment), tightened lines of defense, and ensured continued reinforcements. In a similar fashion, before launching a growth offensive, companies must:

- Develop a strategic plan (a battle plan) to define those actions that will get them to their end objective
- Dispose of all unnecessary inventory and equipment and deploy productive assets (marshal resources) to provide the strongest possible operating base
- Shore up marketing efforts (tighten lines of defense) to improve the flow of information for tactical decisions
- Restructure sources of capital (ensure reinforcements) to provide sufficient cash to meet strategic goals

This chapter offers suggestions for beginning the development of long-term growth strategies by laying out an objective-oriented battle plan, which, in modern-day vernacular, is appropriately called a strategic plan. Chapter 3 looks at ways to tighten a company's operating base that will lead to improved productivity and cash flow. Chapters 4 and 5 focus on marketing and promotion strategies, and Chapter 6 advances ideas for strengthening a company's capital base.

"Strategic planning" may be one of the most overworked, misused terms in modern-day business. Pro forma financial forecasts have been called strategic plans. So have cost center budgets, business plans, capital budgets, financing plans, and sales forecasts. While they include part or all of these supporting elements, true strategic plans encompass much more. To clarify this point, perhaps some definitions are in order.

- A *strategy* is a plan of action based on a series of measures intended to accomplish a specific, long-term goal.
- A *plan* is a method or program in accordance with which something is to be done or accomplished.

- A *strategic plan* is such a program based on a series of anticipated decisions aimed at enhancing the growth of a company's sales and/or profits over the long term.

As described in Chapter 1, the flexibility to make abrupt tactical changes in market penetration and product configurations when cyclical or long-term variations in customer demand and competition dictate underlies all effective long-term strategies. Tactical approaches that enhance rather than detract from a company's flexibility include:

- A proactive (as opposed to reactive) marketing program that encourages variations in product pricing, distribution, and customer service *in anticipation of* changes in market demand and competitive reactions to these changes
- A product mix that maximizes the sale of high-margin items
- A lean organization of highly motivated employees who are capable of shifting direction as conditions warrant
- Internal operating procedures (including effective cash controls) that enable quick responses to varying circumstances
- A capital structure that maximizes leveraging advantages while providing sufficient free cash to invest in new opportunities as they arise

An organization so mobilized can concentrate on developing long-term growth strategies, secure in the knowledge that personnel, marketing policies, product mix, and capital structure can be adjusted to fit nearly any mold. Take, for example, the case of a small furniture distributor, Wicker America. This company had struggled with a 1 to 2 percent growth rate for five years. Although the company was profitable, competitors were forcing deeper pricing discounts in its primary market, Greater Miami.

The president of Wicker America decided enough was enough. She terminated all commissioned sales personnel, hired a sales manager and two salesmen, struck an agreement with a new manufacturer, refinanced the outstanding balance of her line of credit into a five-year term loan, and began advertising in the Orlando and Tampa markets. Wicker America's growth rate soared to 5 percent the first year. In the second year, however, Wicker's president recognized that new markets were opening in Guatemala and Belize and quickly shifted gears.

Since she had insisted that the new sales manager be fluent in Spanish, it took little time to refocus the company's marketing and advertising programs on Central America. Sufficient free cash had been generated over the previous two years to enable the company to risk a joint venture arrangement with a Guatemalan distributor. Sales jumped 10 percent the first year and 15 percent the second. Within five years, 85 percent of the company's profits came from Central American sales.

Although, Wicker America was able to see the opening of new markets and move quickly to capture a major share, most companies aren't so fortunate. They have to plan for the implementation of strategies long before they need to act.

And that's where strategic planning comes in. A well-conceived strategic plan enables a company to test growth assumptions as occasions warrant and then move quickly to capture new markets, discard low-margin product lines, and develop operating policies to exploit virtually any situation. With sufficient flexibility in people, products, facilities, and capital, companies can create opportunities rather than react to those that others have already recognized.

The process of testing alternative strategies can best be accomplished with a forecasting model. This model must be based on the cost/sales/asset functional relationships that a company currently experiences. It should be so constructed that various levels of sales, costs, and assets associated with a series of "what if" scenarios can be tested against one another. Sales, profits, and return on investment resulting from each strategy can then be compared to determine which strategies result in the best overall company performance. Although such a forecasting rationale is equally adaptable to manual and computer-based computations, the complexity and number of "what if" alternatives encourage the use of computer-based spreadsheet programs.

My book *The Small Business Valuation Book* describes the detailed use of a proven-effective forecasting model. Readers who wish to apply this model to their own businesses may seek assistance from the author and his associates. A request on your letterhead sent to ZYX-VU, Ltd., P.O. Box 347, Southeastern, PA 19399, will bring an immediate response.

COMPANY MISSION

The starting point for any strategic plan is the determination of a realistic company mission. The importance of defining an achievable mission can most easily be seen by comparing two examples. In the first, assume that the owner of Movies-for-Rent, Inc., became impatient with stagnant revenues and decided to diversify by offering new product lines—movie projectors, camcorders, and TV and stereo furniture—and by presenting movie-editing seminars.

Competing stores that specialized in each of these product lines had lower overhead and hence were able to price their products below Movies-for-Rent's full cost. Although total revenues increased 10 percent the first year, low competitive prices coupled with the company's expanded debt service obligations kept margins on each of the new lines well below those earned from movie rentals, driving down total company profits.

As a second example, assume that Hollywood Tonite kept to its original mission—renting movies. As revenues stagnated, the temptation to diversify led the owner to prepare a long-term strategic plan. He saw at a glance that although Hollywood Tonite had the lion's share of the video rental market, several nearby stores had already captured major market shares for each of the new product lines that Movies-for-Rent was introducing. He therefore increased advertising for movie rentals and initiated a bonus rental program. Although revenues did not increase as fast as those of Movies-for-Rent, profits soared far above those of this diversified competitor.

Without question, diversification is called for under certain circumstances. When it is consistent with a company's original mission, diversification should add to total profits. However, when diversification into new products or markets is at variance with the original mission, more often than not, total company profits and return on investment suffer.

A company mission may be anything the owner desires. In a recent university study of private companies in the Philadelphia area, business owners were asked to define a mission statement that best described their businesses. In order of popularity, the responses were to:

1. Maximize cash draws for the business owner
2. Provide the best service (or product) at the least cost
3. Sustain a steady growth rate commensurate with available resources
4. Provide steady employment for long-term employees
5. Maximize estate assets for the owner
6. Maintain a socially responsible position relative to employees, the community, and the environment
7. Meet the needs of employees and the community while maximizing profits and return on investment
8. Gain and sustain a commanding market share
9. Provide a constant challenge and mental stimulation for the owner and key managers
10. Be recognized as the leader in a given market/industry

Mission statements may be as broad or as narrow as one desires. In some cases, product or market diversification is necessary. For instance, if a company's mission is to maximize return on investment, it may be necessary to purge unprofitable product lines, or to initiate a high-margin export program, or to make a leveraged buyout of a competitor, or to source components offshore.

In other cases, a company's mission might involve narrow business choices. For instance, gaining and sustaining a commanding market share might mean directing all available resources to advertising and promotion programs, or expanding current facilities for higher production volumes, or initiating labor training programs in the community.

Regardless of the specifics, effective long-term growth strategies call for a finite statement of the company's mission, followed by a strategic plan to achieve it.

GROWTH OBJECTIVES

In addition to a wide diversity of missions, businesses may have different growth objectives. In a dynamic business environment, companies will, over time, experience either increases or decreases in sales and profits. Standing still is not an option. Also, since it seems unlikely that a company would intentionally choose to decrease profits, one can assume that growth of one type or another is a prime objective. Therefore, it is necessary to define precisely the nature of that growth objective.

Although there are many variations, the four most common growth objectives involve market share, sales, return on investment, and diversification (to insulate against business cycles). Improving market share is probably the most far-reaching of the four. Markets may be defined by:

- Geographic boundaries (region, state, city, or neighborhood)
- Product superiority or uniqueness
- Technological advance
- Marketing and distribution originality
- Customer service supremacy

In all cases, market dominance gives companies the ability to control pricing, and hence profit margins, unfettered by competitive interference. For companies that dominate markets, the ultimate consumer, not competitive advertising, giveaways, or price-cutting discounts, is the sole determinant of pricing strategies.

In bad times as well as good, the sustainability of extraordinarily high prices for Mercedes-Benz automobiles sold in the United States is an excellent example of one company's dominance of a particular market—in this case the top-of-the-line luxury car market. The consistently high prices for Sears Craftsman brand power tools are another example of market dominance. In cut-throat home appliance markets, General Electric sustains its market dominance (and prices) by providing twenty-four-hour, seven-day, do-it-yourself repair service consultation.

Many companies regard steadily improving sales volume as their primary growth objective. Although in the long term, strategies aimed at increasing sales at the expense of profit margins can be dangerous, companies with a high ratio of fixed cost to sales ratio, such as hotels, may find this a reasonable trade-off, at least for interim periods.

Sales strategies run the gamut from cutting prices to increasing advertising to improving customer service to speeding up deliveries. More than one retailer (such as Domino's Pizza) has increased sales by offering free delivery service when competitors either charge for the service or do not deliver at all. After-sale service, free or low-cost customer training, "no-questions-asked" return policies, and "two-for-one" sales promotions have proved to be successful sale strategies in specific industries. "Hard-sell" tactics that pinpoint locales or products have also proved to be effective strategies, as in lawn-care businesses.

By focusing on sales objectives, more than one company has increased its market share and, in so doing, achieved market dominance over the long term. The main idea is to pick one or more specific marketing ploys to increase sales in identifiable markets without losing long-term profit margins.

Companies that focus on return on investment objectives usually find it more difficult to develop strategies that can be quickly implemented. In many cases, three to five years is considered normal. The efficient use of assets, as reflected in assets employed and asset turnover ratios, is the key to improving return on investment. Although rising profit margins also help, without steady improvement in asset turnover, it's virtually impossible to obtain significant improvement in return on investment.

Strategic plans that call for the acquisition of new product lines or businesses have, in many cases, been the most successful in meeting return on investment objectives. However, it's important to recognize that such acquisitions must be selected for their contribution to overall investment returns, not merely to meet diversification or sales objectives.

Companies that face wide business-cycle swings in sales and profitability frequently concentrate on strategies that will mitigate the effect of seasonal, short-term, or even long-term dips and spurts in market demand. Those businesses that are affected mostly by national economic swings might find market diversification strategies involving development of new offshore customer bases the best answer. Carefully chosen foreign markets with counteracting economic cycles can go a long way toward mitigating the effects of wide swings in domestic demand.

Similarly, scare materials or energy, high labor wage rates, or erratic sources of supply for parts or components frequently lead companies to diversify both their sources of supply and their production or assembly operations to offshore facilities. Diversification objectives might also take the form of joint ventures with companies that have complementary but cyclically offsetting product lines.

In addition to clearly defining a company's mission and growth objectives, the strategic planning process should earmark specific market niches to exploit or to abandon.

MARKET NICHES

In contrast to large companies with abundant resources, wide product offerings, and diverse marketing organizations, private businesses usually look to one or a limited number of market niches for growth opportunities. The broad-brush, something-for-everybody approach to product offerings or markets proves to be too costly and unwieldy.

As previously pointed out, markets, and hence market niches, may be defined by geography, products, customer base, technology, or distribution channels. In any case, to develop a meaningful strategy, it's necessary to define as precisely as possible those market niches that characterize a company's current sales efforts. Nearly all companies offer more than one or two services or products, or sell to more than one or two classes of customers. The greater the number of either, the higher the probability that one or more are draining cash and other resources without producing acceptable profit margins. These are the products or customers to dump, leaving more resources available for those market niches that produce the highest margins.

During the strategic planning process, it is also likely that one or more market niches that are not currently being exploited will be identified. Tapping these markets may require modification of products or distribution systems, or it could involve a restructuring of the customer mix.

For instance, assume that a baseball bat manufacturer sells exclusively to retail chains such as Kmart, Sears, and J. C. Penney. While exploring alternative markets as part of the strategic planning process, the sales manager learns that Little League teams, secondary schools, and universities buy their disposable athletic equipment (such as baseball bats and balls) in volume through national distributors. Although unit margins on sales to distributors run less than on retail sales, this could probably be offset by production efficiencies resulting from large-volume orders. Furthermore, assume that only one major bat manufacturer sells to this market. If major sales and delivery efforts are redirected to national distributors, advertising expenses should be less and customer returns completely eliminated. Such a redirection of marketing efforts could increase the growth rate of both sales and total profits.

Four criteria should be used to analyze market niches:

1. Market size and growth potential

2. Major competitors

3. Ease of entry

4. Resource requirements

Market Size and Growth Potential

The whole concept of focused marketing rests on gaining major market shares by expending minimum resources. A market's size and growth potential depend on the current and projected demand for a given product. Both the current status of a market and its future potential should be recognized as basic criteria for continuing or expanding market penetration.

When exploring the possibilities for entering a new market, more than one business owner or sales manager has made the common mistake of equating customer demand with customer need. This is always a serious error because seldom, if ever, are the two equal. It may be logically argued that customers "need" a new product or service, but if they are unwilling to buy it, their "need" for it is irrelevant.

An excellent example has been the overwhelming need to eliminate nonbiodegradable plastic from consumer packaging. Environmental studies clearly indicate the need to stop flooding landfills with plastic containers and packaging. With current technology, plastic packaging could easily be replaced with biodegradable material. But manufacturers have been hesitant to incur the added costs of converting packaging machinery. The plastic container industry has deferred the development of alternative products. And federal and state legislatures have been unwilling to meet the need with regulations that ban plastic packaging. Despite market need, the absence of consumer demand for biodegradable packaging is the main reason we continue to stuff landfills with ecologically damaging plastic.

Clearly, customer need is not sufficient reason to enter a new market. There must also be substantial customer demand. In and of itself, however, even strong market demand isn't enough. The strategic planning process must also reveal the nature and extent of competition.

Major Competitors

If the objective of entering a new market niche is to gain a controlling share, picking a niche that already has a market leader could be a very expensive proposition. The odds of winning are much higher in markets in which many small companies compete, but none has a major share. Such a tactic is also far less expensive than unseating an entrenched market leader. However, there are opportunities to gain control of niche markets within in broad markets controlled by a few major companies, such as woodworking power hand tools.

For years, major brands such as Craftsman, Black & Decker, and Skil have controlled the national power hand tool market, with product offerings ranging from circular saws and saber saws to routers, drills, and sanders. Complaints from both do-it-yourself customers and professional carpenters about the awkwardness of using extension cords have fallen on deaf ears. Recently, Skil came out with a rechargeable battery power pack for its line of miniature circular saws used for finishing work and model building. The first company that can translate this concept to full-size tools at an economical price will certainly capture a niche where there is real market demand.

A similar case involves the small battery market for flashlights, portable stereo equipment, and toys. By being the first to enter, GE effectively controlled price and distribution in the rechargeable small battery market, still a minor niche in a broad national market. However, the first company to develop rechargeable batteries that are priced competitively with traditional small batteries should have a clear shot at capturing a significant market share from GE.

The idea behind searching out new niche markets with little, if any, serious competition is to gain pricing and probably distribution control (thereby increasing margins) at minimum cost and in the shortest time period. A strategic focus along these lines will inevitably result in faster growth than pursuing highly competitive markets.

Ease of Entry

As a corollary to competitive saturation, ease of market entry determines to a large extent how long a company can remain in control of a niche market. Low-cost, low-technology, high-volume markets are naturals for new entrants. Unless the manufacturing process or distribution system requires extensive capital investment, many large and small companies will be attracted to such a market.

The tax-return preparation business is a prime example. Literally thousands of micro businesses and hundreds of large firms continually enter and leave this industry. Market demand is always high, capital investment is nonexistent (except perhaps for a personal computer and a tax library), certification is not required, and the technical ability to prepare individual tax returns is easily learned (as witness the large number of H & R Block offices).

It would make little sense to include this market in a strategic plan unless a sales gimmick could be developed. One such gimmick was the filing of tax returns electronically. Another gimmick, initiated by H & R Block, was instant refunds. Although short-lived advantages were certainly achieved in both cases, other competitors soon jumped in with the same offers.

Conversely, attacking a niche market that by its nature has stringent entrance barriers could be a highly desirable strategy. Barriers might be (1) technological, as with laser-optical gun sights or night-vision goggles; (2) regulatory, as with state licensing or FDA approvals; (3) cost, as with capital-intensive products; (4) financing, as with hotels, office complexes, shopping centers, and other real estate-based development projects; or (5) craft, as with mural design, Fiberglas layup, or teaching (such as Berlitz language schools).

The major drawback to strategies aimed at capturing barrier-prone markets is that not infrequently they require substantial capital and dedicated personnel. To the extent that capital and qualified personnel are available or can be obtained without much expenditure of time or money, low-entry markets generally offer disproportionately high profit margins and the chance to capture significant, if not controlling, shares.

Resource Requirements

Of the four major criteria, the resources required to capture new market niches can often be the most difficult to achieve. Few companies have large amounts of excess cash available to promote their entrance. Even fewer have technical or managerial personnel who are capable of adding new assignments to their current responsibilities. And hardly any companies have excess facilities that can be used for new production, storage, or office functions. A shortage of resources, more than any other element, blocks market entrance. This is why flexibility is so important. Companies that have restructured to achieve flexibility in their capital reserves, personnel skills, product mix, operating procedures, and marketing organization will inevitably be in the best position to draw on current resources for new fast-growth opportunities.

Moreover, developing a comprehensive forecasting model based on cost/sales/asset functional relationships puts companies in a good position to determine with a high degree of certainty what resources must be obtained and when they must come on line to meet strategic plans. Without the ability to predict the need for new capital, personnel, and facilities well in advance of moving to new markets, fast growth is nearly impossible.

COMPARATIVE ANALYSIS

Athletes who compete in races keep one eye on the finish line and one eye on other athletes in the race. Original strategies for positioning and pace must be altered during the race as competitors surge ahead or fall behind. This is analogous to the business world. The specific tactics originally planned to achieve our long-term growth strategies must be altered as competitive forces ebb and flow. And to know which tactics to change and when to change them, we must know how our competitors are doing. Blindly following your original plan without considering how your company's market position and pace stack up against competitors' and industry standards can lead to missed opportunities and lost markets.

One of the best ways to judge the merits of tactical decisions is to compare your company's key financial ratios with those of other companies of comparable size, producing similar products, or selling to similar market niches. Making such comparisons with publicly held companies is relatively simple. Annual reports, SEC filings, and a stream of reports from security analysts reveal just how well or poorly a publicly held company is doing. It isn't quite as simple to compare your company with closely held companies, although with a little digging and creative analysis, it can be done.

Four steps are involved in deciding which companies to use as comparison standards:

1. Compile a list of all known companies in your industry

2. Pare this list down to companies that compete in your niche markets—product niches, location niches, distribution niches, and so on

3. Separate publicly traded companies from closely held companies

4. Dig out as many financial ratios and as much raw data as you can about those companies that seem to be the closest match

The first list should be made from sources that supply data on publicly traded companies in your industry. This is relatively simple once you define the applicable Standard Industrial Classification (SIC) codes. Many companies serve more than one class of customer, however, or sell more than one product line or service. In those cases, it's necessary to choose the appropriate SIC code for each industry—whether market-oriented or product-oriented. As a general rule, it pays to make the industry definition as broad as possible, thereby keeping the number of SIC codes to a minimum.

All SIC codes are listed and defined in the federal government's *Standard Industrial Classification Manual*, down to the lowest subheadings. These codes are structured to permit the collection of data needed to produce all the business-oriented statistics published by the government and therefore must be kept up to date and complete.

The easiest and fastest way to begin is at a public library. Most libraries have many reference works containing data on national, regional, and local companies, both public and privately held. In fact, libraries the only practical source of data, short of spending a small fortune on reference-oriented computer databases.

Once the appropriate SIC code has been determined, it's possible to trace companies from other reference works. The following are readily available sources that are easy to tap:

1. *Standard & Poor's Register of Corporations, Directors, and Executives* and *Standard & Poor's Corporation Records*. These directories probably have the most complete catalog of listed and unlisted companies to be found anywhere. The only problem is that they do not distinguish be-

tween public and privately held firms. To make this distinction, use the National Quotation Bureau's *National Monthly Stock Summary* in conjunction with the S & P volumes. This publication can be invaluable for determining whether small, unknown companies are public or private. It lists all companies whose stock has been quoted on the "pink sheets" within the past month. Pink sheets list the bid and ask prices of unlisted stocks as compiled by the National Daily Quotation Service. Of the more than 13,000 small companies that have issued public stock, only about 4,500 are traded on NASDAQ markets. The rest remain relatively unnoticed, with most trades conducted between brokers from pink-sheet advertisements.

Between the S & P volumes and the *National Monthly Stock Summary,* you can get information about company history, listings of subsidiaries, location of principal plants and other properties, business and products, officers and directors, comparative income statements, balance sheet statistics, financial ratios, and a description of outstanding securities. If your library doesn't carry these publications, they can be obtained from:

Standard & Poor's Corporation
25 Broadway
New York, NY 10004

National Quotation Bureau, Inc.
Plaza Three
Harborside Financial Center
Jersey City, NJ 07302

2. Moody's Manuals. In many respects, Moody's five manuals, *Bank & Finance*, *OTC Industrials*, *OTC Unlisted*, *Public Utilities*, and *Transportation*, give a more comprehensive description of companies than *Standard & Poor's Register*. These manuals list both large and small companies whose stock is traded in public markets. Of the five, the *OTC Industrials Manual* and the *OTC Unlisted Manual* are the most helpful. Both provide a range of information about smaller public companies; the first covers those listed in the NASDAQ market, and the second covers pink-sheet companies. The range of data includes company history and background, mergers and acquisitions, subsidiaries, business and products, location of principal plants and other properties, names and titles of officers and directors, financial statements, and a description of capitalization, including financial and operating ratios. Any of the Moody's manuals can be found in libraries or from:

Moody's Investors Service
99 Church Street
New York, NY 10007

3. *DIALOG Information Services.* DIALOG is one of the country's biggest computer database companies; it is reachable on-line through CompuServe and other telecommunications systems. A wide variety of services can be purchased depending on the specific information being sought. One of the most popular is DISCLOSURE II, which is also available from several other on-line data base suppliers. In addition to other data, DISCLOSURE II provides access to the Value Line surveys database. Subscribers to on-line database services can download public company annual reports and SEC 10-K filings directly to their computers.

The major drawback to using on-line database services is that they cost money—and fairly large sums for comprehensive coverage. Except in rare cases, a relatively good selection of potential comparisons can be drawn from the hard copy S&P and Moody's references. If you want to hook up with DIALOG, CompuServe's address is:

CompuServe Information Services
5000 Arlington Center Boulevard
Columbus, OH 43220

Information about accessing DISCLOSURE II can be obtained from:

Disclosure, Inc.
5161 River Road
Building 60
Bethesda, MD 20817
(800) 638-8241

4. *Value Line Investment Survey.* This is one of the most widely used reference services both for individual investors and for stockbrokers. In tracking the financial and business performance of 1,700 publicly owned companies, it presents a one-page summary updated periodically, for each company, including historical trends, historical and current stock prices, a description of the business and product lines, beta, and a wealth of profit, sales, and asset information. It also has a unique evaluation system that rates the timeliness and safety of investing in each company's stock, based on historical trends and regression analysis. Value Line can be found in the reference section of libraries. To subscribe, contact:

Value Line, Inc.
711 Third Avenue
New York, NY 10017

5. Dun & Bradstreet's *Key Business Ratios.* This publication contains fourteen significant financial ratios for more than 800 different lines of business, listed by SIC code. Current ratios, quick ratios, debt-to-equity ratios, and net-income-to-sales ratios are representative of those included. Although this service doesn't identify specific companies, ratios

by SIC code can help establish comparative standards. The major drawback is that the ratios are drawn from relatively large public companies.

Once you have a workable list of companies to compare your company against, the next steps aren't too time consuming—unless, of course, you happen to be looking at an obscure or highly specialized market. Begin by phoning or faxing each company and asking for sales literature, product descriptions, published quarterly and annual reports, statistical compilations, names of directors and officers, and facility locations. It's truly amazing how much information companies are willing to disclose for the asking.

Most active trade associations compile annual or quarterly statistics from member firms. Normally, data for specific member companies is merged into industry averages, which can then be used for comparison purposes. However, some associations do release a modest amount of specific data of a qualitative nature concerning its members. If available, qualitative comparisons can be nearly as valuable as numerical statistics. Some of the key elements to look for are:

- Credit status (easily obtained from Dun & Bradstreet or other credit agencies if trade associations won't provide it)
- Depth and experience of management (based on technical certification and tenure with the company)
- Competitive position and intensity of competition (derived from market size and number of member firms)
- Tenure of the business (not usually available)

Valuable statistics may also be available. Here are the main ones to ask for:

- Employee turnover
- Number of employees
- Average sales
- Gross profit and operating profit as a percent of sales
- Annual capital expenditures
- Annual R&D expenditures
- Inventory turns
- Receivables days sales

Although such data will probably be incomplete and will not reveal performance results from the highest- or the lowest-rated members, it should be enough to permit at least gross comparisons.

Government bureaus can also help. The Department of Commerce (supported by the Department of Labor) collects reams of monthly, quarterly, and annual reports from practically every company doing business in the United States—both public and private. This data is sorted by various levels and sublevels of SIC codes. It can be especially valuable when trade associations either do not publish compilation reports or are hesitant to release data to nonmembers.

The categories of government-compiled statistics are almost identical to those produced by larger and more active trade associations. In addition to sales, employee turnover, and other traditional information, however, the Department of Commerce compiles a virtually unlimited number of statistics in special areas. Here is a sampling that tends to be universally applicable to large and small companies:

- Sales volume compared to inventory purchases
- Number of new employees hired compared to employees terminated
- Square feet of floor space used in production
- Building permits and building starts (for construction industries)
- Various employee benefit statistics
- Employee accident statistics
- Bad debt ratios

The Department of Commerce staffs full offices and libraries in many major cities. They are open to the public, and for the asking you can peruse vast files of data for the current year and for many prior years. Some offices have progressed to computer databases, which are also available for public use.

ECONOMIC/BUSINESS CYCLE INDICATORS

The final step in the strategic planning process—that is, an analysis of pertinent economic indicators—needs to be completed before you develop detailed marketing and financial strategies. Such a macro analysis sets the framework within which a company must operate. Like it or not, we are all subject to the vagaries of recession, inflation, federal monetary and fiscal policies, and currency exchange rates. The first step in any planning cycle must be an analysis of the economic and business conditions that are expected to occur during the plan period. And the most important assumptions underlying such analyses have to do with national economic cycles and industry business cycles.

In fact, without a thorough understanding of a company's current position on both cycles, it's impossible to forecast sales with reasonable accuracy. Although marketing programs, selling techniques, and market demand affect sales levels, very few businesses are immune to cyclical trends. It goes without saying that you should choose only those indicators that apply to your company. It does little good to worry about national unemployment rates if you employ two people. Or to be concerned with building permit trends if you manufacture motorcycles. Or to crank in aerospace industry statistics for ladies' garment stores. However, certain conditions affect all businesses—interest rates, inflation rates, consumer spending, and perhaps business investment, to mention a few.

For those readers who are not familiar with the major economic indicators, a brief review might be in order. The federal government regularly prepares indexes that together make up an analytic system for assessing current and future national economic trends, particularly cyclical expansions and recessions. These indexes are grouped as leading, coincident, and lagging, according to their tendency to change direction before, during, or after the general economy turns the corner—either from recession to expansion or from expansion to recession. The leading indexes reflect business commitments and expectations, the coincident indexes indicate the current stage of the economy, and the lagging indexes identify business cost trends.

The Bureau of Economic Analysis in the U.S. Department of Commerce releases a monthly synopsis of each set of indexes in a press release and in the Bureau's monthly magazines, *Business Conditions Digest* and *Survey of Current Business.*

The whole concept of economic indexes is that profits are the prime mover in a private-enterprise economy and that recurring business cycles are caused by changes in the outlook for future profits. Such an outlook is reflected in the leading indicators and in the ratio of the coincident index to the lagging index (which is itself a leading indicator).

The components of each index are as follows:

Leading Index:

- Average weekly hours of manufacturing production workers (average weekly hours)
- Average weekly initial claims for unemployment compensation
- Manufacturers' new orders for consumer goods and materials industries, in 1982 dollars (manufacturers' orders)
- Vendor performance (percent of companies receiving slower deliveries)
- Contracts and orders for plant and equipment, in 1982 dollars
- New private housing building permits (housing starts)
- Manufacturers' unfilled orders for durable goods industries, in 1982 dollars (manufacturers' orders for durable goods)
- Prices of crude and intermediate materials, monthly change (Producer Price Index)
- Stock prices of 500 common stocks (stock market price indexes and dividends yields)
- Money supply (M-2), in 1982 dollars (money supply)
- Index of consumer expectations (Consumer Confidence Index and Consumer Statement Index)

Coincident Index:

- Employees on nonagricultural payrolls (employment)
- Personal income less transfer payments, in constant dollars (Personal Income)
- Industrial production index
- Manufacturing and trade sales, in constant dollars

Lagging Index:

- Average duration of unemployment (unemployment)
- Inventory-to-sales ratio for manufacturing and trade, in constant dollars (inventory-sales ratio)
- Labor cost per unit of output in manufacturing, monthly change (unit labor costs)
- Ratio of commercial installment credit outstanding to personal income
- Average prime rate charged by banks (interest rates)
- Consumer price index for services, monthly change (Consumer Price Index)

Since World War II, when the government began compiling these indexes, the leading index has consistently declined for nine months and the coincident/lagging ratio for thirteen months before the onset of a recession. Also, the leading index predicts an expansion in the economy four months before it begins, and the coincident/lagging index predicts such an expansion two months before the official turn. Although these indexes are only a rough guide to the direction of the economy, they can be useful in preparing pro forma forecasts and developing strategic plans.

Global economic conditions also affect an increasing number of companies. Those that import materials from abroad, that export products and services, or that have foreign subsidiaries or branches are affected by exchange rates, international financial markets, and economic cycles.

Stock market, commodity market, and currency market trends might also be relevant to the future growth of your company. To the extent that consumer or industrial buying habits are influenced by capital market trends, statistics related to these markets must be analyzed.

The number of sources of national and international economic, financial, and trade data boggles the mind. By far the biggest collector of such data is the federal government. The *Federal Reserve Bulletin, Statistical Abstract of the United States, Survey of Current Business*, and *Economic Report of the President* are popular sources. Eximbank puts out a wealth of data relating to international trade. The Department of Commerce offices in major cities are chock full of data, reports, government booklets, and a plethora of other information.

Many states and a few major cities also provide more localized economic and business data. California, New York, Texas, and Illinois all do excellent jobs, as do New York City, Los Angeles, and Chicago.

Major investment banks publish financial market statistics by the carload. Standard & Poor's, Moody's, Value Line, and Dun & Bradstreet compile valuable statistical tabulations. Money center banks like Citibank and Chase routinely circulate current economic trend information. The sources go on and on.

On the industry side, trade associations and trade magazines are invaluable sources of current data and statistical trends. The *U.S. Industrial Outlook* and Standard & Poor's *Industry Surveys* include data on most industries. And major securities houses like Merrill Lynch, Bear Stearns, and Prudential Securities, publish data on a wide range of industries. Once you start looking, you'll find an endless number of data sources. Just be careful to use only those indicators that relate to your company or your markets.

Chapter 3

Restructuring Strategies

It's hard to visualize a company that after a few years in business doesn't have at least some equipment, machinery, or vehicles that are no longer in use, or slow-moving or obsolete inventory that has piled up, or entire product lines that are losing money (or, at least, not as profitable as others). Many businesses also have excess space—spare offices, unused storage areas, idle production space, and so on. As a preliminary step in the strategic planning process, it pays to make a concerted effort to get rid of all assets or product lines that no longer generate enough income to justify keeping them. This accomplishes two important goals:

1. It frees up personnel for real growth activities.

2. It frees up capital that can be used to implement expansion or development strategies.

Selling unnecessary operating assets is a lot easier and can be done much faster than analyzing and then disposing of entire product lines or business units. It makes sense, therefore, to begin the consolidation effort here. Each of the five classes of assets—production machinery and equipment; office furniture, fixtures, and equipment; vehicles; inventory; and space—lends itself to a different approach.

PRODUCTION MACHINERY AND EQUIPMENT

Nearly every manufacturing company has machinery and equipment it doesn't use. Machinery purchased for a special order that has been completed and shipped. Excess equipment that remains after disposing of product lines. Broken pieces that have never been repaired. Forklift trucks that gather dust after changes in warehousing procedures. Machines that have been replaced with newer, state-of-the-art pieces. Equipment left in storage, in the corner, outside your plant, or at customers' facilities that is no longer needed to produce current product lines. Now is the time to gather these pieces and sell them off.

To get started, take a physical inventory of all machinery and equipment, clearly identifying those pieces that are currently used in production and segregating those pieces that were leased for a special job or borrowed from customers or other companies. Although you can't sell equipment that has been leased or borrowed, you can return it to its owners, thereby reducing lease payments and freeing up floor space.

Production machinery and equipment can be sold either all at once at auction or piecemeal to individual buyers. Private manufacturing companies that need specific pieces for special purposes buy used production machinery and equipment, as do used equipment dealers. The latter normally buy at auctions, the former by specific solicitation. Even in a depressed equipment market, higher prices can be realized by selling individual pieces than by mass sales at auctions. On the other hand, auctions take much less time, thus quickly freeing up personnel, floor space, and capital that can be applied to growth strategies.

An auction requires someone to handle the bidding and administrative chores (aptly called an auctioneer) and a location in which to hold the auction. The auctioneer advertises the sale, notifying interested parties of the place and date of the auction and of the specific pieces to be sold. The selling company must pay for this advertising, plus the auctioneer's out-of-pocket expenses and commission (normally 7 to 10 percent of the cash collected). Several reputable auction firms operate nationally and advertise in local newspapers. Secured lenders are also a good source of referrals.

The most readily accessible market for individual pieces of machinery and equipment is used machinery and equipment dealers. Names and addresses can be found in any metropolitan area telephone directory. Placing advertisements in the "Equipment for Sale" section of local newspapers also brings results. Some cities even have regional advertising tabloids that charge for the listing only when items are sold.

OFFICE FURNITURE, FIXTURES, AND EQUIPMENT

Used office furniture, fixtures, and equipment (FF&E) usually sells much faster than used production machinery and equipment. It seems that people are always on the lookout for FF&E bargains. Prices for individual pieces probably won't be as high as for production machinery and equipment, but at least the turnover is quicker.

Methods for selling used FF&E are about the same as for selling production pieces. Unless a company has a large quantity, however, national auctioneers won't be interested. You'll have to go with smaller, local firms. Also, auction commissions on small sales can run much higher—sometimes as much as one-third of the auction proceeds.

Used office furniture and equipment dealers are a good source for a quick, inexpensive sale. Local dealers frequently offer a flat price for all pieces, although prices are normally very low—about one-tenth of replacement cost. In most cases, companies come out ahead by selling FF&E piecemeal to individual buyers through newspaper advertisements and local circulars.

Used computers, printers, and peripheral equipment can be far more difficult to dispose of. Stiff competition among manufacturers and rapid technological changes have made it virtually impossible to sell used computer equipment for any reasonable price. Computer leasing companies buy recent-vintage equipment but are generally not interested in old models. A few computer exchange outlets that operate in the larger cities take used equipment on consignment. Most companies have better success advertising the sale of specific pieces in local newspapers and circulars.

VEHICLES

Practically everyone knows how to sell a car to a used car dealer or through a newspaper advertisement. Prices are negotiable, and the mechanics of the sale are relatively straightforward. Trucks and other road vehicles tend to be more difficult to dispose of, however, especially older ones. Newspaper "For Sale" advertisements work as well as anything. Occasionally a local auto repair shop will need a truck or car for its own use or for parts. Also, repair shops are a good source of referrals, as the owner of a rural lumberyard learned.

Although it specialized in lumber for do-it-yourselfers, who frequently required home delivery of small quantities, the yard also sold coal, sand, and gravel by the truckload. The battered trucks brought little as trade-ins and were usually junked when new models were purchased. One day the owner of an auto repair shop offered the yard $1,000 for a beat-up coal truck headed for the junk pile. He fixed up the engine and transmission and sold the truck for $1,900. The two entrepreneurs have since turned over four additional trucks that were too far gone to sell on the open market.

Forklifts, off-road vehicles, snowplows, trailers, electric carts, and other miscellaneous vehicles don't usually have much value. If you can get anything for them, the best source of buyers is other companies in the area. However, even if they can't be sold, at least junk them and get them off the premises. Space is a valuable commodity that could be leased or used to expand operations.

INVENTORY

Piles of production materials or stacks of unsold merchandise gathering dust don't create income; however, they do take up valuable space, require employee time to keep track of, and probably increase fire and casualty insurance premiums. Even if the materials may be needed at some indeterminable future date, the cost of maintaining an inventory usually outweighs the advantages of having "just-in-case" materials available. Part of the clean-up process should be to sell as much old inventory as possible. Markets can usually be found for inventory regardless of how old it may be. Even battered goods can be sold at distress sales.

Arranging a bulk sale to a secondhand dealer is certainly the quickest way to dispose of old inventory. Special sale advertisements in a local newspaper also seem to work well for many types of businesses. Employees may be anxious to buy the goods if they are usable. If all else fails, sell them to a junk dealer for any price you can get. Selling the merchandise at below cost might produce a book loss, but if you don't need the goods, cash in hand is better than inventory in the corner. In addition, losses are tax-deductible.

Excess production and office supplies should also be disposed of. Hardly any business is so efficient that it uses up all the odds and ends of its paper, cleaning solvent, computer printer ribbons, machine oil, lumber, and other supplies. These products seldom wear out, and although packaging may be dirty or dog-eared, they could still be worth something to somebody. Try selling them to employees or to other companies in your area. This usually works best for odd lots.

Spare parts for equipment that has been sold or junked and components for products that are no longer carried in inventory should also be sold. Customers that continue to use your old products may be more than willing to carry their own spare parts, especially if they can get them at a discount. Machine shops, distributors, repair businesses, and a variety of other companies in the business of fixing up equipment and machinery can probably use spare parts. If buyers can't be found, try a yard sale.

Turning old inventory into cash, regardless of the amount, is preferable to allowing it to gather dust. Consolidating inventory is as important a housecleaning step as disposing of old equipment and machinery, and generally much easier. Without question, there is a great temptation to rationalize keep old parts and materials on the theory that they may be needed in the future. However, with effective growth strategies in place, if you do need the old inventory, business should be booming and new items can be purchased.

Start cleaning up old inventory and supplies by counting the items on hand. This will most likely reveal parts, supplies, and materials that no one knew were there, as occurred in a small machine shop. In an effort to raise cash, the company listed all old inventory and supplies from its accounting records. The total was a meager $4,000. A count of all inventory in closets, old storerooms, and a distant warehouse uncovered items that everyone had forgotten about long ago, including two old bicycles and a pair of skis. This effort resulted in auction proceeds of $15,000, not $4,000 as originally estimated.

LEASING UNUSED ASSETS

One way to get over the psychological hurdle of fearing to sell space, machinery, or equipment, vehicles because you may need them in the future is to lease them out on short-term leases. Leasing is especially viable for temporarily converting unneeded floor space to cash. The garage that stores unused equipment won't be needed once the equipment is sold. That vacant lot down the street was a real bargain when you purchased it ten years ago; today the property is probably worth much more, and leasing it preserves the asset in case it is ever needed in the future. Perhaps it makes sense to consolidate a manufacturing plant that comprises several buildings and lease out one or more of them. How about that old house purchased a couple of years ago for extra offices that never materialized?

Leasing property frequently brings in more cash than selling it. This is especially true of office or storage space. Leasing real property is like an annuity—the cash keeps rolling in year after year. Leasing out office space is probably the easiest and fastest way to bring in extra capital. Perhaps at one time it made sense to use the space for file storage, conference rooms, a place for auditors to sit, employee exercise rooms, segregated computer rooms, two or three executive offices for expansion, or an employees' lunch room. But looking toward consolidation of assets as a preliminary step for long-term growth strategies, are these conveniences really necessary? When lease periods run out, you can always reclaim the space if you really need it.

Company cars, extra personal computers or other office equipment, surplus testing equipment, or an unused forklift can also be leased out. Given a choice between losing their company cars and leasing them from the company, most employees will opt for the latter. Holding on to extra computers in the expectation that they will be needed if and when additional employees are hired wastes money. Why not also lease computers to employees? Most would probably love to have one at home. If you expect to need that spare forklift for future growth, you can always rent it out on a month-to-month lease and reclaim it when you need it. The same principle holds for other production, testing, or support equipment.

Since the idea of leasing as opposed to selling assets is to keep them available for growth opportunities, it's usually a good idea to keep the lease period flexible—perhaps one year with mutually agreed upon options to renew. A contract clause that allows cancellation with ninety days' notice also adds flexibility.

PURGING PRODUCT LINES

Two fundamental principles underlie any successful business. It must:

1. Produce and/or sell only those products that contribute to the company's overall profitability

2. Produce and/or sell only those products that fit the company's primary mission

With the exception of very small service businesses, every company has underperforming products or product lines. These products are priced below total cost to meet competitive pressures or production costs, and/or that require extra efforts to sell, draining cash and other resources from the principal mission of the company.

A retail store might carry inventory that hasn't turned over in years, yet continues to take up space and management time and effort. This robs the business of much-needed cash that could be better used elsewhere. A manufacturing company might produce a dozen different product lines, of which two or three account for 80 percent of the company's profits. A service business might offer services at customer locations that cost two, three, or four times as much as they would if done in-house.

The tendency is to think of a company as a single unit, not a group of separate businesses. We organize our personnel, arrange financing, and develop plans along a single track. To reverse the field and view a company as a composite of separate, stand-alone businesses is a radical departure. Getting over this hurdle may require the engagement of professional advisors who are familiar with business segment accounting.

A case in point arose not long ago when a small-business client ran into trouble with a bank. The business consisted of two distinctly different activities and markets: (1) a distribution center that supplied disposable and nondisposable products to hospitals and other health care facilities, and (2) a home care segment that rented physical therapy equipment to homebound patients. The company's borrowing base (comprising receivables and inventory) was fully extended, but it still needed additional loans. The bank said no.

As an outsider, I saw that we had two businesses to deal with, not one, and that one (the home care segment) was highly profitable, whereas the other was dying on the vine. My client couldn't see this, arguing vociferously that despite separate personnel, floor space, pricing, advertising, delivery, and credit and collection activities, home care and distribution had to be looked at as one business.

Undaunted, I prepared a business segment analysis of the prior year's financial statement, a cash flow forecast for each segment, and business valuations for two stand-alone businesses. Proceeds from the eventual sale of the distribution center paid off all short-term bank debt, and the client's home care business became even more profitable than forecasted.

The first step in analyzing the potential disposal of unprofitable lines is to grasp the meaning of *business segments*. The most meaningful definition for private businesses is a product line or group of product lines, division, subsidiary, or market (such as exporting) that could operate efficiently as a stand-alone business with minor additions of support personnel or hard assets. They may or may not have synergistic characteristics, and transfers of products, services, or support activities between segments may or may not be desirable.

Once separate business segments have been defined, relevant data for each segment needs to be gathered and assimilated in anticipation of preparing business segment financial reports and probably cash flow forecasts. Some data is easily identifiable by segment—sales (or revenues), cost of sales, customer orders and backlog (if any), inventory, and probably receivables and payables. It may even be possible to identify specific machinery and vehicles (and related costs) dedicated to each segment.

Most companies code payroll records by job function and department. In that case, business segment labor hours, payroll, and numbers of employees can be accumulated. Costs of supervisory personnel should be related directly to the employees supervised.

Assuming that each business segment has dedicated sales personnel, then selling costs related to these employees (such as payroll, commissions, fringe benefits, travel and entertainment, samples, sales literature, and probably advertising expense) can be segregated. The cost of automobiles could also be related to specific sales personnel.

In the administrative expense category, such costs as payroll and fringe benefits of credit and collections employees and payroll clerks, auto insurance, product liability insurance, and the salary and benefits of business segment managers can usually be identified and segregated.

Although general-use assets, liabilities, and debt obligations appear to be unassignable, every attempt should be made to allocate as many items as possible. And the easiest way to do this is with a cost accounting system.

COST ACCOUNTING SYSTEM

Before a product line or business unit can be sold, a selling price must be established, and that calls for a determination of the product line or business unit's market value. To establish market value, the profit contribution and assets of each product line or business unit must be known. Sales, assets, and liabilities are relatively easy to segregate directly from basic accounting records. However, to segregate costs by product line or business unit, a company must have a functioning cost accounting system.

Although there seems to be a common assumption among business owners that cost accounting systems are a luxury reserved for large corporations, this is definitely not the case. Regardless of the size or type of company, the assignment of direct and indirect costs to products (or services) is essential in order to strategically determine which products or services should be emphasized in the marketplace and which should be eliminated.

A basic cost accounting system doesn't have to be complex. Many building blocks, such as payroll and inventory records, are probably already in place. A cost accounting system merely accumulates labor hours and inventory quantities in a disciplined manner, according to the specific products they relate to. Although companies with large volumes of transactions definitely need a computer to gather and sort data, smaller firms can easily install a manual cost accounting system based on existing payroll and inventory control records. The sample worksheet in Figure 3-1 demonstrates a typical format for the product line allocation of sales, costs, assets, and liabilities.

Care should be taken to include only those revenues, costs, assets, and liabilities that can be specifically identified with a product line or that can be reasonably allocated. Many costs and assets do not fit this mold. For example, the salaries and related fringe benefits of the general manager, controller, and other administrative personnel normally cannot be directly associated with a specific product line. The same holds for payments on leases of office equipment and computers, rental payments for an office or production facility, fire and casualty insurance premiums, real estate taxes, and a variety of other administrative overhead-type expenses.

Assets that normally cannot be assigned to product lines include company-owned factories, warehouses, stores, and offices; equipment used for all product lines, such as testing gauges, scales, or shipping tools; and company-owned vehicles used to deliver products or to pick up materials and components.

By segregating those costs and assets directly attributable to product lines, we can prepare separate balance sheets and income statements can be prepared. From these financial statements, cash flow forecasts can be constructed to determine the contribution each line makes to the overall growth strategies of the

Figure 3-1
Sample Worksheet to Segregate Product Lines

	Envelopes	Tables	Gloves	Shovels	Total Company
Income and Expenses					
Sales	———	———	———	———	———
Cost of sales					
Beginning inventory	———	———	———	———	———
Materials	———	———	———	———	———
Labor	———	———	———	———	———
Overhead allocation	———	———	———	———	———
Less: Ending inventory					
cost of sales	———	———	———	———	———
Gross profit	———	———	———	———	———
% of sales	———	———	———	———	———
Direct overhead costs					
not included in allocation					
Plant supervision	———	———	———	———	———
Delivery expenses	———	———	———	———	———
Sales commissions	———	———	———	———	———
Advertising	———	———	———	———	———
Other	———	———	———	———	———
Total direct overhead	———	———	———	———	———
Contribution margin	———	———	———	———	———
% of sales	———	———	———	———	———
Assets and Liabilities					
Accounts receivable					
Inventory					
Raw materials	———	———	———	———	———
Work in process	———	———	———	———	———
Finished goods	———	———	———	———	———
Fixed assets					
Land	———	———	———	———	———
Buildings	———	———	———	———	———
Machinery	———	———	———	———	———
Vehicles	———	———	———	———	———
Total	———	———	———	———	———
Less: Depreciation	———	———	———	———	———
Net	———	———	———	———	———
Total assets	———	———	———	———	———
Liabilities					
Accounts payable	———	———	———	———	———
Accrued expenses	———	———	———	———	———
Total liabilities*	———	———	———	———	———
Net book value	———	———	———	———	———

*If bank loans or other debt obligations can be specifically identified with product lines, such amounts should be included as product line liabilities along with trade payables and accrued expenses.

company. With a cost accounting system in place, managers can begin to weed out either those products that are not producing a profit or raise selling prices to profitable levels.

CORPORATE OFFICE COST CENTER

Those expenses and assets that remain after as much as possible has been allocated to business segments fall into the corporate office or headquarters pool. In some companies, virtually no corporate allocations can be reasonably made. In others, it's possible to allocate nearly all the salaries and expenses of management personnel (except business owners) to specific business segments. To the extent that separate facilities house different business units, the cost of buildings, improvements, and office equipment can be charged directly to the units. If all business segments occupy the same premises, however, it usually makes sense to treat common facilities as corporate office assets.

Some people dispute this approach, arguing that even if buildings and support equipment cannot be specifically identified with a business segment, they should be allocated—perhaps in proportion to the square footage used by each business segment—so that the corporate office cost center has zero assets. This has merit when the resultant business unit ratios are used for establishing product prices or other internal measures. However, it's difficult to see how an allocation of common assets (or costs) assists in determining the contribution of each unit to the company as a whole. If each business is viewed as a stand-alone entity that could be severed from the total company without endangering other business segments, clearly allocated floor space or allocated costs become meaningless.

Theoretically, business segments benefit from a corporate office through the sharing of certain managerial tasks. (In smaller businesses the corporate office comprises the business owner and supporting staff, perhaps a secretary, a controller, and a receptionist.) If operated separately, each business segment would need a general manager and support personnel, thereby increasing total administrative overhead.

In many cases, however, segregated businesses can run efficiently on their own, making a corporate office an unnecessary overhead expense that drains cash. If we look at each business segment separately, corporate office expenses might very well stand out as unproductive luxuries.

The following are typical corporate office expenses that cannot logically be allocated to operating units:

- Salary, fringes, and expenses of the business owner/manager
- Salary, fringes, and expenses of secretaries, receptionists, office clerks, custodians, and so on
- Salary, fringes, and expenses of the accounting/finance function
- Property, liability, and casualty insurance
- Office rent
- Office equipment, maintenance, and telephone expense

- Professional fees—legal, accounting, consulting
- Charitable contributions, goodwill promotion and public relations expenses, overall company advertising

In certain companies, one or more of these expenses might be reasonably allocated, but in most cases they cannot be.

One way to test the reasonableness of corporate office expenses is to compare the ratios of expenses to sales and expenses to equity with the same ratios from public companies in similar industries. Although large corporations certainly have many more levels of administrative overhead than private businesses, theoretically at least, the ratios of expenses to owners' equity and expenses to sales should be somewhat comparable. Several analytical studies of the twenty-five largest industrial companies conducted over the past ten years indicate that the ratios of corporate overhead to owners' equity ranged from 0.3 percent all the way to 9 percent, with the ratio of corporate overhead to sales running from 0.1 percent to 2.7 percent.

Benefits derived from a corporate administrative cost center are difficult to calculate, however, in some companies they can be substantial. Broadly speaking, administrative activities benefit a total company in two ways.

- By filing one tax return as a corporate entity, the company as a whole can garner tax savings by using losses from one business unit to offset taxable income from another unit or by leveraging the company at the corporate level with corresponding tax deductions for interest expense. (Obviously, without corporate debt and interest expense, tax savings won't occur.)
- Intangible, qualitative benefits may be derived from vertically integrated economies of scale, overall management direction, improved communications throughout the company, relationships with external parties (such as banks and the financial community), and so on.

Evaluating Business Segment Contributions

By segregating profits, assets, and liabilities by business segment, a company immediately knows where to concentrate future growth efforts and which business lines should be sold or liquidated. Such an exercise also clears the air about the positive or negative contribution of nonproductive administrative activities. More often than not, once this exercise has been completed, it becomes obvious that corporate administrative costs should be trimmed back. And with financing becoming increasingly costly and difficult to attract, the disposal of cash-draining business segments can have a dramatic effect on both the total company's immediate cash flow and its prospects for achieving strategic growth plans.

A multibusiness company called Multicorp was used for demonstration purposes in *The Small Business Valuation Book*, and is a good example of how business unit valuations form the foundation for restructuring an average company into a clear winner. To get the full benefit of the following evaluation, readers should refer to Chapter 12, "Multibusinesses," in the above book. The average statistics from a five-year forecast of results from the Multicorp business segments were as follows.

FIVE-YEAR AVERAGES

	Catalog	Made-to-Order	Retail Store	Corporate Office	Total Company
Sales	1,324	628	2,395		4,347
After-tax profit	(11)	75	213	(140)	137
Total assets	142	557	2,564	2,037	5,300
Total debt	0	23	600	105	728
Return on equity	0	20%	13%	0	6%
Cash flow for the entire period	(97)	323	835	(711)	350
Present value	(73)	241	597	(581)	184

This data reveals several alternatives for improving the company's profitability and return on investment. The most obvious alternative appears to be the sale or liquidation of the catalog business. To the extent that a selling price in excess of the catalog unit's liabilities could be negotiated, this would be the preferable route. Otherwise its inventory could be liquidated at cost (at a minimum), creating a one-time cash drain of $22 (which represents the excess of liabilities over inventory book value). Figure 3-2 shows the impact of this strategy on the total company.

A second alternative might be to reduce corporate overhead by (1) laying off the corporate sales manager (1992 expense of $75) and (2) subletting building space occupied by the catalog unit ($10 pretax income per year). These two steps in conjunction with the disposal of the catalog unit result in the impact on the total company shown in Figure 3-3 (page 60).

By making three strategic moves—(1) disposing of the catalog business unit, (2) laying off corporate sales personnel, and (3) subletting building space previously occupied by the catalog unit—Multicorp could more than double its market value, from $184 to $414.

Once the profitability, cash flow, and fair market value for each business segment are known, many alternative strategies become available. Those most commonly open to private businesses include options to:

- Sell a business unit
- Liquidate cash-draining business segments
- Purchase a company complementary to the business unit
- Redirect advertising and other sales promotion efforts
- Redesign pricing policies
- Redirect management efforts
- Restructure the administrative organization

Figure 3-2
Option #1: Liquidate Catalog Resale

FIVE-YEAR AVERAGES

	Made-to-Order	Retail Store	Corporate Office	Total Company without Catalog	Total Company with Catalog
Ratios					
Sales	628	2,395		3,023	4,347
After-tax profit	75	213	(140)	148	137
Total assets	557	2,564	2,037	5,158	5,300
Total debt	23	600	105	728	728
Return on equity	20%	13%	0	6%	6%
Cash Flow					
Cash flow for the entire period	323	835	(711)	447	350
Less cash shortfall on liquidating catalog segment				(22)	0
Net cash flow				425	350
Present Value					
Present value	241	597	(581)	235	184
Less present value of tax savings from catalog operating loss				(25)	0
Net present value				210	184

- Refinance debt structures for specific business segments
- Raise new equity capital
- Sell the entire company at a premium price

As previously pointed out, the key to business segmentation is a workable cost accounting system. If your company already has a cost accounting system in place, establishing a chart of accounts commensurate with business segments and recoding transactions to accumulate costs, revenues, assets, and liabilities for each segment becomes a relatively simple matter.

Business segments can be analyzed without a cost accounting system, but the analysis is much more difficult and less accurate. Therefore, regardless of how you keep your financial accounting records and whether or not your company prepares formal financial statements, at least a basic cost accounting system should be installed before implementing a growth-oriented strategic plan. It's the only feasible way to track business segment profitability and cash flows, and in the long run it's well worth the money and effort required to install it.

Figure 3-3
Option #2: Reduce Corporate Overhead

FIVE-YEAR AVERAGES

	Made-to-Order	Retail Store	Corporate Office	Total Company without Catalog	Total Company with Catalog
Ratios					
Sales	628	2,395		3,023	4,347
After-tax profit	75	213	(83)	205	137
Total assets	557	2,564	2,037	5,158	5,300
Total debt	23	600	105	728	728
Return on equity	20%	13%	0	9%	6%
Cash Flow					
Cash flow for the entire period	323	835	(426)	732	350
Less cash shortfall on liquidating catalog segment				(22)	0
Net cash flow	323	835	(426)	710	350
Present Value					
Present value	241	597	(399)	439	184
Less present value of tax savings from catalog operating loss				(25)	0
Net present value				414	184

Once the amount of cash flow contributed (or drained) by each business segment has been calculated and tested over time (generally the shorter of one year or half a business cycle—trending either upward or downward, alternative strategies for disposing of unwanted segments can be evaluated.

Business segments may be disposed of in several ways. Products may be withdrawn from the market, personnel directly attributable to that business segment dismissed, and assets sold. Fire sales can liquidate inventory. Or perhaps a competitor stands ready to buy the inventory in bulk. The biggest benefit, however, usually comes from selling the product line and its associated assets as a going business. This tactic is known as a *spin-off*.

SPIN-OFFS

Selling an entire product line (a division, subsidiary, or business segment) is much like selling a company. The sale includes not only the product's engineering drawings, name, and patents (if any), but also its raw material, work in process, and finished goods inventory; its customer list, order backlog, and receivables; any machinery, test equipment, or vehicles associated with the line;

and land and buildings, if it occupies a separate facility. Not infrequently, buyers retain most of the personnel responsible for the product line.

Preparing for a spin off is relatively simple:

1. Segregate the business to be spun off into a separate corporation
2. Set up separate accounting records so that sales, costs, and therefore profits of the new corporation can be maintained apart from those of the parent business
3. If possible, move all machinery, equipment, vehicles, and inventory needed to produce and sell the products into a separate facility, even if it must be leased specifically for this purpose. (If this is impractical, at least segregate the assets in a separate section of your facility.)
4. Set up a separate payroll system for the new corporation, and pay all supervisors and workers from it
5. Once these steps have been completed, proceed with a normal divestiture

Legally, a spin-off is a sale of assets. The same bulk sales laws that apply when all of a company's assets are sold also apply to spin-offs. The tax recognition of capital gains and ordinary income is also the same. In addition, the tax code's built-in gains provisions might apply if your company has elected to be taxed as an S corporation.

Spinning off a product line, especially if the products are profitable, produces several benefits:

1. The capital raised can be used to reduce outstanding debt obligations, clearing the way for future borrowings
2. If the product line has commercial value, its selling price should exceed the cost of its supporting assets and this incremental cash premium would probably not be realized simply by continuing to sell the products in the marketplace
3. After the spin off has been completed, additional cost-cutting moves should be feasible, such as personnel layoffs, a sale or lease of excess production and storage space, and a lowering of personal property taxes

Locating buyers for product lines is not as difficult as it may appear, especially if the assets are already segregated in a separate division or subsidiary. Very often competitors are viable buyers. If they already have plans to expand into one of the spun-off product lines, buying the entire line is usually much cheaper and faster than picking up an entire company or starting from scratch.

Customers are also viable candidates. Larger companies might be planning to extend their vertical integration and could be eager to acquire a source of supply for components, subassemblies, or spare parts.

People who are currently employed in producing or selling these products are probably the most likely buyers. Management buyouts (MBOs) can be structured relatively quickly, and financing is seldom a problem. Banks, secured lenders, and even certain venture capital firms tend to bend over backwards to accommodate an MBO. It's also possible to finance the deal through an employee stock ownership plan (ESOP).

Spinout IPOs

In recent years, the advent of reverse leveraging [returning the equity of prior years' leveraged buyouts (LBOs) to the public markets] and privatizations (the selloff of government-owned businesses to the private sector), coupled with a strong stock market and a relatively stable economy, have encouraged the use of a creative innovation called the *spinout IPO* as a viable way to dispose of segregated business units. Although several well-known companies have successfully gone this route—including Bally International, Waste Management, Phillips Petroleum, and American Express—it is certainly not a tactic reserved for large corporations. Small businesses can also use the technique effectively.

This is how a spinout IPO works: Assume that a company, YSO, Inc., has several diversified manufacturing divisions, one of which makes refrigerators. As part of its consolidation, and prior to implementing its long-term strategic growth plan, YSO, Inc. forms a new corporation, Freeze-Out Corporation. It then sells its refrigerator division to Freeze-Out, for stock. YSO, Inc. next takes Freeze-Out public with an initial public offering (IPO). Initial shares totaling a 65 percent interest in Freeze-Out sell for $20.

The market judges the investment potential of Freeze-Out on the basis of its own performance and projections, completely separate from the business of YSO, Inc. After the IPO, the parent company still owns 35 percent of the outstanding shares of Freeze-Out but has been relieved of financial responsibility for the business. So everyone wins!

On the downside, however, spinout IPOs can be very costly. All the accounting, registration, and legal costs of a normal stock registration apply to spinouts (see Chapter 13). In addition, a spinout forces a more arm's-length relationship with the parent, especially when pricing goods and services for transfer between entities. This takes extra administrative and accounting effort, and managers tend to become absorbed in these administrative details rather than managing the business.

Still, if the shoe fits, spinout IPOs can be a clever way to dispose of an ill-fitting business unit or product line while simultaneously raising new capital for expansion. It's important to point out once again that spinout IPOs are not restricted to large corporations. Companies of any size with separate divisions, business segments, or subsidiaries can use the technique effectively.

One word of caution: Highly leveraged companies that choose this route should price the public stock issue with care. Investors in today's markets are becoming increasingly queasy about bailing out reverse LBOs. Some make sense; a great many do not. Not many investors will buy the gimmick used by some reverse LBO managers of coming out with a conservative price and then pushing it up after investors have a chance to study the company's financial statements. Such a tactic might work occasionally, but more often it will fail.

Chapter 4

Marketing Strategies

Marketing strategies are the heart of growth-oriented strategic plans. They focus on strengthening marketing organizations, eliminating unprofitable or low-margin products, optimizing customer configurations, evaluating pricing policies, targeting advertising programs, and coordinating new product development efforts. Like other parts of a strategic plan, the marketing segment should be proactive, not reactive, and strategies must be devised with an eye toward expected changes in market demands. While marketing policies should target new customers and new products, they must also focus on strengthening current positions in the marketplace. This entails the development of strategies to gain and retain control over product pricing, distribution systems, and packaging.

Once achieved, market control enables companies to implement innovative after-sale customer service policies, new product introductions, and selective sales tactics commensurate with long-range growth strategies. In the short term, market control enhances the management of inventory levels, credit sales collections, and personnel utilization. This chapter looks at ways to enhance competitive positions under an umbrella of strategies loosely referred to as *focused marketing*.

FOCUSED MARKETING

Focused marketing defines a set of actions designed to maximize the sales volume of the products with the highest gross margin in those market niches in which the company has the largest share and hence the greatest control. Market control is the key to focused marketing. In addition to enhancing the management of product and customer mix, market control leads to the optimization of sales turnover. This, in turn, encourages the most efficient use of sales tools to keep selling expenses at the lowest possible level. Market control is achieved by actions taken in one or a combination of three areas: product mix, customer mix, and after-sale service.

Optimizing product mix involves the selective selling of products that optimally match sales volume and profit margin. Managing customer mix means identifying and concentrating on customers willing and able to pay the highest prices for the quality and quantity of products that can be produced most efficiently. Cost-effective after-sale service ensures repeat sales of the right products to the right customers. Market control strategies coupled with cost-effective selling tactics should yield the optimum profits for practically any company.

The starting point in achieving market control is to specifically define those markets currently being served. Most markets can be defined geographically (by neighborhood, city, or region; national; or global), by type of customer (upscale, budget, prime contractors, chain stores), by pricing strategy (high-end, mid-range, or low-end), by quality standards (top-of-the-line or throwaways), or by product specifications (standard shelf products or made-to-order products).

No company, large or small, can afford to be all things to all customers. Those that try to serve a wide range of markets are generally unable to control any of them. Rather than spreading resources over a broad spectrum, it makes sense to identify those specific markets that offer the greatest opportunity, then structure a marketing plan to control those markets.

In the context of this book, the term *product* refers to services offered for sale as well as tangible products. And when we talk about *product mix*, we are referring to a range of services as well as a range of goods.

CHANGING PRODUCT MIX

Most companies sell more than one product. Obviously retail stores do. Manufacturing firms usually produce at least three or four different products, and often many more. Service businesses generally offer a variety of products, each priced differently. Government regulations, demographic shifts, consumer convenience, distribution networks, product selection, and a variety of other factors affect market demand for one class of products rather than another. Although small businesses tend to believe that they are at the mercy of such uncontrollable market forces and can do little to influence customer preference, this does not have to be the case. Most companies do have the ability to influence market demand at least to some extent, making the management of product mix a very viable strategy for controlling their own destiny.

Take, for example, a generic product like paint. In many parts of the country, ease of cleaning up, quick drying characteristics, and promotional advertising have given latex paints a significant sales edge over oil-based paints, especially for do-it-yourself homeowners. Quite naturally, therefore, paint stores stock more latex than oil-based paints. Stores carry a range of brands from several latex paint manufacturers with customers' choices affected by various sales promotions, advertising, prices, manufacturers' reputations, and availability of colors. Market shares remain fairly constant, controlled primarily by perceived standards, price, and special promotions.

However, assume that a manufacturer promotes an oil-based paint as being easier to clean up, providing better coverage, coming in a broader choice of colors, and boasting greater longevity than latex brands. To appeal to upscale buyers, the manufacturer prices this new paint higher than other oil-based and latex paints. With the proper sales pitch, it's entirely possible that this oil-based line will outsell latex, and therefore change proportionate market shares. Unless the oil-based line fails to perform as promoted, the manufacturer has exerted market control and improved its profit margins simply by changing its product mix strategy.

Another method of increasing market share by shifting product mix is product pruning. In most companies, 20 percent of the products account for 80 percent of the profits, for a very logical reason. Over time, businesses tend to add products as market conditions change, but they seldom remove slow-moving products unless they become technically obsolete. This is especially true in retail and manufacturing companies, but it applies in service businesses as well.

By pruning out, or deleting, all or some of the 80 percent of products that account for 20 percent of profits, companies can achieve several benefits. As product lines are deleted, internal cost reductions should follow, simply because as a result of the pruning process personnel whose activities are dedicated to those products are no longer needed. On-hand inventory of deleted products can also be disposed of. New purchases of materials and supplies will end. And, in many cases, selling expenses can be eliminated.

These cost reductions invariably create greater production efficiency and productivity for the remaining products (which in turn reduces their unit costs). Such cost savings can then be passed on to customers through lower prices for the remaining 20 percent of the products without hurting margins. By lowering prices, the company should realize increased market shares, at least temporarily. Such a temporary advantage can often turn into a permanent one if the company follows price reductions with improved customer service. The same types of cost reductions resulting from the elimination of noncritical products allow customer service personnel to spend more time and greater effort servicing sales of the remaining products.

When products are pruned, total sales drop. This can be a frightening experience, but it should not adversely affect your company. On the contrary, if the deleted products did not contribute to the company's overall profit, the cost of producing and selling them was probably equal to or greater than the sales revenues generated. Therefore, a reduction in sales should bring reduced costs with no adverse affect on either profits or cash flow.

In fact, just the opposite usually occurs. As nonproductive overhead drops, overall profits improve. Margins for the remaining products increase, not only because fewer people are on the payroll, but also because nonpayroll costs vary to a large extent with the number of people employed. Fewer people use fewer supplies, make fewer telephone calls, and require less electricity. Reductions in all of these costs improve overall company profit margins.

Intentionally shrinking the product offering also reduces purchases of materials and supplies. Not only does this save cash that can then be used more effectively to support growth strategies, it also permits purchasing personnel to concentrate more fully on buying the materials needed to produce the remaining products. Such concentrated efforts to search out new suppliers offering lower prices, better terms, or more effective delivery times should further improve margins. Clearly, companies whose products have a high material content will reap the greatest benefits, but service and retail businesses should be able to realize some savings from prudent selection of suppliers.

The pruning of low-margin products should also bring in fresh cash from the sale of machinery, equipment, and facilities that supported these product lines. Whether they are sold individually or through the spin-off of an entire business unit, assets dedicated to products that are no longer sold should be disposed of as soon as possible. The cash raised can then be used to reduce outstanding debt (thereby adding to flexibility) or reserved for the implementation of future growth strategies.

CHANGING CUSTOMER MIX

For the most part, smart customers—that is, customers who focus on getting the most value for their dollar—practice brand loyalty and are willing to pay a higher price for quality items, efficient deliveries, and after-sale service. Optimizing your customer mix can do more to gain market control than virtually any other single action. Moreover, this principle applies to practically any type of business or market. Two cases illustrate how optimizing customer mix works in different types of businesses.

After more than thirty years of selling high-end furniture, the top salesman in a suburban store retired. Subsequently, sales of higher-priced styles slipped badly. The store owner noticed that the three remaining salespeople steered customers to lower-end merchandise. Although price-shoppers responded well, customers looking for value did not, and they often left the store without buying anything. Sales of low-end furniture began to increase, but because such sales generated lower margins, overall profits declined.

As a corrective strategy, the store owner directed one salesperson to handle nothing but high-priced goods, and to pass price-shoppers on to the other two. In six months, sales of high-end furniture had substantially increased—as did company profits—while sales of low-end pieces remained nearly level.

In another case, the owner of an auto repair shop took the time to explain to customers the reasons for their cars' failures and how they might avoid such repairs in the future. Even though the shop's prices were substantially higher than competitors', business boomed. In an interview for a local newspaper, the owner was asked why business continued to boom during the recent recession. He replied, "Because educated customers are smart buyers. Smart buyers, knowing that they are not being ripped off, become loyal customers. And as loyal customers, they are usually willing to pay higher prices for superior service."

Selling to smart customers nearly always increases market share. Most smart buyers are willing to pay for quality products. Customer loyalty is easier to establish with smart customers. Delivery aggravations tend to disappear when a smart buyer understands why the truck didn't arrive on time. And repeat business is much easier to nurture with smart buyers. These factors add up to market control and therefore increased market share.

You can also manage customer mix by discouraging certain types of buyers. One of the objectives of managing customer mix is to concentrate on those customers who generate the highest margin per product sold. Margins are not determined by price alone, although certainly price is a major influence. The costs of convincing customers to buy your products, the expenses of getting products to customers, presale storage expenses, sales commissions, and other selling expenses—all reduce selling prices and therefore margins.

For example, assume that a company sells hand tools to three classes of customers: discount retail chains, privately owned hardware stores, and manufacturing companies. Production cost for all three classes of customer is identical. Manufacturing companies are willing to pay the highest price because they like the quality of the tools, although this class also accounts for the lowest volume. Hardware stores buy a greater volume, but since they aren't as concerned about quality they demand lower prices. Discount chains are mainly concerned with volume and buy large quantities at the lowest possible prices.

Further assume that the company must employ four salespeople to cover discount chains, and two to handle hardware sales, and that all manufacturing sales are house accounts. Also, manufacturing customers pick up from the factory, hardware stores want door-to-door delivery, and chains will buy only through regional distributors.

To maximize margins, the company must compare not only the sales volume generated by each customer class, but the associated selling costs as well. In this example, the cost of getting the product to the chain stores was three times that of selling to manufacturers and one and one-half times as high as that of selling to hardware stores. By emphasizing sales to manufacturers, the company earns more profits with lower sales volume. Although the age-old argument that you must have volume to cover overhead has a ring of truth, without corresponding margin improvements, volume increases alone seldom contribute much toward long-term growth.

For companies that sell industrial/commercial products, a second criterion should also be used to evaluate customer mix: the current status and future potential of customers' industries. If a customer's industry is booming or is likely to boom in the foreseeable future, it's reasonable to expect accelerated demand for your products—be they parts, components, subassemblies, machinery, vehicles, production materials, or supplies. Conversely, customers in declining industries, or those in the throes of recession, will most likely decrease future orders and/or demand price concessions.

In some cases industries may be affected by declining business cycles, only to bounce back, healthier than ever, in a short time (this is the case with most construction market niches). Clearly, it makes sense to stay with customers in this situation, looking toward profitable, long-term relationships even though sales and profits may decline in the short term.

On the other hand, several industries continue to change very rapidly. The telecommunications, computer, and pharmaceutical industries are cases in point.

Customers in these industries that do not have the managerial or technical capability to keep up, or those with balance sheets so overleveraged that they cannot exploit changing market or product requirements, probably cannot be relied upon for future growth potential. They should be de-emphasized as quickly as possible to make resources available for more lucrative opportunities.

Still other industries are in long-term declines, such as the agricultural equipment and traditional energy-generating equipment industries, as well as several segments of the defense industry. Sales to customers in these industries will inevitably decrease over time. To continue pouring resources into these markets that could otherwise be put to more productive use doesn't make sense. The only logical strategy is to begin shifting away from these customers as soon as possible.

Other facets of customer mix should also enter the equation. Will policies that emphasize sales to customers who are willing to buy long production runs of products rather than short runs increase long-term growth? Can you improve margins by concentrating on customers who demand high-quality products that may cost more to produce but sell at higher prices, or just the reverse (the Cadillac versus Ford comparison)? Will expanding your geographical customer base be more profitable than contracting it?

The type of business you have determines how answers to these questions will affect your customer mix. However, regardless of which specific tactics have the greatest impact, focusing on the management of customer mix should enhance the contribution of marketing strategies to achieving long-term growth objectives.

AFTER-SALE CUSTOMER SERVICE

In nearly every industry, competitive pressures are forcing increased emphasis on after-sale customer service. For most businesses, efficient after-sale service stimulates customer loyalty and repeat business, and therefore should be the cornerstone of any focused marketing strategy. Sears and General Electric have both proven time and again that attention to customer service increases sales from previous customers and new customers alike. Generally, the smaller the company, the more important after-sale service becomes.

After-sale service takes many forms, depending on the type of business. You might need an 800 number that customers can use to get technical information or instructions about the product. Perhaps a "no-questions-asked" return policy is appropriate. Some companies find that free or low-priced repair service at customer locations gives them a competitive edge. Others offer free delivery, advance notice of sales promotions, telephone ordering, or customer training.

Regardless of the type of service offered, focused marketing strategies should include more or better after-sale services than competitors offer. This normally low-cost effort can have a marked effect on positioning your company as a market leader. Some businesses have come up with innovative gimmicks for after-sale service that quickly set them apart from their competitors. The owner of a hardware store, for instance, found that providing customers with free saw and knife sharpening not only increased business but brought free advertising through local newspaper coverage. In another case, a computer store doubled software sales by offering customers a free three-hour training class.

Concentrating in growth markets, optimizing product mix, managing customer mix, and creating an after-sale customer service edge are all effective strategies aimed at increasing market control. They won't all work with equal effectiveness for all companies. However, they all merit serious consideration as marketing strategies aimed at long-term growth.

COST-EFFECTIVE SALES TACTICS

Although market control strategies form the foundation of fast-track marketing plans, cost-effective sales tactics are the tools to implement such plans. In price-competitive markets, companies frequently look to price-cutting tactics as a primary means of increasing sales. Practically any business can lower its prices to below the competition's and attract price-conscious buyers. However, this nearly always results in short-term benefits, not long-term gains. When price cutting causes sales to increase at least as much as unit margins decrease, companies benefit—at least, until the competition retaliates. Then, as prices continue to drop, margins wither away, and without corrective action, companies go out of business.

Fortunately, there are ways to increase sales volume without wholesale price cutting. Whether you sell products or services, tactics other than price cutting should result in a healthier company over the long run. The fundamental principle behind cost-effective sales tactics is that the broader the customer base, the greater the probability of increasing market share and improving market control.

Promotional efforts that encourage the same customer base to buy larger quantities achieve short-term results, but unless customers' buying habits can be altered, they will eventually slip back to their old ways. Although sales promotion efforts vary significantly by size of company, geographical coverage, and type of product or service, the following tactics can be implemented in varying degrees by most small businesses. It's important to recognize that these tactics are only illustrative of what can be done. They should, however, stimulate ideas applicable to your business. Examples of selling tactics that should increase profitable sales include:

- Volume pricing
- Incentive returns
- Same-day delivery
- Customer training
- Barter arrangements

Volume Pricing

We are all familiar with how volume pricing works. If you normally buy one pair of shoes for $100 and a sales promotion offers a second pair for $5, each pair actually costs $52.50. Or if customers usually buy one can of oil for $2 and a special promotion offers a case of 12 cans for $18 the price per can drops to $1.50. Volume pricing promotions have been commonplace in retail businesses for years.

Many retail establishments that offer such discounts don't suffer any loss of margin because manufacturers or distributors pay for the promotions. Permanent volume pricing is not as common, however. In fact, without support from distributors or manufacturers, most retailers promote volume pricing only for very short periods. The one exception arises when you exercise pricing control over a specific market niche. In that case, permanent volume pricing may be just the ticket to discourage new competitors from entering the market.

Although service businesses tend to stay away from volume pricing, in certain cases this strategy can work as well for them as for retail establishments. Take an auto repair shop, for instance. One way for it to attract new customers might be to offer customers regular maintenance work— oil changes, lubrication jobs, state inspections, minor tune-ups, and so on) for a second car at half the price for the first car.

Such volume pricing can be extended to many other service businesses as well. Tax return preparers could offer discounts for multiple returns from the same family. Dentists could use the same family-discount approach. Dry cleaners could use two-for-one sales on women's or men's suits. Lawn-cutting services could offer discount pricing for contracts that cover all the lawns in a given neighborhood.

Some volume pricing promotions turn into permanent discounting. Others are effective for short periods. Although such promotions don't add to sustainable growth for all businesses, those that can use the technique often find that it not only strengthens market control but actually increases unit margins over the long term by permitting more efficient use of personnel.

Incentive Returns

Incentive return promotions work well for retail and manufacturing businesses. Incentive return policies are based on the premise that if customers do not like the product they have purchased, they can return it with no questions asked. For years Sears has applied this policy to sales of its Craftsman line of hand and power tools, as well as other selected products. Many major retail department stores have adopted the same policy.

Generally, any business that offers generic rather than proprietary products can use incentive return policies as effective sales tactics. If a product really does meet market demand, there shouldn't be too many returns. However, the fact that stores offer a money-back guarantee induces customers to give the product a chance.

Of course, money-back guarantee promotions can also backfire. A flood of returns could eat up profits from new sales in a hurry. Although this shouldn't happen with quality products that already enjoy market acceptance, it might very well occur with new product introductions. Several retail stores have learned the hard way not to use this promotion for newly introduced low-end Asian imports, for example, because too many are poorly constructed. If the promotion takes hold, stores can get stuck with a pile of useless, broken merchandise.

Same-Day Delivery

Same-day delivery, or same-day service, is an excellent promotional scheme for increasing sales at very little additional cost. As our economy becomes increasingly attuned to a "buy it now, have it now" attitude, we become more and more frustrated with waiting days (or often weeks) for purchased products to arrive or for service to be performed. Companies willing to guarantee same-day delivery have found this to be an extraordinarily effective sales tactic that practically ensures a competitive edge.

Despite the fact that most people regard time as a valuable commodity, few businesses pay any attention to rapid service. Manufacturers, retailers, and service firms want their bills paid on time, but all too often, they do not reciprocate. A postal system that requires four days to fly a letter from New York to Los Angeles and five days to transport a letter ninety miles from New York to Philadelphia seems to reflect the general lack of concern for product delivery service that pervades our economy.

Although sales tactics that promise and then fulfill same-day delivery within a specified area almost always bring in new customers, for some businesses, same-day delivery is impossible. In my consulting business, for example, it is physically impossible to deliver a report to a client the same day the work is performed, and of course clients realize this. But an extension of the same-day-delivery philosophy—that is, to deliver work at a promised time—furthers long-term growth in consulting and other service businesses. If you promise to deliver on Wednesday, or next Monday, or the first of next month, keep the promise. Customers schedule their time around your promises, and since so few businesses perform as promised, those that do reap substantial rewards.

Doing what you say you are going to do when you promise you will do it will inevitably increase service sales as effectively as rapid delivery does in product businesses. It is simply good public relations. Turning it around, when a plumber, electrician, or furnace repairperson promises to take care of your service problems tomorrow and actually does so, the chances are very good that you will call that person again when the service is needed.

Customer Training

Some businesses sell technical products (such as personal computer software) whose use requires a certain level of customer expertise. Many software retailers offer customer training classes, but also charge fairly high prices for them. Beating the competition by offering free customer training classes can be a great way to increase sales.

A case in point arose not long ago with a retailer whose only product was computer software. Competition was fierce, and new stores were opening every week, selling software along with computer hardware and repair services. Even the large department store chains competed. The store's owner began offering free training classes every Saturday morning in Lotus 1-2-3, WordPerfect, and Ventura desktop publishing programs. To gain admittance, customers had to bring at least one guest. The result? A substantial increase in software sales and an invitation from the local division of a large corporation to conduct private training classes for a substantial fee.

Customer training promotions don't have to be free. As long as the fee charged is less than that charged by competitors, customer training is almost a sure-fire way to increase sales in many types of businesses. The best part about customer training promotions is that they cost very little to implement.

Barter Arrangements

As a means of conducting trade, barter has been around since caveman days. Bartering indigenous goods for imported goods is common practice in Latin America, South and East Asia, Africa, and other developing areas, and for small businesses (as well as giants like 3M Corporation), barter is rapidly becoming an accepted means of doing business in the United States. Barter is simply the exchange of one product or service for another. In some cases, part of the purchase price may be paid in cash; however, in most cases, only goods and services are involved.

Barter is an excellent tactic for increasing sales when credit is tight. For example, assume that company A wants to sell office furniture to company B, which distributes cut meat to restaurants. But B is in financial trouble and cannot raise sufficient cash to make the purchase. The two companies strike a barter deal. A sells desks, chairs, and lamps worth $2,500 to B in exchange for various cuts of beef and pork. Company A then makes a deal with two restaurants to take delivery of the meat from B's warehouse and pay A $3,000, which is 10 percent below the price charged by the local meat packer for similar cuts. The two restaurants are happy with the 10 percent discount. B gets its new office furniture. Company A makes an extra $500 profit above its normal margin. It's a win-win-win situation for everyone.

This is a classic example of how barter deals can be used to increase sales. It sounds complex, but it really isn't. A third-party barter deal does, however, require extra effort to locate appropriate buyers for the bartered goods.

Although barter won't always work, on certain occasions it can be used effectively to stimulate sales of other products. Any repair business is ideally suited to barter arrangements. So are personal service businesses. For example, lawyers can exchange legal services for advertisements in local newspapers. CPAs can exchange tax return preparation for office supplies. Medical practitioners can exchange diagnostic and treatment services for office rent or office furniture.

Probably the most difficult part of using barter as a marketing strategy is finding a mechanism for informing potential customers of the type of barter arrangements you will take. Unfortunately, there isn't any easy way to do this. Soliciting barter sales takes creativity and a certain sophistication on the part of customers. Customers who have lived overseas or spent any time doing business in developing countries will, of course, know how barter works. Many others, however, may be leery of barter overtures.

One method that seems to bring good results is to run advertisements in local newspapers, explaining what barter is all about and what type of barter you are promoting. Also, several barter brokerages are being formed around the country that can assist in arranging barter deals. Several trade associations have begun assisting members in locating such houses.

COST-EFFECTIVE SALES PROMOTIONS

Sales promotions form an integral part of any effective marketing strategy and, if properly structured, cost very little to implement. Some expense is usually involved, however, since it's hard to implement a sales promotion without advertising it. One drawback to many sales promotions is that managing them takes a fair amount of time, and in businesses with very few employees, that time just isn't available.

Before spending money to advertise a sales promotion, try to visualize how the mechanics will work and what benefits can be expected. The five-step questionnaire in Figure 4-1 (page 74) should be helpful in making these determinations.

Item 5 deserves special attention. It is all too easy to begin a sales promotion without giving any thought to who will manage it. As with every business activity, someone must be in charge. Someone must have the responsibility for putting all the pieces together and making sure that the promotion gets implemented as planned. And someone must be accountable for the problems and miscalculations that always come up.

In larger companies, sales managers can be assigned the task of managing promotions; however, the smaller the company, the greater the probability that the owner must take the responsibility for:

- Being on the premises to greet customers, if that's part of the promotion
- Coordinating and following up to make sure deliveries are made on time, if that's part of the program
- Personally handling any barter arrangements or questions that arise from customers

SALES ORGANIZATION

Few successful businesses would deny that an efficiently structured sales organization will bolster any marketing strategy and an ill-conceived one will kill it. As in any business endeavor, employee competence and motivational drive usually make the difference between success and failure. This is probably more true in sales activities than in any other function.

Figure 4-1
Questionnaire for Planning Sales Promotion

1. What do you expect to gain from this promotion?
   a. Increased sales from existing customers? How much? For how long?
   b. Increased customer base? How many new customers? Repeat customers? How much sales will they bring in?
   c. To introduce a new product/service? How much sales? What follow-up to the promotion?
   d. To open a new market? Where? What? How big? How long will it take?

2. What sales promotions are involved?
   a. Volume pricing?
   b. Incentive returns?
   c. Customized or same day delivery?
   d. Customer training?
   e. Other? What type?

3. How will you notify the market of the sales promotion?
   a. Circulars? Mailed? Hand delivered? Picked up? How many?
   b. Newspaper advertisement? What newspaper?
   c. Direct mail notification? How many?
   d. Television? Radio? Cassette tape? Video?

4. What is the cost?
   a. Advertising?
   b. Lost production time?
   c. Damaged merchandise?
   d. Rented space?
   e. Special equipment?
   f. Contract labor?

5. Who will manage the promotion?
   a. Yourself?
   b. Sales manager?
   c. Other employee?
   d. Advertising agency? What cost?
   e. Other outsider? What cost?

Whether your business employs full-time salespeople, commissioned agents, or a combination of the two, three organizational matters must be dealt with:

- Sales management
- Sales compensation
- Selling expenses

Of course, if you are the top sales manager or the only salesperson, these topics are a matter of personal discipline. No one can tell you how or when to make sales calls or how much you can spend on selling expenses. And naturally, the question of compensation never arises.

If you employ salespeople, however, you should take certain steps to structure how, when, and where sales calls should be made and how much will be allowed for selling expenses. Regardless of how meticulously a strategic plan is constructed, without firm control over a sales organization, time and money will inevitably be wasted and the achievement of strategic objectives delayed.

The first order of business should be to implement a reporting system for all sales personnel. Each field salesperson should submit weekly call sheets showing each customer's name and address, the reception received, the orders booked, and the potential for obtaining additional orders. The purpose of this report is to hold sales personnel accountable for their time. It's all too easy to become unproductive when on the road. Even full-commission salespeople make unnecessary calls or spend too much time with low-potential customers. A weekly report with prompt follow-up from the sales manager (or owner) won't eliminate unproductive time, but it will reduce it.

The second step should be the implementation of a personnel evaluation system. This doesn't have to be elaborate, but it should be used at least semiannually to compare the productivity (that is, the amount of sales or orders) of each salesperson with that of the others. Internal competition tends to bring out the best in people, and if all employees and commissioned agents know that their performance is being evaluated against that of their peers, they should be motivated to do better. This evaluation system should also serve as part of the compensation review.

If used regularly, customer feedback can be one of the most effective management tools available to control and motivate sales personnel. Most business owners know the identity of their main customers. If they open lines of communication with these customers, with either a regular phone call or a letter, salespeople quickly learn that their customers as well as their boss are watching their performance. Customer feedback can frequently serve as an early warning signal that something is amiss. An example of this occurred when the owner of an electronic game manufacturer made her semimonthly customer calls.

A veteran sales agent had been calling on a customer for four years with stable but unspectacular results. Recently, however, few new orders were being booked. The business owner sensed that something wasn't right but couldn't put her finger on it. This time, when she made the follow-up call, the customer let it slip that the salesman had recently been showing up smelling of alcohol. The owner confronted the salesman and learned that since his wife had died six months earlier, his drinking habit had returned. Under threat of termination, he started a recovery program with Alcoholics Anonymous and soon began booking orders at his old rate.

Compensation

The type of compensation that brings the best long-term results is still open to debate. Many companies that sell "big-ticket" items claim that a combination of a relatively low salary and a substantial commission provides the best motivation. However, micro businesses that cannot afford full time sales personnel usually contract with commissioned sales agents who also handle products from other companies. If you use this method, it's generally a good idea to make your commission rate higher than that paid by other suppliers, thereby motivating the agent to push your products first.

Incentive bonuses also prove to be an effective stimulant under certain conditions. Except in unusual circumstances, however, only noncommissioned salespeople should be paid bonuses. Commission rates should be set high enough to create their own incentive.

Selling Expenses

Sales personnel hate to have the boss watch their expenses. Their age-old arguments never change: "I have to entertain my customers to close the order." "My customers insist that I call on them personally." "How would it look if I took my customer to lunch in a three-year old car?" "All the coach seats were taken. I had to fly first class to keep my appointment." "The few expenses I incur are a small price to pay for all the orders I bring in." The excuses go on and on and on.

These statements may all be true. Nevertheless, out-of-control selling expenses generally indicate that sales personnel are more interested in having a good time or creating a status image than in booking sales. This, of course, can have a deadly effect on the best-conceived marketing plan, so it pays to keep a tight rein on selling expenses regardless of complaints from sales personnel.

Other than advertising and public relations expenses, covered in Chapter 5, the typical selling expenses that need close scrutiny are:

- Travel
- Customer entertainment and promotion
- Company cars
- Sales literature
- Telephone, fax, and telecommunications

Travel expenses

Sales travel expenses are easy to control. Commissioned agents pay their own expenses and should not be reimbursed by the company. Travel expenses for salaried personnel, however, must be closely monitored. All plane reservations and ticketing should be done by a travel agent with strict instructions to book the cheapest discount fare—even if it means changing planes. Sales calls should be planned in advance to take advantage of seven-day and fourteen-day discount fares. Obviously such luxuries as first class or business class fares should be forbidden. Flying coach class may be uncomfortable, but you get to your destination just as fast and just as safely as the person sitting in the front seat drinking free cocktails.

Stringent rules about renting cars should also be enforced. Orders are seldom lost because the salesperson shows up in a compact car. Full-size rentals are more expensive and unnecessary, so insist that everyone use the smallest car available. And don't take any insurance offered by the rental company. American Express, personal automobile policies, or fleet coverage takes care of rental cars.

Stay out of first class hotels. Once again, sales are seldom made simply because sales representatives stay at a Hilton, Marriott, Sheraton, or Hyatt. Have the travel agent book rooms at Days Inns or other budget hotels. The savings can be significant.

It's too easy for salespeople to spend more than necessary when traveling. Keep a tight rein on expense reports. Demand documentation. Insist that everyone follow company travel policies. And have salespeople make round trips whenever possible. In most parts of the country, one-day trips have become relatively easy to arrange, making hotel and dinner expenses unnecessary.

Customer entertainment and promotion

Playing the bigshot may be a favorite game for salespeople, but it can become a very expensive luxury. Picking up lunch or dinner tabs, supplying liquor for sales parties, ordering expensive wine for dinner, and so on, may be great for the ego but seldom enhances long-term sales growth.

Without question, some customers expect to be entertained. Many lower-level purchasing agents find that this is the only time they get a chance to eat out. But once again the temptation to overspend must be nipped in the bud. One of the best methods is to establish a maximum per diem allowance for entertaining—say $25 per day. Let those salespeople who want to play the VIP spend their own money. Another acceptable policy is to pay for fully documented meals but no liquor or wine. These measures might seem extreme, but the essence of a growth-oriented marketing plan is to put your resources where they do the most good—and rarely does entertaining qualify.

Company cars

In this day and age, most salespeople are given a company car as part of their compensation package. A company car is a terrific employee benefit, but it always costs more than one realizes, for an obvious reason: Employees do not give company cars the same care as personal ones.

Here are a few ideas for reducing car expenses:

1. Charge employees a monthly fee for personal use of the car

2. Insist that employees pay part of the fleet insurance premium

3. Have employees insure the car under a personal policy, with partial reimbursement by the company

4. Charge all gasoline and repairs on company credit cards and insist on a monthly accounting of trips

5. Have employees pay for their own gas and repairs, with partial reimbursement by the company

6. Lease the fleet with a open-end lease

7. Lease the cars for four or five years rather than three

8. Use only compact cars in the fleet

9. Charge employees for repairs that result from road accidents

While controlling selling expenses won't contribute directly to sales growth, it will increase profits and conserve cash, both highly desirable short-term results.

Chapter 5

Advertising and Public Relations Strategies

Regardless of the quality of a company's product offering, or its price competitiveness, or its superior after-sale service, the company will have difficulty attracting customers if they don't know about the company or how terrific its products are. Sales calls alone might sustain or even increase market penetration without the help of focused promotions; however, the cost and time involved would probably be uneconomical. An effective advertising campaign coupled with a determined public relations effort will, in the long run, bring better results faster and at less overall cost than selling efforts bereft of these tools.

This chapter explores several results-oriented strategies for maximizing the effectiveness of advertising expenditures and for augmenting advertising campaigns with big-payoff public relations tactics.

Although most large corporations have for years recognized the contributions of both advertising and public relations to their bottom lines, closely held companies seem to be less inclined to spend sufficient money on these tools to bolster what are otherwise effective marketing strategies. We are tempted to treat advertising and public relations as less critical than producing products or calling on customers, especially when sales slacken. This can result in lost opportunities. However, since the impact of advertising campaigns and public relations programs is hard to measure and these programs take several months or years to result in increased growth, missed opportunities are seldom recognized until long after the fact.

Few business owners would argue with the statements that unfocused advertising wastes money and amateurish public relations does more harm than good. On the other hand, most successful business owners would probably also agree that both advertising and public relations can, in the long run, improve market control, thereby contributing to substantial growth in both sales and profits. The trick is to develop programs that are both cost-effective and results-oriented—in other words, that will provide the biggest bang for the buck.

Advertising campaigns should be designed to produce three strategic benefits:

1. Attracting new customers to a market

2. Capturing customers from competitors

3. Providing market intelligence

When coupled with a well-conceived public relations program, advertising dollars may well be the best and most cost-effective way to gain control of markets. To make their advertising campaigns as cost-effective as possible, companies should focus on four specific objectives. They should:

1. Design advertisements to meet strategic marketing goals

2. Select advertising media that achieve the greatest market impact

3. Measure the market impact of each advertising program

4. Keep advertising expenses to a minimum, consistent with the maximization of market coverage

The following sections explore various alternatives for achieving these objectives.

ADVERTISING TO MEET STRATEGIC GOALS

As described in Chapter 4, the primary objectives of long-term marketing strategies are to define and then gain control of those market niches that optimize the company's resources and skills. Such sales tactics as volume pricing, incentive returns, same-day delivery, customer training, and barter arrangements serve as tools to implement strategies aimed at market dominance. Although narrowly focused promotions can assist sales personnel in spreading the word to a limited number of potential customers, a sustainable advertising campaign broadcasts the advantages of a company's products to a large enough market segment to make sales promotions effective.

Whether the objective is to attract new customers to a market, to capture market share from competitors, or simply to obtain market intelligence through customer feedback from sales promotions, an advertising campaign directed to selected classes of customers can, in many cases, create customer demand faster and with less cash outlay than any other technique. Moreover, selective advertising may be the only feasible way to test new markets prior to entry.

In consumer markets, clip-out return coupons continue to be one of the most effective techniques for attracting new-to-the-market customers. When such coupons appear in print media or are received through direct mail solicitations, potential customers have a no-obligation, no-cost opportunity to learn more about the product or service. A high number of returns indicates good potential for making a solid impact on the market. A poor return from an attractive display may mean either that the content of the advertisement was confusing or that the market lacked interest in the advertised product.

Clip-out coupons can also be a very cost-effective method for enticing customers away from competitors. The coupon should be designed to highlight product qualities that are absent from a competitor's line. It should also indicate, discreetly or overtly, that it would be to the customer's benefit to learn more about this product. Comparisons of price, delivery, and quality with competing products are commonly used to make the point.

Several methods of getting the clip-out coupon to the market are available. Direct mailings with return postcards, newspaper and magazine advertisements with a cut-out form, television spot commercials with an 800 phone number, trade show and convention booths with mail-back handouts, and customer registration are all effective approaches. The choice depends on specific circumstances, not the least of which is cost.

The most appropriate method of distributing coupons depends on the type of product, the size of the market, the degree and type of competitive advertising, and the role that customer requests for information play in a company's overall marketing strategy. This brings us to the most critical decision point in developing a cost-effective advertising campaign: What specific short- and long-term objectives do you expect to realize from the campaign?

It's easy to become disillusioned when incremental sales do not immediately materialize. We blame the advertising agency for managing an ineffective campaign because competitors seem to be winning the marketplace war. Or, when business cycles turn down, we stop all advertising, since this is such an easy expense to eliminate. In the end, such reactions only diminish otherwise effective marketing strategies.

Why Advertising Campaigns Fail

Most advertising campaigns fail to deliver the expected results for one of three reasons: (1) the expected results were not concisely defined ahead of time, (2) the time frame within which results could be expected was too short, or (3) the advertisement was inappropriately presented. It seems obvious that spending money on advertising without clearly defined objectives makes little sense. Furthermore, expected results must be quantified. How many responses should come in from a clip-out coupon campaign? How much should sales increase? How much should market share improve?

Improvements in sales volume or market share cannot be achieved in the short run, regardless of how well the advertising campaign is structured and managed. One week, one month, or even six months may be too short a period to realize concrete benefits. Sustainable growth strategies take time to jell, and advertising aimed at short-term results does little to meet such objectives.

Gaining Market Share

Don't fall for the pitch that the more you spend on advertising, the greater the number of customers that will be enticed away from competitors. Over the long run, advertising cannot by itself create customer loyalty. Customers must realize continued, long-term benefits from switching brands or companies. If they don't, any increase in market share will be short-lived.

Strategically, advertising expenditures directed toward increasing a company's share of the market should be viewed as a long-term investment. Permanent market share improvements are impossible to measure over the short term—unless, of course, your product life cycle is short, as with designer clothes or fad toys; in such cases, "permanent" may mean one Christmas buying season, one summer, or one ski season. In any event, to achieve cost-effectiveness, the specific advertising program must correlate with the strategic objectives in a given market.

It is often difficult to judge how much to spend on advertising and what type of media to use. More than one business owner has followed the advice of an advertising agency and that's all right if you can afford it. But experience has shown that left to their own devices, advertising agencies, large and small, believe that the more a company spends and the greater the variety of media, the more effective the campaign. Except for highly competitive, glossy, big-ticket items such as automobiles, this hardly ever works.

The basic rule for making advertising cost-effective is to develop a comprehensive program that meets a company's specific needs but no more. In other words, use only as much advertising as is needed to sustain control of existing markets or to capture new market niches. The ten guidelines shown in Figure 5-1 should provide a helpful reference.

Figure 5-1
Guidelines for Cost-Effective Advertising

1. Use advertising for specific purposes (test new markets, increase a specific market share, gather intelligence about new markets), not to create or sustain a public image.

2. Define precise, quantifiable objectives for each advertising campaign, such as the anticipated number of replies to clip-out coupons or the expected number of new customers.

3. Design advertising programs to target specific focused marketing goals, such as raising prices by 5 percent or increasing sales volume by 10 percent in a given market niche.

4. Manage the advertising campaign yourself—don't turn control over to an advertising agency.

5. Define targeted recipients before starting the advertising campaign (types of customers, geographical coverage, specific competitors).

6. If the goal of your campaign is winning business from the competition, know your competition and compare your products or brand names with those of competitors.

7. Define the time frame within which results can be expected.

8. Segregate short-term expectations from long-term objectives and use different advertising techniques for each.

9. Establish a schedule for the advertising agency to follow, including progress milestones that can be measured.

10. Devise a follow-up procedure to monitor the advertising agency against the schedule.

MEASURING MARKET IMPACT

When asked which medium has the greatest market impact, many advertising executives will quickly point to television spots on highly rated prime-time programs. Coincidentally, these happen to create the biggest agency fees, are one of the most expensive ways to get your message across, and for most companies are anything but cost-effective. The choice of advertising media seems unlimited. Every year new ways are devised to sell advertising. For smaller businesses, however, one or more of the following fifteen choices seem to work best (although not necessarily in the order listed—that depends on the specific company and product line).

1. Product and company brochures
2. Direct mailings to existing customers
3. Direct mailings to potential new customers
4. Newspaper announcements
5. Popular magazine and trade journal ads
6. Billboards or posters—roadside or indoor (e.g., in a sports arena)
7. Television spots—network or local coverage
8. Commercial envelope flyleaves
9. Matchbooks
10. Holiday greeting cards
11. Pencils and pens
12. Calendars
13. Newsletters
14. Telephone Yellow Pages
15. Catalogs

Although media cost is important, defining the target audience is crucial. If you are trying to sell in England, advertising in American telephone directories won't help, but newspaper announcements in the London *Times* might work well. If you have a financial planning or tax return business that serves a local market, it doesn't do any good to advertise on network television. However, a local channel might be just the ticket, as in the following example.

A certified financial planner was just starting her own business. After getting only two clients in six months, she decided to spend some money on advertising. A close friend dared her to invest in a thirty-second spot commercial on a local TV channel. She purchased ten spots over a two-week period.

Trying to cut corners, this entrepreneur devised her own commercial. She stood in front of the camera, told the audience what services she performed, announced that the first interview was free, and flashed her business phone number across the screen. The results were dramatic. Within six weeks she signed up sixteen clients for various types of financial planning work.

In this example, market impact was easy to measure. In other cases, however, results may be camouflaged or benefits may accrue over an extended period of time. Nevertheless, knowing the impact of a specific advertising program on the targeted market is crucial to judging whether to change the approach, continue the same program, or abandon it completely.

To identify the market impact of any advertising campaign, especially one whose benefits may be realized over the long term, a monitoring system should be set up. It doesn't have to be complicated to be effective.—in fact, the simpler the better. Since no prescribed format will fit every situation, each company must creatively design its own method. However, experience has shown that successful measuring systems have two features in common: quantifiable results and milestone events.

Quantifiable Results

The monitoring system must be able to measure quantifiable results against original expectations. In other words, if a direct mail campaign is expected to produce a 10 percent sales increase, you must be able to monitor where the new customers came from. In some companies this is fairly easy. Asking customers what motivated them to buy your products usually identifies whether it was the advertising or some other reason.

In other cases, however, a broader approach must be used, especially to monitor long-term results. Historical records should identify the approximate sales gains that result from industry or national business cycles. Also, if competitors leave the market, sales increases from the absorption of latent demand are normally a fairly obvious result. On the other hand, if sales increase and such uncontrollable factors cannot be identified, then it is reasonable to assume that the advertising campaign was the main stimulant.

Milestone Events

To effectively monitor advertising results over the long term, some type of milestone measurement must be used. For example, suppose the objective is to increase market share by 6 percent over the next three years. It would seem reasonable to assume that an advertising campaign today will have little direct effect two and one-half years from now; however, indirectly it may have a material effect. New customers attracted in the short term may provide repeat business, with a secondary effect of drawing additional new customers later on.

A system for recording new customers should show this number making a big jump for the first six months, then tapering off over the next four or five periods. If an increase does not occur during the first six months, chances are high that the advertising failed to achieve its objective.

CONTROL ADVERTISING EXPENSES

Seven types of expenses, excluding payroll and benefits, account for 90 percent of most private business advertising budgets:

1. Printing letterhead and envelopes for direct mail

2. Postage

3. Media charges—television, radio, newspapers, magazines, etc.

4. Layouts, artwork, and copy

5. Color printing for brochures, etc.

6. Collating and assembling circulars, brochures, etc.

7. Recording and handling replies

A good rule of thumb is that any portion of this work handled by an advertising agency will cost at least 50 percent more, and in some cases ten times more, than if you do the work yourself. The following show the costs of two advertising jobs I did for myself using my personal computer and an old, second-hand offset press compared with quotes received from a small advertising agency.

	In-House	Ad Agency
Case 1: Direct mailing (500 mailings)		
Copy	0	$200
Letterhead and envelopes	$60	70
Print letterhead and envelopes	0	50
Address envelopes	0	120
Stuff envelopes	0	250
Collate and handle replies	0	250
Postage	125	125
Total cost	$185	$1,065
Case 2: Two color, 4 x 6, 3 page brochure (500 copies)		
Copy	0	$500
Layout	0	600
Artwork	0	
Printing (I could not do this myself)	600	1,000
Heavy paper	100	
Total cost	$700	$2,100

These quotes came from a small, local agency, with a minimum of overhead and staff personnel. Fees from large agencies run a great deal higher—probably five to ten times those of a small one. And most large firms won't even look at such a small job.

With state-of-the-art advances in short-run printing equipment and simplified personal computer software, there is little reason to pay exorbitant prices for any type of printed advertising. Although managing media advertising gets a bit trickier, it can also be done without an agency.

Another reason to do your own advertising is that no agency can possibly be as familiar with your company's product lines and customer characteristics as you are. Nine times out of ten, in-house personnel can do a better job than advertising agencies in pinpointing the types of copy and media that will be effective.

Assuming that you can keep the cost down, try a newspaper advertisement if direct mail doesn't work. If that also fails, perhaps a spread in a trade publication will do the trick. Or maybe your best bet is to rely on a strong public relations program (which we'll look at later in this chapter). Without the added expense of the advertising agency's profit, you should be able to experiment until something does work—without spending a fortune.

Equipment and Software

With a few pieces of office equipment, three high-quality software packages, and layout and artwork assistance from freelancers, any business can put together its own advertising. The following equipment should be the minimum configuration for complete independence.

1. *Personal computer.* It should have at least a 200-megabyte hard drive and six million bytes of random access memory (RAM). Excellent IBM (or compatible) or Apple computers run between $2,000 and $4,500 new, and between $800 and $2,000 used.

2. *High-speed laser or inkjet printer.* It must produce excellent, full-color print quality. New ones run $1,000 to $2,500. Satisfactory used models can be found for under $800.

3. *Copy machine.* It should have multiple-copy loading capacity and collating capability. Be sure it produces high-quality copies for long runs. Because of maintenance problems, it's best to lease rather than buy.

4. *Facsimile machine.* Be sure it runs at high speed and is compatible with common brands. A fax comes in handy for relaying documents to media or to advertising agencies for special jobs.

5. *Small offset press.* A used one will do perfectly well. There are plenty of them around for less than $1,000.

6. *Drafting table.* Also, you'll need appropriate supplies for artwork.

In addition to equipment, special computer software must be purchased. Three packages should be sufficient.

1. *A multiprogram desktop publishing package.* Ventura by Corel (under $700) works well with IBM machines. The Macintosh has its own software. It is more expensive but also more user friendly.

2. *A strong word processing package.* Wordstar, WordPerfect, and MS Word (each about $500) are all capable of doing nearly anything.

3. *A compatible telecommunications module.* This is handy for uploading (transferring) data to media and agencies, as needed. Those by Hayes and other manufacturers are acceptable and cost about $150.

It's always preferable to purchase new software rather than copy someone else's (which is usually illegal). With new software, manufacturers provide technical advice and a complete instruction manual. However, in spite of the copyright laws, many people continue to copy computer programs for their personal use or to give to friends. Obviously, copied software doesn't include technical help, warranties, or user manuals.

Quick-Print Shops

For those who don't like computers or who don't want to bother with all this equipment, state-of-the-art quick-print shops offer an alternative. No longer restricted to copy machines, the new breed of quick-print shops have a complete configuration of the above equipment plus much more. The good ones are extremely capable and fast, and turn out very high quality products.

Using quick-print shops will cost more than doing the job in-house, but far less than using advertising agencies. A few have multicolor press capability, and more are adding it every month. Prices for multicolor printing approximate those charged by small printing companies.

Mailing Lists

Mailing lists are another do-it-yourself aid. If you have a good word processing package and a printer capable of handling mailing labels, there is no reason to pay an agency to prepare direct mail solicitations. There are hundreds of reputable mailing list companies across the country that produce lists for virtually any category of company, industry, geographic area, or product designation. Most of the bigger houses provide either hard-copy mailing labels (ready to stick on envelopes) or computer diskettes for making customized labels in-house. The cost of diskettes is about half that of preprinted labels. Metropolitan telephone directories and library reference works are good places to get the names and addresses of mailing list companies in your region.

Mailing lists are expensive, however. A single-sort list that includes the first and last names of appropriate contacts runs between $1,000 and $2,000 for a minimum of 1,000 companies. Preprinted labels are extra.

Media Contacts

Advertising agencies can usually handle media advertising more efficiently than amateurs. Legal collusion between major newspapers, magazines, television channels, and radio stations on the one hand and advertising agencies on the other, makes placing your own advertisements a difficult undertaking. But it can be done. All it takes is perseverance, patience, and an apprentice's knowledge of media language. Two clients taught me the ropes.

A business broker who wanted to place a series of advertisements in a local big-city newspaper decided to conserve cash by managing the placement in-house. Upon calling the newspaper, the broker was told that a blocked advertisement with logo and special trim required a plate. The newspaper recommended that an agency handle the preparation. The broker persisted and eventually found out exactly what was needed. It wasn't a plate at all, but merely a typeset copy that a local quick-print shop could make with its desktop publishing software. It took some pulling, but the exercise saved the broker about $2,000.

For another example, a fast-food client was told by the local television channel that a professionally prepared video was needed. The client borrowed a camcorder and made the video at one-fifth the cost quoted by an agency.

It may not be as easy as advertising through direct mail, but media placement can also be a do-it-yourself activity. Advertising is one expense that can be cut to the bone and still be an effective marketing tool.

SELECTING THE RIGHT ADVERTISING AGENCY

Every metropolitan area has a wide range of advertising agencies. Some are very good; some are very bad. Size doesn't seem to matter. Many excellent agencies are very small, with two or three employees. Other small ones are totally incompetent. The same holds true for the giants: Some are excellent, and others seem to be completely ineffective.

In the majority of cases, it's best to stay away from large, well-known agencies. These firms are just too big and have too many large corporate accounts to be bothered with small jobs. Even if they are interested, most are very difficult to work with because small jobs get pushed down the line to junior people. It's like working with a giant law firm. You may get an initial appointment with a senior partner, but juniors end up doing the work. That being the case, it makes a lot more sense to go with a small agency where the owner handles most of the work. Then when you have problems, the buck has already stopped!

The best way to locate a qualified small agency is through personal contacts. Ask around. Check with local businesses for references. If all else fails, local printing companies can usually point you in the right direction. Be careful going this route, though. It is not uncommon for advertising agencies to pay printing companies commissions on new client referrals, and that increases prices.

PUBLIC RELATIONS

Advertising is one side of the promotion coin; public relations is the other. A well-managed advertising campaign may be all you need, or want, to support marketing strategies. However, in certain industries—such as personal service businesses, advertising won't do the job without a concurrent public relations program. In still other cases, advertising is too expensive, and companies rely exclusively on public relations to promote business.

Public relations is nothing more or less than the creation of a favorable image in the public eye. For many service businesses, its reputation in the marketplace can make or break the company. Health care providers, investment advisory services, physical fitness centers, professional practices, tax return preparers, and many other service businesses prosper or fail because of their public reputation rather than because of any unique service they offer, or don't offer. Although some service businesses try to get their message across through advertising, many more rely on developing and sustaining a favorable reputation in their industry or in the public arena.

If concrete results from an advertising campaign are difficult to measure, identifying specific benefits derived from a public relations program is virtually impossible. Most business owners look on public relations as a method of creating sustainable benefits over long periods of time and make it an integral part of their growth strategies.

Implementing a Public Relations Program

The starting point in any public relations campaign is to establish credentials in such a manner that the public can clearly distinguish the specific expertise that you or your company brings to the table. This can be accomplished in various ways depending on your communication skills, area of expertise, and market dispersion (local, regional, national, or international).

In some businesses (e.g., financial planning, public accounting, life and casualty insurance, auto mechanics), optional certification or licensing establishes a level of competence in the public eye. In other types of businesses, credentials may be effectively communicated through written publications (e.g., letters to the editor; articles in trade publications; articles in bank, insurance company, or tax newsletters) or through group events (e.g., trade shows, public forums, symposiums, panel discussions). Once your credentials have been established, a public relations program can begin.

There are two ways to implement a cost-effective, sustaining public relations program as a part of marketing strategies:

1. Hire a professional public relations firm to design and manage the program

2. Do it yourself

The Yellow Pages for any metropolitan area list local public relations firms. Businesses that need national coverage tend to use firms located in New York, Chicago, Los Angeles, Dallas, or Miami. Companies that sell to regional markets can usually get the best service from public relations firms based in their regional center. For example, publishing businesses usually get the best results from New York firms. Los Angeles is still in the lead for anyone in entertainment or leisure-time related businesses. Houston and Dallas own the market for oil-related industries. Chicago is best for heavy industry, agriculture, and food processing. Public relations firms in Miami do an excellent job for companies with business ties to Latin America.

Nearly all large corporations maintain continuing contracts with equally large public relations firms. Stay away from these. They employ qualified people, all right, but their fees are definitely not cost-effective for smaller companies. Your best bet is an equally small public relations firm, generally a one- or two-person business. Even with a smaller firm, however, a continuing program can easily run $2,000 per month for a twelve-month contract. Project work generally starts at $10,000 and goes up from there.

Be careful, however. There are a few unethical public relations agencies that will take your money without performing any beneficial service. Unfortunately, as in many types of unlicensed service businesses, anyone can claim to be a public relations expert, and more than one business owner has been stung by these shysters. The best way to avoid such a trap is to carefully interview prospective firms and then get sufficient references from banks and clients.

Once you have chosen a reputable firm, you can engage it to work either on a project basis or on a continuing contract. The good ones design public relations programs and make all arrangements for implementation, including television or radio interviews, media promotions, panel participation, or trade show speaking engagements.

Frequently public relations projects overlap with advertising programs. So much the better. A small publisher might run an advertising campaign directed at selling specialty magazines to homemakers and have a public relations firm line up interviews with homemakers to get their reaction.

The two biggest advantages of using a professional rather than doing the work in-house are (1) professionals know specifically who to contact to set up promotions through any medium, and (2) professionals do all the selling and administrative legwork, which can be very time-consuming. The big disadvantage is that public relations firms cost money, and their fees can amount to a big chunk of a promotion budget.

Do-It-Yourself Public Relations

Many business owners find public relations firms an unnecessary expense, preferring to promote the company's image themselves. The biggest disadvantage of going this route is that it takes a fair amount of time that could otherwise be devoted to running the business. Although most people certainly don't have the time or the inclination to implement a broad, sustained public relations program, a favorable image can be promoted in narrow, targeted markets with relative ease.

One example of such do-it-yourself publicity was undertaken by an ex-professional football player who started an investment newsletter business. The four-year-old venture was very successful, with more than 11,000 executive subscribers. As an expansion strategy, the entrepreneur wanted to open a new market: college students in the nation's business schools. He couldn't afford to hire a public relations firm, but he realized that to tap this market, he must spread his reputation as an honest, knowledgeable investment advisor to the college ranks.

The objective was accomplished in three steps. The first step was to arrange a series of three free lectures on personal investing in the evening school division of a local college. The second step involved getting the local newspaper to cover the lectures. The entrepreneur then used this publicity to convince seven business magazines with large student circulations to publish his article about investment projections.

The entire public relations program was handled without spending a dollar, except for minor travel expenses and postage. Within a year a new market had been created that netted over 4,000 student and faculty subscribers.

Some do-it-yourself steps cost a few dollars. Others can be done without any out-of-pocket expenditures. The cost of implementing the publicity ideas shown in Figure 5-2 is at most a few hundred dollars, and the majority can be accomplished with no outlays. Some are particularly adaptable to small service businesses. Others lend themselves to retail establishments. Still others seem to work best for manufacturing businesses.

Figure 5-2
Ideas for Publicity Campaigns

1. Invite a local newspaper to write an article on some unique aspect of the company.
2. Invite television reporters to cover a special event sponsored by the company (e.g., a fund-raising drive, a banquet honoring an employee, or the introduction of a snappy new product).
3. Start a charity book collection drive at local schools.
4. Sponsor a young people's athletic team.
5. Sponsor a civic band or float in a local parade.
6. Donate materials, space, or services to community theater groups.
7. Provide facilities for Boy or Girl Scouts, Rotary, Kiwanis, Toastmaster, or some other public or civic group.
8. Sponsor a paper, glass, aluminum, or plastic recycling drive.
9. Get behind a social cause (e.g., homes for the homeless, food and clothing drives for the poor, or clothing and activity donations for state mental hospitals).
10. Donate used computers, office equipment, etc. to local schools, hospitals, or welfare agencies.

Personal Public Imaging

The main idea of a public relations program is to create a favorable public image. The reverse can also happen—an unfavorable image. Companies selling products deemed environmentally or socially harmful have an especially difficult time maintaining a favorable image. One of the best ways to overcome this stigma is for the business owner or key executives to take active, positive public roles in community or political affairs. Demonstrating public responsibility can frequently overcome at least some of the tarnish. Figure 5-3 (page 92) resents a few ideas that you might experiment with to improve your public image and that of your company with minimal, if any, cash expenditure. Many of these ideas are especially beneficial for professional practices and personal service businesses.

The whole idea behind public imaging is to project a sense of caring about and participation in community events. Obviously, if your market niches are national rather than local, this type of imaging won't buy much. On the other hand, more than one business owner has parlayed local community involvement into national recognition as a political or social leader. And this does improve market recognition on a scale beyond the immediate locale.

Figure 5-3
Ideas for Public Imaging

1. Run for local public office.

2. Speak to local school or community groups about drug abuse, alcoholism, teen pregnancy, and so on.

3. Start a new Rotary, Kiwanis, or other social-help chapter.

4. Become active in a local PTA group (if you have school-age children).

5. Write social or political commentary articles for the local newspaper.

6. Become an active leader in your church.

7. Conduct a lecture series on community topics.

8. Teach at an adult evening class.

9. Lead a fund-raising drive for the United Way, Heart Association, or other charitable organization.

10. Participate in radio and television talk shows.

Well-conceived and conscientiously managed advertising and public relations programs are important tools for implementing long-term growth strategies. Businesses of all sizes and in virtually any industry need to seriously consider either an advertising campaign or a public relations program, or both, to ensure market control. Unfortunately, many smaller companies tend to shy away from both advertising and public relations, assuming that the expense is too much for tight budgets.

Since advertising and public relations are so important for attracting new customers to the market, for enticing customers away from competitors, and for providing market intelligence, it makes good business sense for even the smallest business to find a cost-effective way to use them. Furthermore, with a little effort and creativity, nearly any type of program can be designed and managed in-house, thereby conserving cash while still getting good results.

Chapter 6

Financing Strategies

As business owners, we directly control the development and implementation of our companies' internal restructuring, marketing, advertising, and public relations strategies. However, our success in raising long-term growth capital is a different matter entirely. It depends to a large extent on external forces, such as the condition of the economy, the status of financial markets, and the broad outlook for world capital markets. In addition, the willingness of investors and lenders to put money into our businesses is directly related to how they perceive our future. To the extent that lenders and/or investors view a company as a well-managed enterprise, capable of providing high returns in future years, they will supply capital. Conversely, if a company's future looks bleak, capital suppliers will beat a path out the door.

Although ensuring a company's access to long-term capital is as important in the growth equation as developing marketing plans and getting internal affairs in order, it seems that growth-oriented financing remains a mystery to many otherwise astute business owners. Such puzzlement is probably caused to a large extent by the cloak of mystery surrounding the criteria that financial institutions (and to a more limited extent the investing public) apply to the desirability of investing debt (or equity) funds in a particular company. By camouflaging these benchmarks, lenders and investors discourage many private businesses from taking the actions necessary to attract capital.

The primary purpose of this chapter is to dispel such fears—to demonstrate that business owners and managers do have it within their power to control their own financial destiny, to choose from a variety of capital sources, and to fine-tune their capital funding as confidently as they do marketing strategies.

Experience has shown that the most important contribution financial management can make to a company's long-term growth is to restructure outstanding debt, and in some cases equity, to provide the flexibility so that is necessary to support growth strategies. Without financial flexibility, companies cannot attract new debt and equity investors. And without new capital, most growth strategies cannot progress beyond the planning stage.

The restructuring of current capital is referred to as *recapitalizing a balance sheet*, or merely *recapitalization*. In terms of a company's long-term growth, recapitalization objectives should be to:

- Build free cash reserves

- Enhance the likelihood of attracting fresh debt capital by achieving and sustaining healthy debt-to-equity ratios
- Increase the probability of attracting fresh equity capital by improving return on investment ratios

It goes without saying that recapitalization techniques apply mainly to companies that have been in business for several years, not to first-stage businesses that are probably still striving for sustainable customer bases and profitable product lines. After five or six years, however, companies have moved through first- and second-stage development and matured to what is referred to as the *third stage* of growth.

Not infrequently, third-stage companies find the capital structure that was appropriate during their earlier years outmoded. Operating needs change. Venture capitalists must be paid off. High interest rates drain cash. Perhaps overseas opportunities are blocked by outdated banking relationships. These and many other factors lead to serious consideration of recapitalization as an integral part of long-term growth strategies.

Many of us, however, find it difficult to face up to such a decision. Confronted by daily operating crises, it's easy to postpone refinancing until time permits a thorough investigation of alternatives. Solid relationships with current lenders and investors lull us into a sense of false security. Meeting loan covenants without much difficulty blinds us to changing needs. Cash flow remains sufficient to continue our bonus programs, even though payables and receivables may be stretched. Developing exciting new product or marketing strategies lends an air of surrealism to our future. Why bother with a mundane and obviously complex recapitalization?

The answer is relatively simple: Without a sound financial base, long-term growth objectives are impossible to achieve. Maximizing a company's liquidity and hence flexibility is the only way to meet the radically changing conditions that will inevitably occur in the future. Financial complacency only stymies the implementation of strategic growth plans and, in the end, destroys the company.

Apart from pressure from obstreperous financial institutions, there are a variety of reasons why companies recapitalize their balance sheets. A few of the more common motives are to:

- Decrease debt service payments
- Raise substantial capital for a specific purpose, such as a business acquisition or a major overseas expansion
- Minimize tax liabilities
- Improve book value prior to offering a company for sale
- Survive tough economic times

If relationships with lenders or investors are already strained to the breaking point, however, you probably don't have any choice but to recapitalize. To help you decide whether to recapitalize your company, Figure 6-1 lists several conditions that point in that direction.

Figure 6-1
Checklist for Recapitalizing

It's time to consider recapitalizing when:

1. Monthly sales are declining, have leveled off, or are not accelerating as rapidly as planned.
2. More than 2 percent of receivables have slipped beyond sixty days.
3. Trade payable payment terms are stretched far beyond receivables collection periods.
4. Inventory is increasing faster than sales.
5. Employees are not fully occupied with productive work.
6. Bank relationships have deteriorated beyond repair.
7. Published financial statements show your company's profits and ratios deteriorating.
8. Your company's debt-to-equity ratio exceeds 3 to 1.
9. The value of assets securing term loans has increased.
10. Lease payments are higher than debt service would be; or the reverse.
11. Strategic growth plans require additional capital, but all assets are fully pledged.
12. Additional capital is needed to develop a new product and bring it to market.
13. Growth plans call for the acquisition of a going business or major product line.
14. Major improvements need to be made in a management incentive program to motivate key employees.
15. You want to sell the company.
16. Either debt service or dividend payments are draining cash that is needed to finance increasing sales or expansion plans.
17. Your bank is about to call its loan.

If your primary objective is to reduce debt service payments or to inject new capital for operating needs, the quickest and least expensive ways are to:

- Renegotiate current loans
- Go after foreign bank loans or guarantees
- Sell major hard assets and lease them back

When recapitalizing for major expansions or when restructuring a company in anticipation of selling it, fresh equity capital makes more sense than new debt obligations. Attracting equity investors takes more ingenuity and time than attracting lenders, but significantly greater amounts of cash can be raised. Two of the easiest and least costly ways to raise equity capital are through employee stock ownership plans (ESOPs) and joint ventures, both of which are covered later in this chapter. Two other sources of relatively large amounts of equity capital—venture capital funds and common stock issues—are dealt with in Chapter 13.

RAISING OPERATING CAPITAL

Mature companies that still carry a high level of short-term debt usually find that it makes sense to convert as much of the balance as possible to long-term notes. Assuming that solid relationships have been nurtured, most banks should be willing to convert at least part of your short-term obligations to longer-term notes. Obviously, the longer the term, the better. Five years is a good place to begin negotiations.

To the extent that such a conversion can be made, soft collateral (receivables and inventory) that previously secured short-term debt can be freed up for operating needs. While monthly principal and interest payments must be made on the term notes, at least part of a company's cash outflows have been pushed into future periods, when stronger growth should make repayment easier.

On the downside, however, two conditions make such a conversion a risky tactic. In the first place, interest rates for new long-term loans will almost certainly be higher than those for short-term credit. There aren't very many banks around that will wait longer for their money and still charge the same rate. Second, a bank (or other lender) will most assuredly demand additional collateral for a term loan. If hard assets are already pledged against mortgages or other long-term debt, the only choices may be nonbusiness assets and personal guarantees.

Foreign Bank Loans and Guarantees

The opening of branch offices by major international banks has become common, especially in major international trade centers like New York, Los Angeles, San Francisco, Miami, Chicago, Dallas–Fort Worth, and the Baltimore–Washington corridor. British, French, Japanese, German, Mexican, and many other foreign banks have strategically positioned branches to tap the growing financial needs of American companies engaged in international trade. Most foreign bank branches do not have full-service capability; however, they do consider loans placed through their main U.S. offices. In addition to handling international financing needs, these banks compete in domestic U.S. markets, although so far they have not captured a significant share.

Instead of making direct loans, many international banks prefer guarantees (called *standby letters of credit*), which can then be used as collateral for a term loan with your local bank. Although nearly all American banks accept L/Cs as collateral (provided they have a relationship with the foreign bank placing the L/Cs), there is a catch: Borrowers must collateralize the standby L/C. Fortunately, foreign banks tend to be more creative in the types of assets they accept as collateral.

Since most of these banks have branches all over the world, assets located offshore may be the best bet. American banks won't touch offshore assets, but foreign banks are quite comfortable with them. A second home in the Caribbean, investments through a Swiss bank, gold holdings in Hong Kong, and trust assets in a tax-haven country are examples of offshore assets that could be pledged.

Sale/Leaseback of Major Hard Assets

The sale and subsequent leaseback of a company's assets (referred to as a *sale/leaseback*) can be an effective financing method for companies with a heavy concentration of hard assets (machinery, equipment, real property). Since only hard assets can be sold and leased back, manufacturing companies are the main beneficiaries; distribution, retail, and service businesses usually find other types of financing more appropriate.

Contrary to some promotions from leasing companies, leasing equipment can cost more than borrowing the money to buy the asset. The sum of payments over the entire lease period normally exceeds the sum of principal and interest payments on a comparable loan. On the other hand, companies benefit from sale/leasebacks by receiving an instant cash infusion (from the sale of the assets) and by amortizing lease payments over a longer period than most term loans carry.

One serious disadvantage of recapitalizing with sale/leasebacks is that the spread between the value of the hard assets being sold and the loan they collateralize (if any) must yield enough free cash to make the transaction worthwhile. if that if the case, the fresh cash infusion could be a viable way to repay unwieldy bank loans and simultaneously increase cash reserves.

Any of these methods (extended repayment terms for outstanding debt obligations, foreign bank term loans and standby guarantees, and sale/leasebacks) of cleaning up old obligations and raising modest amounts of new capital works reasonably well. However, none of these strategies will raise the amount of new capital needed to finance a business acquisition or a major capital expansion. Those ventures normally require equity capital.

RAISING CAPITAL FOR MAJOR PROJECTS

Financing strategies that call for more than $1 million in new capital usually involve new equity rather than debt. A rule of thumb in financing circles is that the more capital a company needs, the greater the possibility of raising it through the equity route. While selling a partnership interest is about the only feasible way for micro businesses to raise new equity, manufacturing, distribution, and retail companies with sales in excess of $10 million enjoy a far broader choice.

Companies that already have stock in public hands might consider a public bond issue. In the 1980s, billions of dollars were raised for business acquisitions with low-grade, high-interest bonds, commonly referred to as "junk bonds." Such possibilities still exist, although public acceptance of low-grade bonds isn't close to what it was during the 1980s. If public bond issues appear to be a viable alternative, any reputable underwriter can offer advice about how, where, and when to make the issue. However, privately held companies usually find public bond issues far too expensive, even if they could attract investors—which most cannot. The following discussions, therefore, are limited to financing major projects with capital other than bonds.

Paying off loans with equity capital raised through a public stock offering is the single most effective way to increase operating cash. It also increases a company's capital base, thereby enhancing flexibility. A public stock issue is also one of the best ways to finance large projects, such as the liquidation of long-term bank debt, the expansion of plant and equipment, the acquisition of a going business or major product line, or the financing of a major research project. Typically, initial public offerings (IPOs) range between $5 million and $20 million. Chapter 13 describes several options available to companies interested in making a public stock offering.

EMPLOYEE STOCK OWNERSHIP PLANS

An employee stock ownership plan (ESOP) is a creation of the Internal Revenue Service, originally intended as an employee benefit plan. Over the years, however, companies have found additional uses for ESOPs, one of which is as a convenient way to raise low-cost capital for refinancing higher-interest loans or for funding expansion programs. The fact that the federal government actually contributes capital to a company is a feature that no other financing method can match. Either of two types of ESOPs can be used: an unleveraged ESOP or a leveraged ESOP.

Unleveraged ESOP

An unleveraged ESOP is funded entirely with company money. At first glance this doesn't appear to bring in additional capital. Indirectly, however, it does. Since contributions to ESOPs are tax-deductible, these funds are immediately returned to the company's coffers. No cash goes out the door, and, in effect, the IRS contributes about 35 percent. For example, assume that the annual payroll is $1 million. The company contributes 10 percent, or $100,000, to the ESOP. The amount of taxes saved by the transaction totals 35 percent of $100,000, or $35,000. The company would not have had the use of this money without an ESOP. Therefore, the IRS has indirectly put $35,000 into the company.

Leveraged ESOP

A leveraged ESOP works the same way, except that leveraging principles allow even more money to flow to the sponsoring company. In addition to receiving contributions from the company, the ESOP borrows from a bank or other lender to buy shares in the company. Employees get company stock, and the company gets the bank's money without taking out a loan and with practically no collateral. Although banks normally insist on guarantees from the company, they do not require that additional assets be pledged. Annual tax-deductible contributions pay the principal and interest on the loan.

Leveraged ESOPs enable the sponsoring company to borrow money at a significantly lower cost than it could with a straight bank loan, mainly because of the tax treatment of loan repayments. Annual contributions to an ESOP that repay the principal of the ESOP loan are tax-deductible, up to a limit of 25 percent of payroll. This means that the loan gets repaid out of pretax earnings, an impossibility with a bank loan. Two other tax benefits are also available:

1. Contributions to an ESOP that are applied to interest payments are tax-deductible in full.
2. Dividends paid on preferred shares sold to the ESOP and either used to retire the loan or distributes to participant accounts are tax-deductible in full.

An extra feature kicks in when the ESOP owns more than 50 percent of a company's stock. At that point, lenders may exclude 50 percent of interest earned on ESOP loans from taxable income. Theoretically, this should encourage significantly lower interest rates.

Refinancing with an ESOP

Although an ESOP makes an attractive benefit package for employees and is a convenient way to structure a management buyout, companies benefit most by using ESOP financing as a recapitalization strategy. Figure 6-2 shows a comparative calculation of the after-tax cash effect of borrowing through an ESOP and a conventional term loan. The assumptions in this example are:

- A $1 million loan
- Interest at 10 percent
- Annual payments for seven years
- An effective tax rate of 35 percent
- An annual payroll of $600,000
- Maximum annual contributions of 25 percent of payroll, or $150,000

Figure 6-2

			Conventional Loan		ESOP	
Year	Principal	Interest	Tax Savings	After-Tax Cash Effect	Tax Savings	After-Tax Cash Effect
1	$142,857	$100,000	$35,000	$207,857	$85,000	$157,857
2	142,857	85,714	30,000	198,571	80,000	148,571
3	142,857	71,429	25,000	189,286	75,000	139,286
4	142,857	57,143	20,000	180,000	70,000	130,000
5	142,857	42,857	15,000	170,714	65,000	120,714
6	142,857	28,572	10,000	161,429	60,000	111,429
7	142,857	14,285	5,000	152,143	55,000	102,143
	$1,000,000	$400,000	$140,000	$1,260,000	4490,000	$910,000

With an ESOP, the actual cost of the loan is nearly 28 percent lower than with a conventional loan. This savings of $350,000 occurs because companies may deduct from taxable income contributions used to repay the principal of an ESOP loan. For companies with payrolls high enough to make ESOPs worthwhile, these IRS-developed benefit plans are hard to beat. Given the right circumstances, an ESOP remains one of the least expensive and most beneficial ways to raise limited amounts of capital. There are restrictions, however.

ESOP Restrictions

Neither the IRS nor the SEC regulates how much stock or what percentage of ownership can be sold to an ESOP. On the other hand, two constraints indirectly affect the size of the ESOP:

1. The portion of a company's contribution used to repay the principal of an ESOP loan is limited to 25 percent of annual payroll. However, the deductibility of contributions for interest payments is unlimited.

2. The ESOP loan cannot extend beyond fifteen years. Banks prefer a maximum of ten years, although some go further.

Assuming that ten years is the best you can get, the maximum amount of capital that can be raised through an ESOP amounts to 25 percent of the company's annual payroll multiplied by ten years, or two and one-half times annual payroll. If full tax deductions are not important or if a bank will go beyond ten years, there is no maximum.

To gain tax-qualified status, the ESOP must meet certain of the following requirements.

1. The primary purpose of the ESOP must be the benefit of its participants; it is an employee fringe benefit.

2. The primary investments of the plan must be in the employer's stock, common or convertible preferred for leveraged ESOPs, and any type of securities for nonleveraged plans.

3. Each employee must have voting rights equal to allocated shares.

4. Employees must have the right to receive plan distributions of company stock.

5. Closely held companies may prevent terminated employees from retaining ownership.

Although an ESOP won't work for every company, if the circumstances warrant, it can be a convenient, inexpensive way to at least partially refinance outstanding bank debt.

JOINT VENTURES

Strategic alliances have become the most popular form of business combination. Although many of the bigger combinations focus on combining resources for high-tech R&D projects (e.g., the Boeing/Airbus alliance), raising capital continues to be an essential function of many alliances (such as the CMS Energy–Dow Chemical venture, formed to raise public debt for a joint cogeneration facility).

The most popular form of strategic alliance is the *joint venture*. Typically, two companies form a new operating entity (partnership or corporation), to which each partner contributes something. Domestic joint ventures offer a convenient way to finance strategic growth while spreading the risk of expansion into new markets among two or more joint venture partners. Most small business joint ventures involve a large corporation that contributes capital and perhaps facilities, and a small company that contributes technology, inventory, or perhaps a marketing organization.

On a broader plane, strategic alliances encompass a full range of corporate agreements, from full ownership control (as in mergers or corporate spin-offs) to partial ownership and contractual control (as in joint ventures and minority investments) to pure contractual control (such as cooperative agreements, R&D ventures, and cross-licensing).

The whole purpose behind any type of strategic alliance is to bring the resources (nearly always different resources) of two or more companies to bear on a specific project. Although the project may involve raising capital, technology development, distribution, manufacturing, or something as straightforward as combining advertising programs, the following discussion focuses on the capital-raising features of joint ventures.

Although a wide variety of problems can and generally do arise with joint ventures, a carefully constructed contractual arrangement that spells out the responsibilities of and contributions from each party should minimize the severity of future disputes. Despite the fear of losing valuable assets by sharing closely guarded patents and proprietary know-how with a partner, companies of all sizes have found joint ventures an acceptable alternative for financing major facility expansions and development projects.

A good example of how a small and a large company can both benefit from a joint venture occurred when Freechase Corp., a privately owned company, needed an additional 100,000 square feet of production space to manufacture its new line of products in quantities sufficient to meet expected market demand. A U.S.-based division of Mitsubishi Corporation wanted to market the line.

The two companies formed a joint venture, with the Mitsubishi division providing manufacturing space in return for exclusive marketing rights. Freechase got its facility without incurring additional debt, and the Mitsubishi division added a new product line and an assured tenant for its facility. In this situation, a joint venture brought benefits superior to those of any financing scheme Freechase could have devised.

Not all joint venture financing comes from the larger partner's cash reserves. Tax, regulatory, and accounting restrictions frequently dictate the use of public debt issues or mortgage loans as more economical choices. Joint venture partners with immediate access to foreign exchanges may choose to float Eurobond issues. Foreign-based partners can often tap government funding that has been specifically designated to subsidize investment in American property and businesses.

Offshore Joint Ventures

Joint ventures are also a popular strategy for financing overseas expansion. Many countries prohibit foreign companies from raising capital through local banks or capital markets. To circumvent these barriers, American and host-country companies form a new joint venture company, which then has a legal right to raise varying amounts of local capital as the occasion warrants. A joint venture with a cash-rich foreign company is especially attractive when entering a depressed economy, such as Eastern Europe or the Commonwealth of Independent States. Local capital may not be available under any circumstances, so that the only way to finance entry is with cash supplied by a foreign partner.

In the Caribbean, Mexico, and Central America, many joint venture partners are equally small local manufacturers or distributors. In this case, financing can usually be arranged through the U.S. government, host-country government agencies, and foreign banks. Although exceptions certainly arise, these capital providers tend to favor American firms that will bring jobs and management know-how to local companies.

Special programs have been established to finance these investments (see Chapter 15 for various sources of foreign direct investment financing). Not infrequently, an American parent company can set up a facility without incurring any debt on its books and without using any of its own funds. Multilateral and host-country development banks, Eximbank-affiliated agencies, and other U.S and foreign government subsidy programs make joint venture investments extremely lucrative, especially in Latin America and the Caribbean.

Studies by the Department of Commerce and several export trade organizations point to three prominent ways U.S. companies benefit from financing through foreign joint ventures. Such alliances enable them to:

- Qualify for local export trade credit
- Access local capital markets
- Limit initial capital investment, and therefore risk

Some companies, especially smaller ones, arrange joint ventures with host-country subsidiaries of large U.S. corporations. The smaller company usually carries the marketing and production risks, while the large company brings trade or investment funding to the table.

Local export credit assistance

Qualifying for government export credit in such countries as Japan, South Korea, Taiwan, Britain, Germany, or France is reason enough to form local joint ventures. These countries and many others support lucrative export/import trade credit facilities that are easier to use and have much broader coverage than those available from Eximbank in the United States. However, most government trade credit programs require that local companies participate in the transaction. East Asian programs tend to be more liberal about financing foreign companies, but even here, a local partner can be invaluable as a qualifier and arranger.

Accessing local capital markets

More than 60 countries support over 175 active stock, commodity, and financial futures and options exchanges; however, listing on most of them is restricted to the country's companies. Even though new trading instruments such as global depositary receipts are finding their way onto more world exchanges, melding international companies with local markets, most stock exchanges in less developed countries continue to require local licensing and incorporation. Forming a host-country corporation with a local partner is one of the easiest ways around this obstacle.

Multilateral financial aid programs (sponsored by the World Bank and the International Monetary Fund) and bilateral aid agencies [such as the Overseas Private Investment Corporation (OPIC), the U.S. Agency for International Development (USAID), and the U.S. Trade and Development Program] also provide foreign direct investment capital, but generally require equity participation by host-country companies. To ignore such lucrative avenues because of ownership constraints makes little sense, especially when a joint venture could open the doors.

Joint Venture Structures

Joint venture partners may share equally or unequally in the ownership of the new company and/or in the responsibility for carrying on its business. They may also share the profits and losses of the venture proportionately (which is used) or disproportionately to their ownership holdings.

Some joint ventures are not intended to produce independent profits or losses but rather to generate longer term gains for each of the partners, as in arrangements to share technology and market intelligence. In most cases, however, a joint venture is a separate operating entity.

The care taken in drafting a joint venture contract often determines whether the arrangement will be beneficial or detrimental to one or both parties. Since the parties to the contract may be from different countries, accustomed to significantly different negotiating techniques, contract language, and local interpretation of contract phrases, the most beneficial contracts are normally negotiated and drafted by intermediaries representing both sides. Intermediaries may be management consultants, investment bankers, attorneys, government bureaucrats, or a combination thereof.

Since no two joint venture contracts are the same, any attempt to illustrate universal contract language or a universal format would be futile. A few common rules do prevail, however. If followed, they should ensure a mutual understanding by all parties of the contract's terms and conditions. With the exception of references to language provisions, the following rules apply equally to domestic and international joint ventures. Adherence to these rules won't guarantee a successful marriage, but ignoring them will certainly strengthen the possibility of a near-term divorce.

Common Rules of Joint Venture Contracts

1. *Multilingual.* For joint ventures involving a foreign partner, the finished contract must be both in English and in the language of the foreign partner. Even if personnel from the two companies are conversant in each other's language, legal contract terminology tends to have different

meanings in different countries. It's crucial to reach agreement on the interpretation of all contract clauses under each party's local laws and customs.

2. *Objective of joint venture.* Whether the objective of the joint venture is to market specific products, to build a manufacturing plant, to manage the operations of a facility, to export, to transfer technology and know-how, or to provide financing for a project—it should be clearly stated in the contract.

3. *Expiration date.* All joint venture contracts should have a definite expiration date, regardless of how far into the future it may be. Along with defining the life for the joint venture, the contract should spell out specifically how the venture's assets and liabilities—including inventory, receivables, plant and equipment, trade liabilities, and unpaid loans or other indebtedness—will be distributed upon dissolution.

4. *Specific activities.* The joint venture's activities may require that specific functions be performed by one or both of the partners, such as managing the operation, arranging financing, marketing, engineering, or liaison with government officials. Regardless of the number of duties assumed by each partner, each should be thoroughly described. The contract should also include specific responsibilities for settling claims, lawsuits, and any other legal or contingent matters that may arise during the operation of the joint ventures as well as for paying all taxes, license fees, permit fees, and so on.

5. *Sharing profits and losses.* The contract must contain definitive language that spells out how the profits losses of the joint venture will be allocated to each partner. It should also describe how, when, and to whom cash will be distributed, and how compensation to the parties will be determined.

6. *Board of directors.* A board of directors or other policy-making body must be defined. Veto rights, withdrawal rights, new or additional equity contributions from partners, eventual transfer of ownership interests at the liquidation date, and other policy matters should be defined.

7. *Escape clause.* In the event that one or both partners wish to withdraw from the venture, contractual provisions must spell out their right to do so, circumstances under which withdrawal will be permitted, what forfeiture or compensatory allowances will be paid, and any other items germane to the agreement.

Although joint venture agreements utilize contract sections similar to those in partnership agreements, joint venture agreements take on an added level of complexity. Now the parties must agree on such arcane issues as:

- The relationship between the newly formed joint venture entity and its participating owners
- Initial and ongoing capital contributions

- Control of the venture
- Conflict resolution procedures
- Termination provisions

Relationship with participating owners

The discussion of the relationship between the venture and its parents should include the amount of each party's contribution to the new entity and its description—capital, technology, machinery, processes, facilities, distribution network, management know-how, and so on. The downward relationship from parents to the venture entity may be quite simple when each partner contributes only corporate assets. However, sharing management responsibilities can make the relationship significantly more complex. For example, one partner may provide accounting services for the venture, and the other partner may be responsible for venture personnel recruitment and evaluation. Or one may manage legal matters and the other handle insurance coverage.

The transfer of assets, capital, or technology from the venture back to the parent companies can also be convoluted. For example, a manufacturing venture might sell products or components to one or both parents. Or perhaps develop a technology that will be used by one or both partners. Or supply a marketing or distribution network to handle the sale of products from one or both partners. Or receive royalties from patents belonging to one partner or the other. Such relationships must be clearly spelled out in the joint venture agreement to avoid future disputes.

Capital contributions

Even a matter as clearly defined as capital contributions must be expanded upon in the agreement. Three areas need to be covered:

- How much initial capital each party will contribute to fund the venture
- Which party has the responsibility for providing working capital as needed
- For international ventures, which party will solicit financing from government agencies, local development banks, foreign banks, and/or local capital markets

On the surface it would seem that ventures between large and small companies should delegate responsibility for initial capital and ongoing funding to the larger of the two; however, this may not always be desirable. A case in point arose when a small U.S. manufacturer, Horkel Products, Inc., formed a joint venture with a large British telecommunications company to establish an assembly facility in Barbados.

The British company agreed to provide initial capital of $5 million and to fund ongoing working capital needs. However, to take advantage of certain provisions in the U.S. government's Caribbean Basin Initiative, Horkel arranged bank guarantees from Eximbank and trade credit with U.S. banks for exports back to the United States. The British partner managed export credit needs for shipments to the European Community.

Similar situations can arise with domestic joint ventures. One such case involved a joint venture between a small installation contractor and General Electric's turbine division to build a generating plant in California. GE financed the equipment and installation with a public bond issue of $10 million. The installation contractor arranged for a bank line of credit to meet its own working capital requirements.

Control of the venture

Disagreements over management control of a newly formed company have caused more than one joint venture to bend, if not break. If such control followed ownership percentages, there would probably be much less difficulty, but in joint ventures this seldom happens. When a large corporation brings capital to the table and a smaller company brings management or technical expertise, generally ownership control rests entirely with the large company and management control with the smaller company.

Most companies experienced with joint ventures would probably agree that 50–50 partnerships rarely work. Each partner has its own venue, its own strategies, and its own operating style. To expect agreement on all decisions is asking too much. One party or the other must be responsible for daily operations, and these responsibilities must be provided for in the contractual agreement.

On the other hand, regardless of which partner has management control, the other party will certainly want a say in major decisions. This is especially true when management control rests with the minority shareholder—that is, the smaller company that did not contribute initial capital. This problem can easily be resolved by granting the majority partner contractual rights to block major decisions affecting the newly formed company. Typically, such decisions include:

- The sale or disposal of venture assets
- Changes in the venture agreement
- The hiring and firing of key management personnel
- The acquisition of capital equipment
- Corporate finance matters, such as the acquisition of new debt or equity capital and the concurrent pledging of venture assets
- Major tax strategies
- Distribution of profits

Conflict resolution

Disagreements are bound to arise in any joint venture. The contractual agreement must clearly spell out how conflicts between the partners that cannot be negotiated quietly and quickly will be resolved. Mutual approval of major decisions certainly helps, but additional provisions may also be required.

Ventures conceived between two companies of approximately equal size (that make similar equity contributions) often provide for a separate committee made up of senior people from both companies to act as a medium for dispute settlement. Such a committee should be separate from the joint venture's board of directors, with no authority over the operations of the venture. Its sole purpose is to meet periodically to resolve those major conflicts between the partners or between venture managers and one or both parent companies that the board of directors cannot resolve.

Arbitration is another possibility. Every joint venture agreement should specify conditions that could lead to arbitration, how an arbitrator will be appointed, and the finality of an arbitrator's decision. When agreement cannot be reached through normal channels, the agreement may stipulate the buyout of one partner by the other, similar to provisions in a standard partnership buyout agreement.

Termination

Every joint venture should have a specific life span spelled out in the contractual agreement. Provisions may also be included to extend the life of the venture, provided both parties are amenable. However, if the extension options are not exercised when the termination date arrives or when conditions occur that give rise to a termination, the venture dies. Specific provisions in the agreement should identify how the venture's business will be wound down, how assets (including cash balances) will be distributed, and what liability each partner will assume for future claims against the venture that may arise after it is disbanded.

Occasionally, the agreement provides for an independent third-party overseer (perhaps an attorney or a major accounting firm) to supervise liquidation proceedings. In some instances it may be desirable to transfer the assets of the venture to a trust and let the trustee liquidate the business and distribute assets. Regardless of the mechanism used, provision must be made to end the joint venture.

Part 2

Special Situation Growth Strategies

Chapter 7

First-Stage Start-up Businesses

You dream of having your own business has become a reality. An office, storefront, or shop has been leased. Business cards and letterhead have been designed. Announcements have been sent to friends, relatives, business neighbors, and your local newspaper. A telephone has been installed. Office equipment, tools, and perhaps vehicles have been purchased or leased. The myriad details have been taken care of, exactly as spelled out in one of those "how-to-start-a-business" books. Following your bank's advice, you even consulted with a Small Business Administration SCORE representative. Now what? Where are the customers? How do you let the market know you are in business? What strategies should you employ to build your business into a viable operating entity, capable of competing in the marketplace for many years to come?

This chapter addresses those questions and others in the context of strategies to develop and sustain a competitive business, regardless of industry or location and regardless of whether it was started from scratch or as a franchise. Over the last thirty-three years I have been fortunate enough to have had the opportunity to start thirteen separate companies—some in retail, some in services, some in manufacturing. All but three were domestic companies. Those three were in Europe and the Caribbean. Of the domestic businesses, two failed miserably, one struggled on for five years and finally folded, and the rest grew into viable contenders, later to be sold. The lessons learned—both good and bad—form the basis for the recommendations presented in this chapter.

To set the stage, the following discussions assume that a business has already transcended its introductory stage—in other words, that it is currently:

- Operating out of a business location—office, shop, warehouse, or storefront
- Making and/or selling products that have been market-tested
- Following the advice of professional advisors (at least an attorney and an independent accountant)
- Utilizing the balance of its "seed" capital to fund operations

A business with these characteristics has survived the introductory stage and is now said to be in its *first stage* of growth. Three overriding issues confront entrepreneurs once their companies have entered this stage:

1. How to let the public know about the company and its products

2. Which sales techniques to use for direct solicitation

3. Where to get first-stage financing to purchase inventory and supplies, to pay the rent, and to meet payrolls while the business goes through its initial growing period

Strategic resolutions to each issue should be short-term; that is, they should be specifically designed to produce growth over the next twelve to eighteen months, in contrast to the long-term growth strategies suitable for more mature businesses. Although this may seem short-sighted, pragmatically it is very logical.

According to several university and federal studies, of the more than 80 percent of all start-up businesses that fail, three-fourths go under in the second or third year. Seed capital, owner enthusiasm, and market newness carry them through the first year, and in some cases the second year. By that time, if their product hasn't caught on and if new first-stage financing isn't in place, their initial capital has probably been depleted and the product/market newness has worn off. It is during this second or third year that short-term strategies must be adopted to carry the company into its second stage of growth.

Although opinions vary as to the sequencing of first-stage financing and sales promotion, this is a moot point—a "chicken-and-egg" debate. In truth, obtaining new financing and promoting new sales must be done in tandem; one without the other is useless. However, since we must begin somewhere, we will arbitrarily look first at ways to increase sales, then discuss various sources of first-stage financing.

PROMOTING SALES

First-stage marketing strategies should focus on sales promotions that will attract immediate customers and selling methods that will ensure repeat business. Chapters 4 and 5 looked at a wide range of focused marketing tactics, cost-effective advertising campaigns, and comprehensive public relations programs. Most of the recommendations were aimed at gaining market control as the primary goal of long-term growth strategies.

First-stage companies can also benefit from similar sales and promotion activities, but with a focus on short-term rather than long-term benefits. The do-it-yourself publicity ideas listed in Figure 5-2 are good examples of promotion strategies that can effectively introduce the company's name and its owner's reputation to the marketplace. Those ideas were the following:

1. Invite a local newspaper to write an article on some unique aspect of the company.

2. Invite television reporters to cover a special event sponsored by the company (e.g., a fund-raising drive, a banquet honoring an employee, or the introduction of snappy new product).

3. Start a charity book collection drive at local schools.

4. Sponsor a young people's athletic team.

5. Sponsor a civic band or float in a local parade.

6. Donate materials, space, or services to community theater groups.

7. Provide facilities for Boy or Girl Scouts, Rotary, Kiwanis, Toastmaster, or some other public or civic group.

8. Sponsor a paper, glass, aluminum, or plastic recycling drive.

9. Get behind a social cause (e.g., homes for the homeless, food and clothing drives for the poor, or clothing and activity donations for state mental hospitals).

10. Donate used computers, office equipment, etc. to local schools, hospitals, or welfare agencies.

In addition, low-cost advertisements could be run in:

- Playbills and other circulars used for local school functions like theatrical presentations, lecture series, band concerts, graduation exercises, and special-purpose fund-raisers
- Door-to-door fliers
- Mailbox "stuffers" announcing special sales
- Church bulletins
- Neighborhood weekly newspapers

The idea is to concentrate on low-cost promotions in restricted market areas. With limited financial resources, most first-stage companies cannot afford to advertise in more than one or two specific market niches. It's important, therefore, to select those niches or geographic areas in which promotions will bring the fastest results for the least cost.

Direct Mail

Although some businesses achieve remarkable results from direct mail solicitations, for most first-stage companies this approach is too scattershot for immediate results. It is also much too costly unless a market can be defined with absolute precision—which most cannot be. Take, for example, the miserable results that a first-stage company selling heating and air conditioning equipment in rural New England achieved from a direct mail advertisement. The owner of 21st Century Air Management Technologies and Installation Corporation (a.k.a. A-M-T) was convinced that a direct mail advertisement to all homeowners in three contiguous Zip codes would certainly bring a flood of new orders. A one-page mailing went out to 180,000 homeowners.

The purchased mailing list, postage, printing, and handling costs totaled $49,922.50. After six months, no sales could be directly traced to this solicitation, and in fact, A-M-T's sales during this second year of its operation actually decreased from the meager first-year level.

Referrals

Owners of professional service businesses (legal services, accounting services, consulting services, and so on) learn early on that referrals can be an excellent source of new business. Although retail, manufacturing, and distribution businesses tend to disregard this avenue, it can be an extremely lucrative sales promotion method for many of them as well. Nothing spreads the name and reputation of a business and its products faster than word-of-mouth referrals.

For instance, when a new restaurant or a new store opens, initial customers are primarily curiosity seekers, perhaps drawn to the establishment by local advertisements. Follow-up advertising may bring in new customers for several months, or even a year or more. Eventually, however, the newness wears off. the initial advertising has done its job. Now, referrals must take over to sustain the business. Satisfied customers tell their friends and neighbors, and soon a new customer base has been established. Referrals actively solicited from satisfied customers can in many cases catapult a business into substantial growth.

Poster Advertising

Poster advertising can also be used effectively to promote start-up businesses, although it's important to select only those displays that match your budget—some can be very expensive. Poster advertisements displayed in public buses, in tour buses, in shopping malls, at trade fairs, at major conventions, in retail establishments, and in many other locations get your company's name and products in front of a large segment of the public.

Here is an interesting example of how posters placed in retail establishments pushed a building contractor to new heights. J. C. Cody Contractors, Inc., had been in business for about fourteen months. The company had just completed its last residential-home contract, and no new jobs were in sight. Mr. Cody hired a small advertising agency to design and print a full-color 36" × 48" poster (total cost $5,042) depicting workers finishing a new house and the homeowner's family (with two small children and their dog, of course) anxiously waiting to move in. He got permission to place the posters in seven area supermarkets, five quick-print shops, and two hotels, and near a refreshment stand at the local minor-league baseball park. Within two months, Cody had signed contracts to build twelve new houses, all a direct result of the posters.

Subcontract Businesses

Subcontracting businesses are companies that make products or provide services to a customer's specifications under contract to that customer. Although products may be involved, they are not proprietary products. In a broad sense, therefore, subcontract companies can be considered service businesses. Such businesses include machine shops, packaging and production services for publishers, printers, certain transportation services, payroll preparers, and specialized building trade contractors (bricklayers, certain landscapers, excavation contractors, and so on).

Subcontracting businesses can spend a fortune on what should be effective sales promotions without reaping any short- or long-term benefits. Not having a proprietary product to offer, these companies must rely on quality of performance, timely delivery, and competitive pricing to get past their initial stage, and promoting such features in a very restricted market can be tricky.

In the end, advertising does little good, and most companies rely on referrals to build their customer base. Since referrals come from satisfied customers and start-up subcontractors can handle only a limited number of customers at one time, first-stage growth generally builds slowly. In most cases, initial customers come from an owner's personal network of contacts in the industry. Building on these personal relationships, high-caliber performance leads to an industry reputation, which in turn brings more referrals. Unfortunately, there isn't any shortcut to this process.

Direct Sales Calls

For most entrepreneurs, direct selling is the most difficult way to get new business, yet very few companies can get by without it. Those who have been in business for several years have usually honed their techniques to make sales calls as efficient as possible. Newcomers, however, often spend countless hours and significant money on trial-and-error sales pitches. Although each type of business and market requires customized selling techniques, the direct sales guidelines in Figure 7-1 (page 116) should help as a beginning step.

CONTROLLING MARKETING EXPENSES

There seems to be a common tendency for owners of first-stage companies to push the panic button when sales aren't increasing in the second or third year at the rates projected in the original business plan. The natural reaction is to assume that some facet of the marketing effort has been slighted: not enough advertising, too few salespeople, skimpy customer entertaining, inappropriate sales literature, and so on. To correct these shortcomings, higher advertising budgets get approved, more salespeople hired, more lavish entertaining arranged, and new sales literature printed—all costing a significant piece of the company's still-meager budget. This is usually the wrong way to go. In most cases, it's not how much you spend on selling products, it's how effectively the money is spent on efforts with measurable results (see Chapters 4 and 5).

Since it is unlikely that your first-stage company has excess cash reserves just waiting to be used, the spend-more-to-make-more approach is seldom a satisfactory solution. While efforts should be made to focus marketing expenditures where they will do the most good, controls must also be initiated to manage the money available for these programs. The most effective controls are tightly constructed monthly budgets, with expenditures forecasted by specific expense category. It's especially important to keep a tight rein on travel and entertainment expenses. They seem to get out of hand the fastest.

It is just as easy (and just as wasteful) to add office workers to support sales personnel. Secretaries, order clerks, computer operators, and customer service

Figure 7-1
Guidelines for Direct Sales Calls

1. Do sufficient research to identify potential customers who appear to need your product (or service). This means pulling together names, addresses, and telephone numbers of companies in your market area that use the types of products you are trying to sell. Calling on companies that do not use your products only wastes time, energy, and money.

2. Get the name, address, and telephone number of the specific individual responsible for purchasing the types of products you are selling. It won't do much good to talk to the marketing manager if you're trying to sell computer programs, or the general manager if you're selling office supplies, or the controller if you're selling machine tools.

3. Know your sales pitch before calling. No one has time to chit-chat about superfluous subjects. No one cares about how you feel, nor do they care to tell you how they feel ("How are you today?" goes over like a lead balloon). One sentence describing your product and why the listener should buy it is all you'll have time for. If you continue beyond one sentence, either you'll be thrown out or you'll lose the interest of your potential customer. When buyers want to hear more, they ask questions. If there are no questions, there's no interest.

4. Don't attempt to close an order at the first contact—either by phone or in person. If the person is interested, ask what would be a convenient time and place for you to return and elaborate on your product offering, including prices, delivery schedules, and quality guarantees.

5. Focus on the benefits to be gained from using your product, not on its price. Explanations of product pricing and delivery options should wait for a second contact. If you are forced to the wall, try to keep your description of your pricing structure general. Examples of responses to pricing questions that tend to get you off the hook are "Unit prices depend on the quantity purchased and the delivery schedule." "We can design payment terms to your convenience." "Our prices are structured to your needs."

6. Follow up all potential leads with another call, a letter, or a sample of your product (if possible). The secret to building a first-stage business base through direct sales is to continually follow up with any potential customer that seems the least bit interested in your product or service.

---

specialists may be welcome additions in mature companies reaching for expanded growth, but they are a luxury few first-stage companies can afford. At this early stage it's much better to spread work among all office personnel, regardless of the specific activity it may relate to.

Many first-stage companies have found that incentive programs for sales personnel can be used to control marketing expenses. If they are intended as a cost control mechanism, however, incentive programs must be based either on the attainment of budgeted expense levels or on company profitability. Start-up businesses with few employees can often use the profitability approach because everyone has a hand in controlling expenses and, to a lesser extent, in satisfying customers. If you have ten or more employees, however, or if you have more than two full-time salespeople, the chances are good that budgetary incentives will be more effective. The main reason is that sales personnel have direct responsibility for selling expenses but little control over other company costs.

One rather unique approach to controlling marketing expenses was used by a computer repair company that had been in business for eighteen months. One salesman and the owner handled not only all sales chores but repair services as well. To control the marketing expenses, the owner struck a bargain with his salesman: For every new customer the salesman brought in, he was allowed an extra $1,000—either to spend on selling expenses or to pocket for himself. At the end of the year, it was agreed that if total company sales exceeded forecast, the salesman would receive a $5,000 bonus. If sales fell below forecast, he would pay back to the company $1,000 for every $10,000 in the sales shortfall.

Over the next three years, sales grew on average 22 percent a year. Since each year was over forecast, the salesman pocketed his $15,000 bonus—plus he made an extra $10,000 (out of a total of $18,000) from the $1,000 allowances—the balance was reinvested in extra travel and entertainment expenses.

FINANCING ALTERNATIVES

By the time your company reaches its first stage of development, it has probably consumed most, if not all, of its original seed capital. Although business may be looking up, sales are not generating enough free cash to buy the inventory needed for further growth. And, of course, the amount of cash you have taken out of the business for personal living expenses has probably been negligible.

Except in very rare circumstances, a new business needs about three years of steady growth before it generates free cash in sufficient amounts to live on. Working capital to keep the business growing must come from outside the company. Financing must be obtained from banks, other lending institutions, or investors, or the company will stagnate and quickly die.

Determining Cash Requirements

Before you approach a bank or other financial institution, it's necessary to prepare a financing plan (often referred to as a working capital plan) focusing on future cash flows. The cash shortfall between receipts and expenditures tells you how much must be borrowed and when it must come in. The more detailed the estimate, backed by reasonable operating and market assumptions, the higher the likelihood of getting the loan.

Many start-up businesses never get further than the initial stage because they are unable to define in clear, concise terms the amount of financing they need to move forward. Without succinct identification of cash requirements, no bank or other institution will consider lending to a first-stage business. The starting point for developing a first-stage working capital plan is to identify those expenses that will be incurred over the ensuing twenty-four months. Next, develop a conservative sales forecast. Both expenses and sales should be forecasted for monthly intervals; if practical, it's even better to use weekly intervals for the first few months.

The construction of such a working capital plan differs slightly for manufacturing, retail, and service businesses, although each uses a similar format. Since estimating cash requirements for manufacturing companies is the most complex of the three, this is a good place to begin.

Manufacturing working capital plans

Manufacturing businesses typically have the following types of cash expenditures:

- Production materials and supplies
- Payroll, payroll taxes, group insurance, and workers' compensation
- Rent for production/warehouse/sales/administrative facilities
- Utilities and telephone
- Business insurance
- Transportation and freight
- Advertising and sales promotion
- Market research
- Product development
- Tools
- Other operating expenses to produce and sell the product or service

Although there are no universal rules for forecasting cash requirements, nearly all financial institutions suggest the following procedures:

1. Estimate cash expenditures for the shortest practical time period. Months are better than quarters; weeks are better than months. Estimates of daily expenditures, however, are impractical.
2. Project cash collections from credit sales conservatively. Since very few companies meet trade payable obligations in less than thirty days, estimate a thirty- to sixty-day collection period.
3. Summarize weekly cash expenditures and receipts by month for one year.
4. Construct a separate inventory schedule showing expenditures for purchases and payroll and clearly identifying corresponding sales of inventory. This is called an *inventory flow schedule*.
5. Estimate the turnover of trade payables very conservatively. In other words, instead of using trade payables to finance working capital beyond thirty days, assume that all obligations will be paid within thirty days of receipt of the invoice. If you can negotiate extended credit with some suppliers, that's extra cash.
6. Specify all expenses necessary to produce and sell the product, including overhead expenses such as rent, utilities, insurance, and taxes.
7. Exclude expenditures for the purchase of production equipment, machinery, delivery vehicles, or automobiles. These items should be acquired with long-term funds, not working capital. However, include payments against all lease obligations.

8. Segregate your salary or draw from other expenses.

Figure 7-2 (page 120) illustrates one format for projecting a four-month cash flow for a first-stage manufacturing company.

In this example, Mack Manufacturing needs two types of working capital loans:

1. A one-year term loan of $400
2. A line of credit (referred to as a "revolver") based on a borrowing base of 85 percent of monthly sales and secured by accounts receivable

The term loan would be secured by a lien against inventory and a second position against all other free assets. A personal guarantee will also probably be required. Although some business owners with close personal contacts at commercial banks might be able to get open lines of credit, revolvers are far more common.

Cash flow projections from Mack Manufacturing Corp. demonstrate that without any loans the company would have a shortfall for the four months of $78, $33, $63, and $42, respectively, resulting in a cumulative bank overdraft of $208 at the end of four months, calculated as follows:

	Jan.	Feb.	Mar.	Apr.
Beginning bank balance	5	(73)	(106)	(166)
Cash receipts from collections	15	90	110	120
Expenditures	106	200	269	267
Less: Principal payment	(12)	(76)	(94)	(102)
Interest expense	(1)	(1)	(2)	(2)
Net operating expenditures	93	123	173	163
Total cash available (shortfall) without loans	(78)	(33)	(63)	(42)
Ending bank balance	(73)	(106)	(166)	(208)

It clearly would be less costly to fund Mack's working capital needs with equity capital rather than loans. Unfortunately, most first-stage companies cannot attract new equity and are forced to go to a bank.

Retail working capital plans

Cash sales, fewer employees, less expenses, and faster inventory turns make working capital plans for retail companies much less complex than those for manufacturing businesses. However, most retailers do not enjoy the high profit margins that manufacturing companies. Furthermore, without receivables as loan collateral, bank borrowing becomes more difficult.

Figure 7-2
Mack Manufacturing Corp.

CASH FLOW FORECAST
For the Four Months Ended April 30, 1991

	Jan.	Feb.	Mar.	Apr.
Beginning receivables	25	135	175	195
Sales	125	130	130	140
Less: Collections	(15)	(90)	(110)	(120)
Ending receivables	135	175	195	215
Beginning trade payables	50	100	125	105
Purchases	70	75	80	100
Less: Payments	(20)	(50)	(100)	(90)
Ending trade payables	100	125	105	115
Cash Receipts				
Collections from sales (15%)	2	13	16	18
Bank loans—revolver	107	110	110	119
Bank loans—term loan	400			
Total receipts	509	123	126	137
Cash Expenditures				
Principal payment on loans	12	76	94	102
Interest expense	1	1	2	2
Payment of trade payables	20	50	100	90
Payroll and payroll taxes	12	12	12	12
Employee health insurance and				
workers' compensation	3	3	3	3
Building rent	3	3	3	3
Electricity	2	2	2	2
Fuel	1	1	1	1
Water	2	2	2	2
Telephone	3	3	3	3
Business insurance	5	5	5	5
Operating supplies	7	7	7	7
Office supplies	3	3	3	3
Equipment lease payments	2	2	2	2
Transportation and freight	2	2	2	2
Advertising and sales promotion	7	7	7	7
Market research	6	6	6	6
Product development	10	10	10	10
Other operating expenses	2	2	2	2
Small tools	3	3	3	3
Total expenditures	106	200	269	267
Cash Surplus (shortfall)	403	(77)	(143)	(130)
Less: Owner's salary/draw	4	4	4	4
Net Cash Surplus (shortfall)	399	(82)	(147)	(134)
Beginning bank balance	5	404	322	175
Net cash surplus (shortfall)	399	(82)	(147)	(134)
Ending bank balance	404	322	175	41
Bank Loans				
Term loan	400	400	400	400
Revolver				
Beginning loan balance	0	99	133	149
New loans—85% of sales	107	110	110	119
Less: Principal payments—85% of collections	12	76	94	102
Ending loan balance	99	133	149	166
Total loan balances	499	533	549	566

Figure 7-3 demonstrates a typical cash flow forecast format for retail businesses.

Figure 7-3
Rex Retail Corp.

CASH FLOW FORECAST
For the Four Months Ended April 30, 1991

	Jan.	Feb.	Mar.	Apr.
Sales	0	50	100	125
Beginning trade payables	0	40	90	100
Purchases	40	80	110	130
Less: Payments	0	30	100	120
Ending trade payables	40	90	100	110
Cash Receipts				
Collections from sales	0	50	100	125
Bank loans	175	0	0	0
Total receipts	175	50	100	125
Cash Expenditures				
Interest on bank loans	0	1	1	1
Payment of trade payables	0	30	100	120
Payroll and payroll taxes	5	5	5	5
Employee health insurance and				
worker's compensation	1	1	1	1
Building rent	3	3	3	3
Electricity	1	1	1	1
Fuel	2	2	2	2
Water	0	1	0	1
Telephone	3	3	3	3
Business insurance	6	6	6	6
Operating supplies	3	3	3	3
Office supplies	3	3	3	3
Lease payments	2	2	2	2
Transportation and freight	3	3	3	3
Advertising and sales promotion	10	10	10	10
Market research	1	0	1	0
Other operating expenses	2	2	2	2
Total expenditures	45	76	146	166
Cash Surplus (shortfall)	130	(26)	(46)	(41)
Less: Owner's salary/draw	4	4	4	4
Net Cash Surplus (shortfall)	126	(30)	(50)	(45)
Beginning bank balance	5	131	101	51
Net cash surplus (shortfall)	126	(30)	(50)	(45)
Ending bank balance	131	101	51	6
Bank Loans				
Term loan balance	175	175	175	175

Note that without credit sales and the high inventory carried by manufacturing companies, Rex can get by with a term loan of only $175. If sales don't pick up in the next two or three months, however, the company may need necessary to return to the well for an additional term loan.

Term loans are frequently easier to arrange for retail establishments than for manufacturing companies. Resale inventory can be liquidated for at least its cost, making this asset ideal loan collateral. In manufacturing operations, liquidation proceeds from raw material inventory are far less certain, causing lenders to discount its collateral value. However, personal guarantees will probably be required for Rex as they were for Mack.

Service business working capital plans

The major differences between working capital plans for service businesses and those for retail companies are related to inventory and payables calculations. Although most service businesses purchase supplies and other items on credit and thus incur trade payables, the amounts are generally small and can be treated as cash purchases in the plan. In addition, since service businesses rarely maintain inventories of anything other than miscellaneous supplies, this asset cannot be used as loan collateral. On the other hand, as Figure 7-4 illustrates, the amount of capital required in first-stage service businesses is significantly less than in either manufacturing or retail businesses.

For most service businesses, first-stage borrowing from a bank is nearly impossible without the owner's pledging personal assets. With the exception of furniture, office equipment, and perhaps an automobile, all of which will probably be financed with installment loans, service businesses don't have the hard assets, receivables, or inventory to interest banks. This means that they need more equity capital to get started. On the other hand, it normally takes service businesses a lot less time to get up and running than it does retail or manufacturing companies.

PRIMARY SOURCES OF SHORT-TERM CREDIT

Regardless of your type of business, it is likely that first-stage credit is a serious problem. Since you don't have a proven track record, you have probably already been turned down by a couple of banks—maybe more. But don't despair. Creativity is now the name of the game. The trick is to locate a financing source willing to gamble on your ability to grow the business and at the same time not charge exorbitant interest or fees.

There are four primary sources of first-stage working capital:

- Commercial banks
- Venture funds
- Investment clubs
- U.S. government agencies

If possible, it's a good idea to avoid borrowing from commercial banks. Not only do they shy away from first-stage working capital loans, they also demand unreasonable amounts of collateral for any type of loan. Although commercial banks may be the only choice, other financing sources that look at first-stage funding from a different perspective are certainly preferable.

Figure 7-4
Sival Service Corp.

CASH FLOW FORECAST
For the Four Months Ended April 30, 1991

	Jan.	Feb.	Mar.	Apr.
Sales	0	25	30	60
Cash Receipts				
Collections from sales	0	25	30	60
Bank loans	100	0	0	0
Total receipts	100	25	30	60
Cash Expenditures				
Interest on bank loans	1	1	1	1
Payroll and payroll taxes	8	8	8	8
Employee health insurance and workers' compensation	2	2	2	2
Building rent	1	1	1	1
Electricity	1	0	1	0
Fuel	0	1	0	1
Telephone	6	6	6	6
Business insurance	3	3	3	3
Office supplies	8	8	8	8
Lease payments	2	2	2	2
Transportation (automobile)	3	3	3	3
Advertising and sales promotion	10	10	10	10
Market research	3	3	3	3
Other operating expenses	2	2	2	2
Total expenditures	50	50	50	50
Cash Surplus (shortfall)	50	(25)	(20)	10
Less: Owner's salary/draw	4	4	4	4
Net Cash Surplus (shortfall)	46	(29)	(24)	6
Beginning bank balance	5	51	22	(2)
Net cash surplus (shortfall)	46	(29)	(24)	6
Ending bank balance	51	22	(2)	4
Bank Loans				
Term loan balance	100	100	100	100

For clarity, the following discussion matches various types of businesses with the most likely funding sources by focusing on four broad market groupings:

1. Businesses offering products or services in industries experiencing rapid growth

2. Businesses operating in stable industries that have opportunistic local markets

3. Businesses that are now or expect to be selling internationally

4. Businesses engaged in selling products or services in highly fragmented, local markets that place a cap on the growth of the individual company

Rapid Growth Markets

Several health care market segments, housing and transport for the elderly, top-of-the-line travel and leisure activities, advanced telecommunications, and alternative fuel sources represent rapid growth markets. First-stage short-term financing for companies selling into these markets is more competitive and easier to arrange than for companies in less glamorous markets.

All risk-oriented, high-return financial sources—venture funds, foreign merchant banks, high-net-worth individuals, and so on—finance companies in rapid growth markets. Their early success in the computer industry encouraged these risk-oriented investors to examine other high-growth markets. Throughout the 1970s and 1980s, small venture capital firms became large investment complexes. More funds became available. The euphoric explosion on Wall Street encouraged even greater risk taking in first-stage, rapid-growth businesses.

In the mid-1990s this high-risk investment fervor has cooled somewhat. The focus of many venture firms has shifted toward more conservative first-stage risks. But vast stores of venture capital are still available, and businesses in high-growth markets still find small venture funds a ready source of working capital.

Venture capital is not cheap, however. Risk-taking investors typically demand annual returns of 30 to 40 percent, on average, over a five-year period, plus substantial investment appreciation. The payoff comes from either future refinancing or public stock issues. Obviously, venture funds seek out high-growth markets because companies in other industries cannot provide such high returns.

Complete listings of venture capital firms may be found in most libraries. *Pratt's Guide to Venture Capital Sources*, published by Venture Economics, is the best source. In addition, a directory of members may be obtained from the National Venture Capital Association, 1655 North Fort Myer Drive, Suite 700, Arlington, VA 22209, (703) 528-4370.

Stable Industry, Growing Local Market

Small but growing local markets usually are created by either new product introductions or vacuums created by competitors withdrawing from the market. An example of the latter occurred in the banking industry during the last half of the 1980s. As regulations governing intra- and interstate bank expansion loosened, a wave of bank mergers eliminated a flock of neighborhood and rural-area banks. Evaluating this vacuum as a potentially high-growth niche market, investors formed new banks (generally quite small) to serve small businesses and individuals.

In certain parts of the country, waste management is another example of a growing niche market. Environmental pressures that forced the development of technologies to convert liquid and solid waste to socially beneficial products enabled several start-up companies to develop technologies and facilities for converting trash to alternative energy sources. Local investment clubs (actually a hybrid of venture funds) were formed to provide first-stage working capital for companies involved in these opportunistic local markets. Many such clubs began as limited partnerships, soliciting investment funds from high-net-worth individuals and local businesses. Others arose when existing venture funds made an effort to diversify their holdings.

Today, such investment clubs remain the best source of capital for stable, local market businesses. Just as with venture capital funds, however, expect to give up an ownership share, perhaps even a controlling interest, and plan to take your company public in five to seven years. Most libraries carry the *Directory of Venture Capital Clubs*, which lists private investment clubs formed specifically to invest in first-stage ventures.

International Markets

Companies selling internationally or expecting to take this step in the near future should look to both foreign and U.S. government agencies as primary capital sources. Selling internationally may mean exporting products. It may entail selling services overseas, as with global construction companies. Or it may mean establishing a physical presence on foreign soil. First-stage working capital financing takes three forms: trade credit, guarantees, and short-term debt.

Most cash ultimately comes from commercial banks, but loan collateral must be raised from third parties. Such collateral comes primarily from two sources: guarantees and loans from the United States Export-Import Bank (Eximbank), and letters of credit (L/Cs) and loans from foreign banks. Eximbank offers a wide range of financial assistance programs. Some are funnelled through the SBA, others come direct from Eximbank. Trade credit may be extended to foreign buyers, who in turn issue L/Cs to be drawn against by exporters for working capital.

Eximbank also issues guarantees that can be used as collateral for working capital loans from commercial banks. On occasion, Eximbank lends short-term funds directly to exporters, although these are very difficult for first-stage companies to obtain. A quick phone call to Eximbank will trigger a flood of information about how to apply for financial assistance.

Fragmented and Mature Local Markets

Without question, the choice of sources of first-stage working capital is the most limited for businesses in fragmented, mature local markets. Businesses serving these markets include machine shops, contractors, auto repair shops, specialty food stores, professional practices, and so on. Most first-stage working capital must be raised through commercial banks, difficult as that may be. Depending on the location and the current status of federal funding allocations, additional loans might be obtained directly from the SBA; however, these have become increasingly scarce.

Rather than funding a small business directly, the SBA prefers to issue guarantees as collateral for commercial bank loans. Although criteria frequently change, as of this writing, the SBA guarantees 90 percent of small-business loans up to $155,000 and 85 percent of an additional $500,000. Interest rates are limited to 2.25 to 2.75 percentage points over prime. In addition, the SBA charges a placement fee of 2 percent of the amount of the loan.

The SBA guarantees term loans, with repayment extending to twenty—five years in some cases. Typically, however, to placate recalcitrant banks, the SBA limits repayment terms for working capital funding to five to seven years. SBA offices, located in most cities, have application forms, and an appointment with a SCORE representative is part of the application process. Also, to qualify, the applicant must have been turned down by at least two banks.

Unfortunately, not all commercial banks lend against SBA guarantees. For best results, first locate a bank that is willing to participate, then contact the SBA. The application process generally moves quickly and smoothly if you have a participating bank already on board.

Chapter 8

Consulting and Other Professional Services

Although the growth strategies in this chapter are tailored to consulting and other business-oriented professional services, many apply equally well to nearly all professions—the law, accounting, health services, architecture, financial planning, engineering, and so on. References to consulting businesses are used for ease of discussion and to clarify points, but readers should bear in mind the similarities with other professional practices.

Consultants and other professional advisors complain as much about how difficult it is to get new clients (or patients) as they do about being overworked and underpaid. They don't mean that they can't get any clients. They mean that the work they get isn't the type they really want, or that they can't bill as much as they think the job is worth. Getting the right clients at the right fee seems to be a problem for both new and experienced practitioners. The absence of a well-conceived strategic plan can be blamed for this condition as much as anything else.

As pointed out in Chapter 2, the first step in strategic planning is to precisely define the mission of the company. In consulting, that means first defining the skills and knowledge that you have to sell, and second, identifying those long-term growth markets that demand such expertise. The more specific you can be, the higher your probability of attracting the right clients.

Most of us have substantial knowledge in more than one discipline. For certain types of engagements, however, it is not enough to be competent—one must be an expert. In 1982 Hubert Bermont put it succinctly in his book *The Complete Consultant* (published by The Consultant's Library, Washington, D.C.): "I find that most people who aspire to consultancy are totally unaware that they have to be tops in their field to qualify. *Mere competence is not enough.*" He further claimed that clients will not pay for mediocrity and that five or ten years in a specific field of endeavor does not necessarily qualify one as an expert.

A small percentage of active consultants specialize in market niches that require state licensing as evidence of professional proficiency. Even without such certification, however, we can differentiate ourselves from the mediocre. Bermont is correct when he acknowledges that mere tenure in a particular field is not enough to qualify one as an expert. It takes more than that. It takes verifiable credentials of accomplishment. It takes personal credibility to inspire clients to listen to what we say and then follow that advice. And in order to attract new clients, we must communicate this knowledge base to the marketplace.

Since credentials and credibility are valuable only if they relate to skills demanded by the market, the starting point is to identify those skills that are marketable. This should not be difficult. We all know what we do well and what we stumble over. We try to sell the former and hide the latter. Such is life in professional services. It does help, however, to articulate the two or three skills in which we feel most qualified by jotting them down on a piece of paper. More often than not, such codification helps us funnel our abilities into definable market niches. Once you have identified those services that are marketable, it's time to move on to implementing a marketing program that meets your strategic objectives.

DEVELOPING CREDENTIALS

If one facet of business-oriented professional services sets this industry apart from other entrepreneurial pursuits, it is the overriding emphasis on marketing. Other business owners enjoy the option of delegating sales responsibilities to employees with proven sales aptitude. Such employees may not know how to manufacture the product or perform the service they sell, but they know how to get orders. Professional advisors, on the other hand, have nothing to sell but themselves. No employee or outsider can do the job for us. We must do it ourselves.

Far too many ex-executives with a wealth of valuable management and technical talent but a dearth of sales ability have tried to start consulting businesses. They struggle to make a go of it—sometimes for years—but never quite seem to make it, never quite reach the pinnacle of their ability. Beginners in the field all too often believe that if they call themselves consultants (or financial planners, or tax advisors, or investment counselors) and run a few promotional spots, clients will beat a path to their doorstep. Seldom do such tactics work. Instead, they must get out in the marketplace and peddle their wares. If they don't, they won't be in business very long.

As a starting point, professional advisors in any field must establish undeniable credentials. Public recognition goes a long way toward opening client doors. Acknowledged expertise smoothes the road to new clients even if you lack selling flair. Although strong marketing efforts are still required (there is no substitute for active solicitation), if you do not have publicly recognized credentials, the obstacles to getting new bookings may be insurmountable.

How does a person establish specialist credentials? For some it takes years. Others accomplish the feat in short order. No pat answer applies to everyone. Each person must search out the most effective means, recognizing personal, geographical, and market limitations.

Obviously, if your skills can be certified, then by all means get the certification: a license, award, professional designation, degree, and so on. Clients love to see a string of letters after your name. If certification doesn't apply, join some authoritative trade or professional organizations serving your specialty. It always looks good to have a few memberships tacked onto your letterhead.

A focused, high-impact publicity program that promotes you as a master in your field works wonders. And there is a wide variety of methods at your disposal. If you do not feel competent to make initial media contacts, hire a small publicity firm to do it for you. This gets expensive, but the recognition a publicity program brings is well worth the cost. A publicity program establishes your credentials by promoting you as an authority, an advocate, a supporter, or all three.

Become an Authority

To become known as an authority, you have to convince the public how much you know about something. Your audience probably doesn't know as much about the subject as you do; therefore, keep your presentations simple, but with enough authoritative jargon to get the point across. Here are some ideas:

1. Publish a newsletter with current developments in your field (but postage is expensive)

2. Write articles for business and trade magazines

3. Conduct an adult evening school course in a related field

4. Write a book about your specialty (this works wonders if you can find a publisher that knows how to market your type of book)

5. Present a seminar on a topic related to your marketable skills

6. Get on the lecture circuit (but it's hard to get started without previously established credentials)

7. Teach part-time at a local college

8. Participate in trade conferences and shows as a speaker or panelist

9. Volunteer consulting services to a local SBA office

Become an Advocate

An advocate takes a stand for something (public duty, human rights, the homeless, the environment) or against something (drugs, poverty, corporate greed, pollution, taxes). Although becoming an advocate doesn't directly establish expert credentials, indirectly it does. By expressing your views on a public topic, you demonstrate knowledge and experience in a specific subject. More important, the audience focuses its attention on you as an individual.

When a potential client remarks, "Didn't I see you on television last week? You really presented good arguments," you'll know how effective advocacy can be. Of course, advocates also run the risk of offending. Nevertheless, effective public imaging must present you as strong, confident, and experienced, willing and able to argue points persuasively, regardless of your point of view.

Some positive ways to get public exposure as an advocate are:

1. Write "letters to the editor" to your local newspaper

2. Actively participate in civic, community, and socially conscious organizations

3. Get on a TV talk show

4. Be interviewed on network radio

5. Donate your time to youth groups, poverty rehabilitation programs, elderly assistance groups, or literacy training

6. Get quoted in newspaper and magazine articles

7. Organize community action groups—recycling projects, governmental awareness programs, anti-crime groups, crisis assistance, or youth involvement

Become a Supporter

Becoming a supporter carries the same risks of offending as becoming an advocate. But then, you can't please everyone all the time, just as you can't sell all services to all types of clients. It doesn't pay to offend too many people, however, so it's best to carefully choose which causes to support and how strongly to support them.

As with advocacy, publicly supporting something or someone doesn't directly establish your credentials in the market niches you're after, but it does bring you into contact with influential people who can indirectly point you to clients. I have found that extending support in the political arena works extremely well for certain market niches. It would have been impossible to penetrate either government contracting or international markets without reciprocal support from public figures.

Here are a few ideas for becoming a supporter:

1. Run for local office

2. Appear on TV and radio in support of local officials running for elected office

3. Acknowledge support for state representatives when specific issues come up for vote

4. Write opinion letters to your congressional representatives

5. Get to know top-level bureaucrats in the Washington offices of the SBA, Eximbank, Department of Commerce agencies, and procurement bureaus

6. Get elected (or appointed) to the local school board or planning commission

7. Write a commentary for the Op-Ed page of your local newspaper

Focusing on all three approaches—becoming an authority, an advocate, and a supporter—provides maximum publicity coverage and seems to bring better results than choosing one over the others. In addition to developing credentials and personal contacts, publicity and public relations programs should be designed to portray you as an honest, forthright person who possesses all those good attributes that everyone admires but few of us really have. This can be as important as establishing credentials once you get through a prospective client's door.

PERSONAL DEMEANOR

We cannot all be super salespeople with a knack for closing orders on the first try. Most practitioners must rely on other talents. Once you have established technical proficiency credentials and a forthright public image, your next step is to convince prospective clients that you do indeed perform your work in a professional manner. And this is best accomplished by looking the part. The image portrayed at the first meeting with a prospective client very often determines whether an engagement evolves or whether the meeting is a waste of time.

Regardless of a person's position in a client's organization, it's extremely important to treat that person professionally. This means dressing the part. It also means exhibiting all those good characteristics you have tried so hard to publicly establish—honesty, loyalty, thoroughness, confidence, commitment, and confidentiality. Honesty, loyalty, and thoroughness need no comment. The other three, however, probably need further explanation.

Clients want to be certain that professional advisors are confident of their ability to do the work and that the results of the engagement will be what the client expects. Confidence cannot be stated: it must be felt. It's easy to tell whether people have confidence in what they do, even on the phone. An air of expectancy, enthusiasm, and assurance leaps out. Conversely, it's just as easy to spot lack of confidence.

Professional advisors must exude confidence. Use whatever means are necessary to convey to clients that you are the best and only person to do the job. No one else can come close to producing the results that the client needs. For some engagements I have gone so far as to guarantee the results the client expects; that is, I guarantee to keep working at the assignment until the client is satisfied, at no additional cost.

Clients also want to know that professional advisors will be committed to the engagement. The last thing anyone wants to hear is that another client takes precedence over this engagement. Clients like to feel that they are number one with you. Yes, they want to know that you have many other clients as proof of your abilities. But once their project begins, they want everything else put aside. They want your full, undivided, committed attention.

Total confidentiality is a must. Clients must be assured that the financial, product, market, competitive, design, and other information you glean from their business remains sealed in your files. Successful professionals learn early in the game to respect a client's privacy. Complete and total confidentiality must be conveyed strongly and persuasively at the first meeting.

In the end, personal chemistry can do more to attract new business than anything else. Although "personal chemistry" is certainly an overworked cliché, as far as repeat business or future references go, the best results come from client representatives with whom we have established a good rapport, a meeting of the minds—a good personal chemistry.

ADVERTISING PROMOTIONS

Personal service business owners, including consultants, seem to get more mileage from effective publicity and public relations programs than from traditional advertising techniques. Many people continue to wince when they see advertisements from physicians, lawyers, financial planners, public accountants, psychologists, and others regarded as professionals.

Traditionally, for some unfathomable reason, it has been considered unprofessional to blatantly advertise personal services, to actually solicit business. However, professional advisors in all fields are learning fast that advertising does bring in clients and that clients don't regard such tactics as unprofessional, provided the advertisements are in good taste—that is, they get the message across without being offensive. Spot television commercials, conservative newspaper spreads, and well-placed mailings are a few examples of techniques that can be used effectively.

Most consultants do not seem very adept at advertising their own wares. It's easy to critique a client's advertising and promotion campaigns. When it comes to putting on our own show, we seem to fall apart. Perhaps modesty prevents us from blowing our own horn. Or maybe some of us still regard advertising as unprofessional. Or perhaps we just don't understand the techniques of promoting ourselves. Whatever the reason, consultants as a group do a horrible job.

Advertising professional services isn't that difficult, as long as you follow these basic principles:

1. Keep the presentation low-key, conservative, and tasteful
2. Use desktop publishing for most of the work (it's a real cost saver, and you can be as creative as you wish)
3. Match your advertising campaign to long-range strategic objectives (go after the markets you want to develop)
4. Target specific market niches (stay away from general advertising)
5. Measure results and modify the campaign if it is not effective

Once they get rolling, consultants have proved to be very effective at coming up with creative advertising campaigns. Here are a few advertising media that members of my consortium have used effectively over the years.

1. Direct mail to lawyers, public accountants, financial planners, and other business-oriented professionals
2. Full-page newspaper advertisements
3. Highway billboards
4. Television and radio talk shows
5. Television and radio spot commercials

6. Advertisements in trade journals, business magazines, and community affairs bulletins such as school catalogs and community theater playbills

But selecting a medium is only part of the answer. Before running an advertisement, we need to determine what to say. An effective advertisement has these four components:

1. *A positive promise of benefit.* "Want to save taxes? We'll make it happen." "Looking for financing? We'll arrange it for you." "Need to control your costs? We can do it with computers!"

2. *A clarification of credentials.* "Twenty years in the business." "Over one hundred satisfied clients." "We guarantee to maximize your refund."

3. *Proof of credentials.* The best proof is testimonials from satisfied clients.

4. *A response mechanism.* Telephone number; return coupon; questionnaire response.

Impact advertising is intended to achieve a specific goal. When writing the copy, bear in mind the specific goal that you are trying to achieve. Are you aiming for walk-in business? 10,000 coupon responses? an avalanche of phone calls? Choose only one goal. Focus the advertisement on achieving one specific response. Of course, if the advertisement is successful, be prepared to handle the responses as efficiently and expeditiously as possible.

It's also important to direct the copy to the right audience. In the merger and acquisition consulting field, for example, do you want large corporations, small businesses, midsize companies, or individuals? Advertising that appeals to one audience will probably not appeal to the others. It also helps to address an audience of one, not one hundred or one thousand. Make the copy single out one individual or one company, not the masses.

Finally, regardless of the medium, it's crucial to prepare advertising copy that defines the specific, unique service you are trying to sell. The more specific you get, the higher the probability of a response. "Consultant experienced in all phases of international work" probably won't bring one reply. "Unique financing sources available for facilities expansion in the European Community" stands a much better chance.

Focused Marketing

It seems that most professionals shy away from the principal tenet of long-term growth strategies: focused marketing. As described in Chapter 4, focused marketing means achieving the best mix of high-margin products and customers, in specific market niches, with the most cost-effective selling techniques. In the consulting field, the key to focused marketing is the optimum mix of billable hours, hourly rates, and selling expenses. Market control is the key to focused marketing, and market control is achieved by concentrating sales efforts on those niche markets that best suit your strategic objectives.

When business slows, the temptation is great to go after any work that nets billable hours, regardless of the type of engagement. This is a deadly practice and can get you into all kinds of long-term difficulty. One of our consortium members who specializes in merger and acquisition (M&A) work learned that lesson the hard way. When the credit crunch hit, Jon had trouble booking new M&A jobs and began soliciting business start-up clients. Accustomed to very high closing fees for M&A work, Jon was shocked to learn that start-up jobs didn't command more than $75 per hour. Nevertheless, an impact-advertising campaign resulted in more than twenty new clients in less than six months. In short order, all his billable hours were fully spoken for.

Out of the blue, another consortium member asked Jon if he was interested in taking on an assignment in England, at Lehman-scale rates (discussed in Chapter 10), for a client interested in buying a business in the $50 million range. Fully loaded with start-up clients (at $75 an hour) Jon couldn't handle the job. Four years later, he was still doing start-up jobs—and was much poorer for it.

Market control can be achieved by taking action in one or a combination of three areas: by optimizing the mix of services performed (don't get overloaded in one market niche), by focusing on the most lucrative client mix (don't get saddled with slow payers or complainers), and by paying close attention to post-engagement follow-up—methods not dissimilar from those described in Chapter 4 for other types of businesses.

Optimizing service mix means selectively selling those services that maximize both billable hours and hourly rates. The most lucrative client mix comprises clients who are willing and able to pay the highest price for the services that you can produce. Post-engagement follow-up offers the most efficient means of assuring repeat business and glowing references.

Some practitioners argue that it is impractical to concentrate marketing efforts on those services that yield the highest fees. Doing so would leave vast gaps in available time or reduce gross billings (as in the case of my consortium associate). There just aren't enough high-fee clients around to be that selective.

Obviously such arguments have merit for those who follow the traditional path of concentrating in markets without positive growth potential, as so many professionals are apt to do. However, it's impossible to gain market control by being one of several hundred professionals offering the same service to the same clients, with nothing unique to separate your business from the pack. Moreover, you will never attain market control by trying to be all things to all people.

To stand a chance of gaining control of your market, you need to have special talents that set your business apart, to broadcast these talents through effective marketing methods, and to specialize in a few high-growth, cutting-edge markets. Consultants who are interested in defining and penetrating these high-growth markets could benefit by picking up a copy of my book *Cutting Edge Consultants: Succeeding in Today's Explosive Markets* (Prentice-Hall, 1992).

SELLING TECHNIQUES

We all have talents and limitations in using different types of selling techniques. Some of us do best with written communications. Others prefer telephone solicitations. Still others work best in face-to-face meetings. Two truisms relate to selling consulting skills: (1) at least one-third of our available hours should be dedicated to marketing our services to new clients, and (2) the worst marketing mistake is to use selling techniques that don't fit with our abilities.

Traditional advertising media—newsletters, direct mail, and so on all work under certain circumstances. Assuming that your verbal communications skills are up to par, telephone solicitation and direct meetings can also be effective. Both generally start with cold calls, the hardest of all selling techniques, and frequently the least productive.

Cold Call Selling

I stopped making cold calls several years ago when I finally realized that this was not my forte. On the other hand, a close friend has become an expert in using this tactic. He is so successful that it's now about the only method he uses. Other consultants have told me that if you have the right personality, cold calls do work. Here are a few tips they have passed along over the years that seem to form the nucleus of successful selling:

1. *Plan the call.* Before you pick up the phone or knock on a door, know precisely who to ask for. You won't get far talking to the purchasing manager if you are soliciting a financing engagement. Also, plan your sales pitch. Once you get through to the right person, you have about thirty seconds to make a pitch. Have three or four sentences prepared that get your message across.

2. *Ask for the order.* No one has time to chat with a stranger. Keep the conversation short and to the point, and wrap it up with a direct request for an engagement. (Although this is a deadly tactic for selling most types of products and services, it can be done effectively in professional service businesses.)

3. *Target markets.* Professional advisors are seldom hired for open-ended engagements. Today's clients want a specific problem solved. Do enough research to identify the companies that are most likely to need your specific service. If you can find who it is, talk to the person responsible for getting the problem solved.

4. *Ask for recommendations.* If the person you call doesn't want your service, ask for recommendations to managers within the same company or other companies who might need your help. If possible, get the prospect to make an advance telephone call on your behalf.

5. *Use indirect leads.* Lawyers, public accountants, financial planners, and bank loan officers all have clients/customers with problems. Consultants should call on these people for leads.

6. *Show concern.* Talk about the prospect's personal concerns, financial problems, personnel shortcomings, increased competition, declining orders, and so on. Be genuine. Show compassion. Convey a sincere desire to help.

7. *Do not talk about yourself.* Focus attention on the prospect. Stay away from your own interests, unless asked. Then keep the answer short. Let the prospect do the talking. Learn whatever you can in the time allotted.

8. *Leave sales literature.* Business cards, company brochures, advertising fliers, and a newsletter (if you have one) are all reminders that you called. Structure the literature to provide evidence of your ability to handle specific types of engagements.

9. *Follow up.* This is the most important step. Never, regardless of your reception, allow a prospect to get away with only one call. Always go back a second time, even if you are turned down cold the first time. Persistence pays.

Hard Sell or Soft Sell

Although not a raging argument, the question of "hard" versus "soft" selling tactics continues to arise. Some consultants feel that hard sell tactics are unprofessional, although such arguments smack of sour grapes. Doctors, lawyers, public accountants, dentists, architects, and many other professionals use hard-sell tactics consistently. A hard sell is effective if it is properly structured. As with sales promotions of any kind, presentations should be accepted as professional if they are done in good taste.

This doesn't imply storming the doors of prospective clients, discourteously refusing to take no for an answer. On the contrary, a soft entrance can lead to a dynamic sales pitch. Self-confidence, expert credentials, honesty, and commitment (all vital professional service characteristics) can be most effectively conveyed through a dynamic, hard-hitting sales pitch—but keep it short.

Some also view persistent follow-up calls as a poor approach, believing that prospects will be annoyed if they are continually assaulted with follow-up calls and mailings. Perhaps that's true in some cases. In most cases, however, persistence pays off. Follow-up calls one, two, or even three years after the initial contact will probably yield at least a few new clients.

Some people are incapable of projecting a dynamic image and find it difficult, if not impossible, to use hard-sell tactics. If the shoe fits, turn to the soft sell, which can be equally effective in certain markets and with certain clients. It seems that the larger the client company, the more susceptible representatives are to soft-sell techniques. Internal politics play a major role in landing such engagements. Political acumen, indirect referrals, and external references all influence the success or failure of a sales call. Hard-sell tactics with such prospects nearly always fail to generate anything but headaches.

Using hard-sell tactics when your personality exudes conservatism not only backfires, it can make you look silly. It's far better to structure marketing campaigns that accentuate your strengths. If this means a slower growth rate or more hours dedicated to marketing, so be it. We can do only what we are capable of doing.

Jumping the "That's the Way It's Done" Hurdle

When trying to penetrate the government contracting segment of the aerospace industry several years ago, I met what seemed to be an immovable obstacle. Well-thought-out recommendations fell on deaf ears. Solutions used by many companies in other industries were stifled with the statement, "That will never work here. The way we're doing it [the method, procedure, evaluation, negotiation] is the way it's done in the aerospace industry. You can't change it."

Such blinders are not restricted to the aerospace industry. Companies the world over use this same excuse. And consultants the world over have two courses to follow: Give up and walk away, or jump the hurdle. There are two ways to make the jump:

1. Get the client company's ranking executive to direct employees to follow your lead

2. Prove to these employees the wisdom of your solution by demonstrating its effectiveness

Clearly, the latter course brings better results for the client. Here's how one consultant beat the odds when hired to help a midsize freight hauler develop its strategic plan.

One of the consultant's strategic recommendations was that the client enter the intermodal freight business. He saw a skyrocketing market for hauling both imports and exports and believed that the company's resources justified the move. The client's vice president of traffic was obstinate, claiming that intermodal freight could never be introduced competitively because it just wasn't the way things were done in that industry. The consultant convinced the board to budget $100,000 for a small advertising program to test his case. Within four months, calls for intermodal service were flooding the client's switchboard, exonerating the consultant.

Engagements limited to solving purely internal problems frequently present a greater challenge, mainly because employees fear for their positions in the company. Creative techniques for bringing clients' employees into the fold seem to work best when the employees know that implementing your solutions won't jeopardize their jobs. A simple statement to this effect from the boss usually does the trick.

COMBINING FORCES

Consultants who practice by themselves, without an office staff or partners, face an uphill battle in growing their business. The limited number of available working hours and voids in their knowledge base will invariably restrict how fast and how far sole practitioners can grow a business. This same restriction applies to lawyers, physicians, dentists, public accountants, and nearly all other professional practitioners.

To compensate, growth strategies must include means of circumventing the limitations of operating a business on your own. One of the best ways to accomplish this feat is to structure your organization in such a manner that you can tap the services of other professionals as necessary, without losing your independence as a sole practitioner. Networks, consortiums, and informal partnerships effectively accomplish this goal. These arrangements are also terrific ways to get a new business off the ground. Not only do they provide clients a broader skill base and a greater number of experts to handle the workload, these combinations enhance marketing strategies designed to reach a much broader range of market niches than a sole practitioner could achieve.

In addition to augmenting marketing and production capabilities, combining forces often results in significant cost savings on office rent, automobile leases and insurance, secretarial and office payroll, office equipment and supplies, telephones, research libraries and databases, computer software, and many other incidentals. Furthermore, combining forces can enhance the effectiveness of advertising campaigns.

Long-time practitioners are bound to raise the age-old objection, "I'm not going to let other consultants (or lawyers, or accountants, or dentists, or physicians) talk to my clients or even know who they are. They might steal them from me!" We must have some kind of proprietary interest in our clients to feel this way. We also must suffer from an intense inferiority complex to believe that client loyalty is so shallow. Nevertheless, one of the occupational hazards of the consulting business (and other professions) seems to be that practitioners do not talk with one another, much less share marketing information.

This is a shame. So many benefits arise from broadening our capabilities that to ignore consortiums, networking, or informal partnerships because we fear losing the clients we have seems like a horrible waste. I have used all three combinations in my consulting career and swear by the results. As a sole practitioner, it would have been impossible for me to grow in the market niches I wanted without the help of many other consultants.

For sole practitioners, one huge benefit of combining forces is the image a larger business presents to a potential client. A united front makes the company appear bigger than it really is. This can be an important marketing ploy when competing with larger firms. A sole practitioner trying to compete with Andersen Consulting, Boston Consulting Group, or McKinsey & Co. can hardly be expected to control a market niche. The same consultant with the ability to draw on the diverse talents of several other consultants stands a much better chance of winning jobs.

Impact advertising campaigns and well-conceived publicity efforts quickly let the marketplace know that you are not alone, a one-man band, with limited resources and work schedules. A comprehensive advertising campaign touting the virtues of the group conveys a strong support organization, varied talents, broad resources, and the ability to handle major engagements. Pragmatically, this is the only way a sole practitioner can build a profitable business within a reasonable time frame.

Informal Partnerships

Informal partnerships seem to be especially popular with sole practitioners, both during the start-up period and after they get established. No formal partnership agreement needs to be executed. Partners do not share business liabilities, income, or expenses. No partnership tax returns are filed, and no state or federal identification numbers are used. An informal partnership is not a legal entity.

Although each partner continues to operate independently, they share client workloads. When you work on one of your partner's jobs or deal with one of your partner's clients, you act under your partner's name, not your own. The client billing goes out on your partner's invoice, not yours. Your partner collects from the client and then reimburses you for work performed.

This sounds more complicated than it is. Informal partnerships proliferate in the consulting industry, as well as the accounting, health care, and legal professions. Most clients don't realize that the partnership is informal. It appears to be a true partnership or an employer/employee relationship. In reality, you sell your services to your partner as an independent contractor.

I now use informal partnerships when I consult for other consultants, which has evolved into a major part of my business. For example, a consultant friend recently needed help sourcing foreign financing for a client. I helped him locate appropriate sources, assisted in developing negotiating strategy, and put the consultant in touch with a competent overseas attorney. The consultant billed my hours and then paid me. I earned income. My partner satisfied his client in a timely manner. The client got the job done on schedule. Everyone was a winner.

Informal partnerships do not have to be among practitioners serving the same markets. Nor are they limited to arrangements between two or more consultants. Informal partnerships between consultants and public accountants, investment counselors, financial planners, and lawyers (in certain specialties) work well.

Administratively, informal partnerships must stay informal, without legal trappings. Partners must remain free to handle their own businesses. Nevertheless, there should be a brief written document spelling out the relationship between the parties. It should identify how various matters will be shared: billings, occupancy expenses, insurance programs, personnel, getting out positions, and so on. The agreement should be nonbinding, however. As soon as two or more independent-minded entrepreneurs use the law to keep a partnership together, it inevitably falls apart.

Consortiums

Consortiums offer another popular choice for sharing workloads. A consortium is a temporary alliance of two or more firms in a common venture. Consortiums work best among businesses with different capabilities serving the same market niches. Small firms specializing in international assignments or those concentrating on extended-engagement turnaround clients rely heavily on consortiums to fill in skill gaps. The production side of these engagements demands such a diverse mix of specialized skills, personal contacts, and management acumen that a sole practitioner, or a small firm, seldom has access to all the needed resources. The solution is to call on a consortium of consultants to offer clients a breadth of capabilities.

A good example of how consulting consortiums work in troubled company engagements occurred recently. A sole practitioner took on an extended turnaround engagement that required the assumption of a general management role at the client's location for six months. A number of issues needed resolution during this period—refinancing, tax planning, personnel recruiting, computer systems installation, the divestiture of a subsidiary, and the acquisition of a distribution company.

Obviously, a single consultant can't be expert in all these areas. While calling on consortium members to help with the M&A work, tax planning, and refinancing, the sole practitioner handled the balance of the work. Each consulting firm maintained its own identity and billed the client separately, although the billing could easily have been consolidated in one invoice. The billing practice depends entirely on client preference.

Consortiums are a terrific strategy for increasing billable hours, and hence cash flow, with minimal marketing effort. Consortiums also represent one of the fastest ways to develop a public image as a quality company capable of handling large as well as small jobs. As a temporary alliance, a consortium can be formed without any formal agreement or legally binding contract. It's just a matter of searching out professionals that augment your specialty and informally agreeing to sell and perform complementary services together.

Networking

Networking is very similar to consortiums except that the identification of each of the firms included in the network is not used as a marketing tool. For instance, lawyers, financial planners, tax advisors, computer specialists, and so on, are finding it increasingly beneficial to network with consultants. Only the particular capabilities of each specialist are marketed, and each member markets the skills of all other participants. The basic idea in networking is to offer clients a complete service capability that crosses many disciplines without incurring payroll costs or the complexities of a partnership.

Each network participant advertises full-service capability. When a job calls for special skills other network consultants can be called upon to perform the work. The customer can be billed either by each company performing work or by the firm booking the order, who then pays each participant.

Consulting firms that serve large regional or national markets can use networking to share the workload in different parts of the country, thus reducing or eliminating travel expenses. In this case, networking becomes a referral service, and the company booking the order gets a referral fee.

Regardless of which format is used, sharing workloads brings in higher billings and opens larger markets than consultants could possibly serve individually. Networking, consortiums, and informal partnerships tend to attract much larger engagements, hit a broader base of potential clients, and penetrate a wider range of market niches, without the implicit or explicit constraints of formal business combinations.

Chapter 9

Recovery Strategies for Overleveraged Companies

When debt service payments can't be made, expected sales don't materialize, and creditors threaten to cut off supplies, the future does indeed look bleak. This hardly seems like the appropriate time to think about growth strategies. Yet, in the end, companies that recover from severe cash shortages often grow faster, generate better profit records, and throw off more cash than stable, well-financed businesses. The key to changing an overleveraged, cash-poor company into a thriving, growth-oriented business is cash management.

Cash management, of course, is nothing more than planning cash requirements and then controlling operations against those requirements. The better the planning and the tighter the controls, the more cash a company will have for expansion. The difficulty faced by many small businesses that are already in the soup, as it were, is that banks and other creditors will not grant them sufficient breathing space to develop cash management procedures. The objective of this chapter is to demonstrate that overleveraged companies can create the breathing space they need to restructure operations, retake command of their own destinies, and go on to develop a meaningful strategic plan for achieving long-term growth.

Although details vary considerably, the general profile of an overleveraged business, which in the absence of drastic new actions to increase cash will run headlong into disaster, is one who fits the following description.

- Short-term debt has been used to increase owners' salaries and bonuses or for the acquisition of long-term assets.
- Bank refuses to grant further short-term credit and probably demands a reduction in currently outstanding loans.
- Suppliers and other creditors threaten to curtail shipments or cut off services.
- Employees spend more time complaining than working.
- Customer base is shrinking, or at best stable.
- Accounts receivable balances have stretched well beyond due dates.

Under these conditions, there isn't enough cash to meet daily operating needs, business falls off, and survival hopes dim. The odds of attracting fresh capital are probably zero, yet new cash is crucial to survival. Therefore, by one means or another, the extra cash needed to turn the corner must be retrieved from the rubble. Only then will it be possible to begin considering growth strategies. Accordingly, this chapter pinpoints the few bargaining chips still remaining that the business can use to improve cash flows by deferring cash expenditures and, in some cases, by bringing in modest amounts of fresh capital.

No one should assume that the turnaround road is free of potholes, however. More than one company has tried to implement recovery plans and failed. Overloaded bankruptcy courts attest to the number of businesses that have bitten the dust in the recent past. However, many of those who took appropriate steps to improve their cash management practices have, in fact, survived.

Nearly any business owner who has successfully brought a company from the brink of extinction to a growing, profitable business would probably agree that the commitment required to achieve such a feat could not have been made while personal assets remained at risk. The psychological burden imposed by personal guarantees stifles the kind of risk taking necessary to turn a company around. Therefore, it only makes sense to safeguard your personal assets before implementing recovery strategies. If the worst happens and you have to file for protection under the bankruptcy code, you certainly want to prevent a business creditor—bank or otherwise—from taking your house, car, investments, and personal treasures.

Strategies to Protect Personal Assets

The very first step should be to retain an attorney skilled in personal bankruptcy law—not because you expect to file personal bankruptcy, but because personal bankruptcy falls under state, not federal, laws (unlike corporate bankruptcy), and a personal lawyer can advise you on creditor/debtor laws in your state. A personal bankruptcy lawyer can also outline specific steps that will protect your assets and the right time to take them. The timing of such actions is as important as the steps themselves.

There are two ways to protect personal assets: keep them in a safe location where creditors cannot reach them, or, better yet, don't hold any valuable assets in your name.

Transfer Title to Personal Assets

If you don't own valuable assets no one can take them from you. If you have nothing to lose, you can deal with recalcitrant creditors much more aggressively. Also, if you have nothing to lose, you don't have to worry about spending thousands of dollars on legal fees defending yourself in court.

As a beginning, if your company is currently operated as a partnership or sole proprietorship, incorporate it. A corporate shield won't protect business assets in all cases, but it is certainly better than holding title in your name. Corporations are easy and quick to form without an attorney. Several Delaware companies specialize in forming corporations for out-of-state residents for approximately $200. The next step is to transfer the ownership of your company's shares to someone else. A spouse is the easiest choice and avoids any complications from the IRS. Adult children are also a satisfactory solution. Other relatives or close friends could be the answer, assuming that you trust them.

Another possibility is to transfer the stock to a trust. To be completely safe, the trust must be irrevocable, and as grantor, you cannot be the trustee or the beneficiary. Does this mean loss of control over the business? Technically yes. But private business owners have been using this technique for years to protect their investment. As long as the trustee can be trusted, you can still set company policies indirectly.

Although not foolproof, multiple corporations also afford reasonable protection for business interests. If you hold a controlling interest in each corporation, you still run the risk of seizure previously described; however, the more complicated it is for creditors to get at assets, the less likely they are to persist. The idea is to spread business assets among various corporations. Each corporation should be owned in varying percentages by your spouse, your children, relatives, friends, and yourself. Some of these companies could be incorporated offshore in tax-haven countries, and others located domestically in different states. Such a scheme tends to dissuade all but the most persistent lawyers from dabbling in your affairs. And if they do try to break all the corporate shields, they will find it very costly indeed.

Once business assets and ownership interests are secure, it's time to turn to other personal assets. Following is a partial list of personal assets that creditors, lawyers, and the IRS love to get their hands on:

1. Residences—either houses or condos
2. Real estate investments—land, farms, vacation homes, rental property
3. Bank savings accounts
4. Bank investment instruments—certificates of deposit, money market accounts, etc.
5. Individual retirement accounts (IRAs) and other retirement or pension entitlements
6. Life insurance policies
7. Stock brokerage accounts
8. Stock and bond certificates
9. Limited partnership shares
10. U.S. savings bonds
11. Automobiles
12. Valuable collections—stamps, coins, antiques, jewelry
13. Valuable personal property—fur coats, diamond rings, paintings, sculptures, libraries, furniture

No assets are immune from seizure as long as you own them. Granted, it's more difficult for creditors to lay claim to some of these assets than to others, but if someone tries hard enough, you can lose everything. In most states, property held jointly by spouses cannot be claimed in settlement of a lawsuit against one spouse. But this is not always the case. Take a residence, for example. In some states, a court may award victorious creditors a claim against your share of the residence. When it is sold, the creditors get your equity share.

Joint bank accounts aren't foolproof either. Some lawyers go so far as to analyze account transactions over the past three years to determine how many of the deposits came from you. If they exceed 50 percent of the expenditures from the account, some courts allow plaintiffs to take half the balance. They can also lay claim to 50 percent of any savings account or other investment held jointly with a spouse.

To be on the safe side, the best policy is to transfer all valuable assets to an outsider. Keep a small bank account for emergencies, but transfer everything else to a spouse, children, a trust, or relatives, as with your company stock. It's better to be safe than sorry.

Place Assets in Safekeeping

If for some reason transferring title to assets isn't practical, the only other alternative is to place as many assets as possible in safekeeping. A bank safe deposit box is all right for certain valuables, but remember, it can be opened by third parties under a variety of circumstances. A much better alternative, although somewhat convoluted, is to assign valuable assets to a trust, as previously recommended for company stock certificates. As long as the trust is irrevocable and you are not the trustee or the beneficiary, the trust shield will be difficult to penetrate.

As an added precaution, set up an offshore trust in a protected, risk-free bank. Although the IRS and the Department of Justice have penetrated the bank security of many tax-haven countries, a few still remain as safe havens for assets, (assuming, of course, that the assets were not obtained through illegal means—even the staunchest tax-haven countries will attach criminally acquired assets).

Switzerland is no longer a safe haven, since the Swiss government and banks have bowed to U.S. government pressures. The same holds true for Bermuda, the Bahamas, the Netherlands Antilles, Luxembourg, and several other countries previously regarded as safe havens. Liechtenstein is still a good location, but difficult to get to. For American residents, the Cayman Islands remains a favorite tax haven and safe haven. Also, Grand Cayman is only a one-hour flight from Miami.

Nearly every Fortune 500 company maintains bank accounts in Grand Cayman, as do many wealthy individuals. During the past few years, a rapidly increasing number of private business owners have begun using Cayman trusts to protect their assets and earn tax-free income at the same time.

Although it is becoming increasingly difficult to find complete protection for personal assets, a tax-haven country is still one of the best ways. The more complicated and costly you make it for creditors to locate and seize your assets, the less likely it is that they will even try. Surprisingly, even the IRS has limits beyond which it will not continue the chase. When you are trying to right a distressed business, personal financial security and peace of mind can make the difference between success and failure. Once your personal assets are secure, you can put aggressive cash management procedures in place to turn the company around and implement new growth strategies.

CASH BUDGETING

The most useful cash management tool for overleveraged companies is the cash budget. After you have taken measures to reduce costs as much as possible, if there still isn't enough cash to go around, it's necessary to implement a cash budget (if you don't already have one in place). As a first step, estimate as realistically as possible how much cash will be coming in the door from receivables collections and new sales. These cash receipts can then be allocated to employees and to those creditors that are most crucial to the company's survival, deferring everything else.

The smaller the budget time interval, the tighter the control, and the easier it is to take care of the most important creditors first. The further out a cash budget extends, the greater the chances that contingencies will pop up. In most cases, a forecast of two weeks should be fairly accurate. Begin with all cash balances in bank accounts and add the total cash receipts expected over the next two weeks. Next, subtract the weekly gross payroll and employer payroll taxes (but not amounts due yourself or other officers and shareholders) and building rent (if it's due). These expenses are the most crucial and must be paid regularly to stay afloat. Any remaining cash can then be used for paying bills.

Gross payroll must be covered, not just the amount of the payroll checks. Amounts withheld from paychecks belong to employees. Legally, you can get by without paying almost every creditor and still survive for a while. But payroll taxes must be paid to the IRS or you, other stockholders, or corporate officers can be fined or even jailed. It's almost as important to pay the rent. Eviction is the last thing a company needs during the turnaround period.

Although it is certainly important to make interest and principal payments on bank loans, bear in mind that it takes banks a long time to enter a foreclosure action—usually six months or more. That gives you at least some breathing space to negotiate deferred payment terms. In the meantime, cash normally used to repay loans can be applied to other creditors.

Once cash has been allocated to payroll and rent, the remaining amount can be used to pay bills. This calls for a schedule listing supplier invoices, past due taxes, utility bills, professional fees, employee expense accounts, and any other invoices that have been received.

SCHEDULING SUPPLIER PAYMENTS

The whole purpose of allocating available cash is to ensure that your company has enough cash to continue in business. Obviously, if there was more cash coming in than going out, there would be no reason to perform this exercise. But when a company owes more money to creditors than it receives from customers, something must give. And the underlying assumption in recovery strategies is that creditors have more flexibility to withstand cash shocks than your distressed company does. Therefore, creditors must help in the bailout by extending additional credit.

To assign payment priorities, it helps to list all bills on hand, regardless of source, and lay them out by invoice date—in other words, create an aged listing of accounts payable. The bigger the company, the more invoices it has to handle, and keeping track of how much has been paid to each creditor can become very confusing without a weekly-updated listing. Simultaneously, try to forecast incoming cash and new bills for each of the next four weeks to provide ammunition for negotiating new payment terms with creditors.

Next, sort the bills payable each week in priority sequence. For example, bills for electricity, telephone, fuel, and so on, must be paid on a regular, recurring basis or the business will cease to function. These critical, recurring bills are at the top of the list and get paid first—after payroll and rent.

Utility and telephone bills all have a billing date listed on the invoice. A one-time cash saving can be achieved by not paying these bills the first month, then continuing to pay them one month late. Utility companies won't complain too much as long as they receive payment before the third-month billing goes out. This gives you an extra thirty days to pay the first bill and saves that much cash. The same approach can be used for paying lease rentals and credit card charges.

Once critical bills have been taken care of, normal supplier invoices can be scheduled for payment. Obviously, some can be stretched further than others. Regular suppliers can usually be convinced to accept sixty day terms, maybe longer. Invoices for infrequent purchases can be stretched a lot further without permanent damage—some as long as six to nine months. The key is to pay only those bills that are critical to keeping materials and supplies flowing. Eventually, if conditions really get tough, even longer terms will have to be negotiated. Here are a few tips for delaying or negotiating long-term supplier payments.

Material and Product Suppliers

When push comes to shove, suppliers of materials, supplies, and purchased services always get paid last, after payroll, recurring bills, taxes, and in some cases debt service. This back-door approach to getting additional credit won't win any friends, but when you are fighting for survival, that should not be a concern.

When creditors are told that their payment has been delayed, their first reaction is to cut off further deliveries until old invoices get settled. Obviously, this cannot be permitted if those materials or services are required to keep the business running. The rest can wait, but negotiations with critical suppliers should begin immediately. Larger suppliers will usually settle for a flat amount each week, or each month, until old invoices have been liquidated. Try to negotiate new purchases on forty-five- to sixty-day terms. This may not work, but by adhering to a payment schedule for old invoices, you might get it. At least get thirty-day terms, not CODs.

Most suppliers tend to be reasonable and recognize that it is in their best interest to keep a customer going so that additional sales can be made. Suppliers very seldom foreclose or force a liquidation bankruptcy because they know that they will end up with less than the amount owed. Moreover, the loss of a customer might do more damage over the long run than not getting paid for old invoices.

Small Local Suppliers

Next in line behind critical suppliers come those small, local companies that rely on regular invoice payments to stay in business—small repair shops, the independent bookkeeper, service stations, independent grocers, pharmacies, the local newspaper, small subcontractors, and so on. These are micro businesses whose owners you may see or talk to every day. Taking care of them as soon as possible not only makes living in a community easier and more pleasant, it helps a company's public image. And that can pay big dividends later on. After all, when times improve you should be good business partners once again.

Service Suppliers and Government Agencies

Suppliers of employee benefits deserve to get paid next: group insurance carriers, automobile fleet insurance companies, state unemployment and workers' compensation funds, employer social security payments, and other employee-related expenses. Federal and state estimated income taxes; sales and use taxes; property taxes; legal, accounting, and other professional fees; noncritical large suppliers; and nonessential outside contractors (e.g., janitorial service, equipment maintenance contracts, equipment leases, and so on) round out the list. Chances are, however, that if there is enough money to pay these creditors, this whole exercise will be unnecessary.

Following is a priority listing that can be used as a quick reference for scheduling the payment of old bills and selecting those vendors that rate the most intense negotiating effort:

1. Payroll and employee withholding taxes
2. Building/office rent
3. Utilities and telephone
4. Interest on bank loans
5. Principal on bank loans
6. Purchases of materials and services crucial to keeping the business going
7. Small service and retail businesses, usually local
8. Employee benefits
9. Federal and state income and other taxes
10. Noncritical purchases and services

LEVERAGING BETTER PAYMENT TERMS

Negotiating better payment terms is always easier if a company has some bargaining chips. The party with the most to lose or the most to gain is always on the defensive; therefore, the secret to successful negotiating is to develop leverage that forces the other party into one or the other of these positions. Other than not meeting payroll, only two conditions might create circumstances more detrimental to a company on the brink of failure than to a creditor: (1) being evicted from the building that houses the business, and (2) not receiving critical materials and services to keep the business going.

Not much can be done about either situation. A business must be housed, and it must have materials and services to make and sell products. That's why landlords and critical suppliers top the payment priority list. Some leverage can be achieved, however. Most lessors would rather work out an extended payment arrangement than go to the expense and aggravation of a formal eviction. In many parts of the country, occupancy rates for commercial and industrial real estate have plummeted in recent years. As long as the renter's market holds, deferring rent payments for at least several months should be a real possibility. That's not a permanent solution, but it does provide some breathing space.

As a trade-off, a landlord may want higher monthly payments over the balance of the lease period. In a crisis situation, that's a small price to pay for conserving cash up front. It might also be possible to negotiate the same rental and merely add the deferred period to the end of the lease. A six-month rent deferral is not uncommon, and many lessees get much more.

It might be possible to leverage critical suppliers to gain better terms. The threat to go to a competitor usually brings even the most recalcitrant supplier to terms. In most cases, a supplier has more to lose (the overdue amounts plus legal costs to sue) or gain (future sales) than a debtor company does. At least making suppliers think that's the case is a good negotiating ploy.

Assuming that you have taken reasonable precautions to safeguard your personal assets, the worst thing that can happen is that you will be forced to liquidate the business. Granted, this can be a blow to any entrepreneur's ego. It might also reduce personal income for a while. However, once the liquidation is over, you can always begin again. As long as creditors believe that they have the most to lose, you are in the driver's seat. The ultimate creditors' threat is to force the company into bankruptcy. By making it clear that this won't hurt and that other plans for the future are in the works anyway, such leverage vanishes abruptly.

LEVERAGING THROUGH THE BANKRUPTCY CODE

The threat of bankruptcy can also be an effective negotiating strategy. In fact, many small businesses find that such threats will get them practically any terms they choose. The reason is simple. Unsecured creditors know that once a company has filed a Chapter 11 bankruptcy, one or both of two situations will happen:

- They will eventually receive at best a small percentage of what is due (five or ten cents on the dollar).

- They will have to wait for an extended period (possible several years) before receiving any payment.

If creditors don't understand these facts of life, it won't take long to lay out the ground rules. Following is a brief explanation of the federal Bankruptcy Code that might be helpful when using this tactic.

Types of Bankruptcies

Four types of bankruptcies apply to small businesses and their owners.

1. *Chapter 7—Liquidation Bankruptcy.* A Chapter 7 filing can be initiated by a business owner or by creditors. Its purpose is to liquidate assets, at auction or otherwise, and divide the proceeds among creditors. Liquidations are usually completed within ninety days of filing.

2. *Chapter 11—Reorganization Bankruptcy.* A Chapter 11 filing means that the creditors of a company cannot take any action to force payment of debts while the company works out a court-approved plan of reorganization. The present management continues to run the company while the reorganization plan gets worked out. This plan normally results in unsecured creditors getting a fraction of what they have coming and releases the company from all further claims.

3. *Chapter 12—Family-Farmer Bankruptcy.* Chapter 12 applies only to a family-owned business that earns at least 50 percent of its income from agriculture. Also, its debts must be under $1.5 million.

4. *Chapter 13—Wage Earner Bankruptcy.* Chapter 13 is designed for individuals with a steady source of income and total debts of less than $450,000, of which the unsecured portion cannot be more than $100,000.

The Risks of Filing Chapter 11

While a Chapter 11 filing can be an effective way to force a restructuring of bank debt and to reduce the amounts owed creditors, it's important to understand the major snares in the system. Two legal points are unique to bankruptcy law:

1. The fundamental principle under bankruptcy law is that an individual (business owner, officer, or shareholder) is presumed guilty until proven innocent—just the reverse of other laws. It is the court's duty, under law, to protect and save the company—not the company's owners or officers.

2. A company protected by Chapter 11, prodded by creditors and a trustee, has the right (it's really an obligation) to recover *preferential payments* from insiders. If the debtor is a corporation, an insider is defined as any director or officer of the corporation or any person who has responsibility for or authority over company expenditures.

Preferential payments are any payments made to an insider within twelve months prior to filing at a time when the corporation is insolvent (i.e., liabilities exceed assets). By definition, the company is considered insolvent for ninety days prior to filing, regardless of its balance sheet accounts. Preferential payment judgments against insiders order them to reimburse the company for any payments made to them for any reason during the twelve-month period prior to filing (assuming that the company is insolvent during this period) or for any payments made in the ninety days preceding filing (regardless of solvency). Such payments include salaries, bonuses, dividends, travel expense reimbursements, insurance premium payments, pension plan contributions, and any other payments made by the company to or on behalf of the insider.

Insiders are always at a severe disadvantage. By law, they have no right to these payments and must return them, even though they may own the company. That's how an individual is presumed guilty under the bankruptcy laws. So think twice before electing a Chapter 11. Shareholders and company officers could end up much worse off, personally, than before.

Threatening Bankruptcy

Obviously, bankruptcy must be considered a last resort. In many cases, however, the mere threat of a bankruptcy filing exacts concessions from creditors. This game gets nasty, but if less onerous strategies fail, nearly anything is better than going under.

Threatening to take the company into bankruptcy works especially well with suppliers that have sold material or services to the company for many years. It also works effectively if purchases have been sizable relative to those of a supplier's other customers. In either case, suppliers should be better off if they retain your company as a customer than if they force it into bankruptcy. If suppliers really believe you'll take the company to the ropes, most will negotiate a long term payment schedule and/or other arrangements.

Another effective tactic is to offer to settle old bills at a fraction of the balance. Knowing that in a reorganization plan they will probably have to settle for five or ten cents on the dollar and spend substantial effort and time meeting with creditors' committees and bankruptcy attorneys, many suppliers will grudgingly take thirty, forty, or fifty cents on the dollar just to keep the matter out of the courts. With a continuing business relationship, they can probably recoup their current losses through additional business or higher prices later on. Once a company enters bankruptcy, the game is over.

Some companies have negotiated supplier agreements to take future deliveries of materials on consignment and pay for them only when the goods are sold. Although suppliers must wait for payment, at least the sale has been made and payment will come eventually. This is certainly a better alternative than seeing the company fold.

The threat of filing a Chapter 11 can also provide effective leverage when dealing with employee groups or collective bargaining units. Many small-business owners have been able to exact unsecured term loans from unions to keep the company alive. From the employees' point of view, almost anything is better than letting the company go into bankruptcy and probably losing their jobs.

On the other hand, the threat of Chapter 11 won't help with state or federal agencies. Seeing a business survive is not an objective of the IRS, state unemployment funds, environmental protection agencies, or other bureaucracies. Politicians pay lip service to saving jobs, but seldom will government agencies grant concessions to make this happen (at least for small businesses; giant corporations like Chrysler, Lockheed, or the "too big to fail" banks are a different story).

Banks are also tough to negotiate with. As secured creditors, banks know that they have top priority in a Chapter 11 filing. They also know that if their collateral value is at least equal to the outstanding loan balance, they can always recoup their loans by foreclosing and liquidating the collateral. On the other hand, with the exception of secured lenders, most banks do not have the internal organization to handle or monitor a liquidation. And therein lies the only viable bargaining chip.

Negotiating Debt Reductions after Filing Chapter 11

Once a company files for protection under Chapter 11, a different type of leverage is involved. Now, the company's leverage lies in the threat to go all the way to a Chapter 7 liquidation, in which case virtually no one wins. Such leverage becomes especially valuable when negotiating with banks and other secured creditors. As secured lenders, banks retain the highest position in the priority of creditors under the Bankruptcy Code. They have the least to lose under a Chapter 11 filing. If there is any chance at all that the company can reorganize itself out of bankruptcy, secured lenders should get paid in full.

A Chapter 7 liquidation is a different matter entirely. The proceeds of a liquidation sale hardly ever come close to collateralized loan balances, and lenders know this. Therefore, once in Chapter 11, companies have a significant amount of leverage to force better payment terms simply by threatening to liquidate.

It doesn't take much negotiating to parlay this leverage into a new loan agreement. The main conditions to shoot for are:

- An extension of the due date
- A moratorium on principal payments
- A moratorium on both interest and principal payments for several months or years
- A conversion of short-term loans to long-term debt.

TRADING DEBT FOR EQUITY

In some cases, overleveraged companies have been able to convert partial loan balances into equity shares in the company. Trading debt for equity works with both unsecured creditors and lenders. The size or type of business doesn't make much difference. Both small and large companies have used debt-for-equity swaps as a viable recovery strategy. Small suppliers seem to be more amenable to this tactic than larger ones, however.

As previously discussed, large suppliers generally prefer to extend payment terms or even reduce old invoice balances in exchange for a quicker payment. On the other hand, small suppliers frequently see an opportunity to influence a customer's sourcing decisions if they have a piece of the action. Since few small businesses have enough spare cash to lend customers, a debt/equity swap that doesn't cost them a penny (other than old, unpaid invoices) could be an attractive option.

Employees react even better to an equity share in exchange for back pay or for relinquishing future vacations, raises, or benefits. When pushing the panic button, companies can ill afford employee vacations. Employees who were not needed to do the work would probably already be gone. If the company could afford additional employee benefits, it wouldn't be negotiating deals with suppliers and banks. Since most employees understand these facts of life, they should be amenable to swapping retirement plan contributions and other cash expenditures scheduled to be made on their behalf for equity interests in their employer.

Finally, although lawyers, consultants, auditors, other professionals, and outside contractors with overdue accounts will probably not be interested in foregoing their payment in return for an equity share, it can't hurt to ask. You can do a lot worse than sharing ownership with a qualified management consultant.

EQUITY CASH FROM CUSTOMERS

Many businesses have large as well as small customers. The larger the customer or the more important your company is as a critical supplier of materials, parts, or even finished products, the greater the leverage for making an equity deal. Quite often, customers view a minority interest in a critical supplier as a very attractive investment, provided the supplier sells a product or service that is either unique and valuable in and of itself or a critical component of the customer's supply line.

The latter situation occurred with a machine shop that was the sole supplier of small turned titanium parts used in race car transmissions. Its major customer commanded 30 percent of the transmission market. As inflation pushed production costs to new highs, competition pounded the company's customer base and kept selling prices low. Its line of credit was fully utilized, and it was still short of cash. The machine shop owner warned this major customer that the company had to reduce its bank borrowings to get some operating flexibility. He suggested that fresh capital was needed to continue supplying these transmission parts and that a 25 percent equity interest in the company was an acceptable trade-off. The customer agreed. Two months later all short-term loans were paid off and the company had $150,000 in cash reserves. Furthermore, it is still supplying these vital transmission parts.

An investment from a customer may not be a palatable alternative, but it works in certain situations. Be sure to draft a supporting agreement that stipulates the terms of a full buyout when conditions improve. The last thing most of us want is to be locked into customers indefinitely. Economic and market conditions are dynamic, and as conditions change, companies need the flexibility to shift customers or product lines as needed to maximize market control. It's hard to do this when customers own part of your business.

EQUITY CASH FROM SUPPLIERS

Equity investments from suppliers are usually easier to swallow. But why would a supplier be willing to invest in a small-business customer? There are many reasons, a few of which are:

1. In exchange for long-overdue payments for purchases
2. As a method of locking up a customer's future purchases
3. To lock out competition
4. For potential investment appreciation
5. To influence management decisions
6. As the first step in the eventual buyout of the entire company
7. To protect sales to a valuable customer that is in financial difficulty
8. To forestall bank foreclosure or other interference with a customer's operations

A company has substantially more leverage for getting equity capital from suppliers than from customers, especially if the supplier is another small business. All you have to do is delay payments on account and blame the delay on cash flow shortages. It's done all the time, and there is very little a supplier can do about it, short of cutting off future deliveries. Assuming that the supplier is not also in trouble, a cash infusion for a minority interest could be a very attractive proposition.

Getting equity money from a supplier has become an accepted practice for many businesses. In addition to liquidating onerous debt, such investments provide a means of ensuring a continued supply of materials or continuing services at prices equal to or less than prevailing market prices. After all, if a supplier (now investor) overcharged, the market value of its investment would decline.

DEFERRING DEBT PAYMENTS

Commercial banks have portfolios full of problem loans, many of them to small businesses. Virtually all commercial banks follow a basic principle: The most important item on the agenda is to get loans repaid in full. Moreover, most of them, especially smaller banks, are not equipped to dispose of foreclosed business assets. They do not maintain close contacts with auctioneers, nor do they have problem-loan experts on the payroll to help a customer through the tough spots. In fact, this would be a conflict of interest, and banks are usually careful not to be accused of interfering in a customer's business.

This lack of skill in collecting collateral, coupled with their primary objective of getting the loan repaid, puts banks in a vulnerable position—to your advantage, of course. The lowest-risk action for banks is to help customers get over short-term cash crunches so that payments on the loan can be resumed. One popular way of achieving this is by deferring loan repayments.

For instance, assume that a company has a revolving line of credit that fully absorbs its receivables borrowing base. A slackening in the market has hurt business and reduced the company's cash flow. By granting deferred payments on the revolver for, say, six months, the bank, in effect, grants a new loan—namely, the unencumbered receivables collections. This extra cash can then be used to buy materials, meet payroll, and cover other operating expenses.

In more cases than not, such a cash infusion is enough to get a business back on line. If your company has been a good customer in the past, it's in the bank's interest to see you through. In most cases, banks view the granting of deferred payments as the lowest-risk action (although at times it takes some negotiating to make recalcitrant bankers see the light). Of course, interest will still be payable each month, but that's less painful than also paying back the principal.

BORROWING FROM NONBANK SOURCES

Banks aren't the only source of loans. You may be able to tap friends and relatives for short-term help to see your business through a cash crunch. However, this is usually a bad policy and can create more animosity than it's worth. Mixing friendship with business seems to put undue strains on all parties and in the end is not a satisfactory solution. Friends, relatives, and business associates generally love to give advice and verbal support, but when you ask for a loan, friends are no longer friendly and relatives seem to get greedy. For some people, however, this remains a viable source of short-term cash.

As an alternative to borrowing from friends and relatives, why not try selling them minority shares in the business? For some unexplained reason, buying a share in a business seems less onerous than lending it money. For those inclined to go this route, here are a few rules that should help avoid family quarrels or misunderstandings:

1. Make the transaction formal. If you have a corporation, actually issue the stock certificates. Otherwise, at least draft a simple agreement spelling out the ownership split.

2. Execute a written document spelling out when the investor will be paid off. Be sure to specify a getting out date so that the family investor knows that his or her money isn't tied up forever.

3. Specify what return the investor will get—cash returns, appreciation, use of the business facilities or products, free services, and so on.

4. Try to structure the deal so that the family investor gets the benefit of any business tax loss as a personal deduction (e.g., through an S corporation or limited partnership arrangement).

5. Ask for the minimum amount of money needed right now. Identify exactly what the money will be used for, and then use it for that purpose.

The Small Business Administration is another possible source of emergency capital. However, the SBA has fallen on hard times. Because of personnel budget cuts and funding allocation shortfalls, the SBA has not stepped in to help very many small businesses in distress.

OTHER DROP-DEAD TACTICS

Here are a few other tips to consider as last resort measures. They may not be very palatable, but they have been used effectively by mainly micro businesses to get out of cash binds.

Borrow on Personal Credit Cards

With credit card companies eager to attract new customers, lines of credit totaling $10,000, $30,000, or more are not uncommon. Try negotiating with credit card issuers for higher limits. Then use credit cards to purchase materials and services rather than buying on open account. Most credit card issuers allow thirty days before beginning to charge interest. For cardholders willing to pay exorbitant interest, it is possible to take years to pay off a larger balance while continuing to charge new purchases. This amounts to an additional open line of credit—albeit at a very high interest rate.

Borrow from the IRS

Although neglecting the payment of employee withholding taxes can result in substantial fines or jail terms, delaying tactics on other taxes will, in effect, place the IRS in the role of lender. One way is to delay the payment of estimated income taxes. Another is to file an annual tax return but not enclose a check for taxes due. Of course, in both cases interest and penalties will be attached, and eventually the taxes will have to be paid, but in the meantime the business has the use of extra cash. It always takes time for the IRS to catch up, and using this cash for six to twelve months might get the company over its cash crunch.

Take Out Personal Loans

Many business owners opt for this alternative right in the beginning, as soon as cash gets tight. Although it may be a solution in some instances, using personal loans to fund a business can be dangerous. All owners, shareholders, and corporate officers should be careful to protect personal assets. When the proceeds of personal loans are used for the business, assets securing these loans are no longer protected. If the business eventually fails, everything could be lost, not just the business.

Yet, time and again, business owners take the plunge. Home equity loans are especially popular because a fairly large amount of cash can usually be raised. As we all know, however, when business cash dries up, mortgage payments can be just as difficult to meet as business debt service payments.

Protecting personal income and assets should be considered part of protecting a company from creditors. In small businesses, the two are inseparable. Bankruptcy laws apply to individuals as well as to businesses, and it's bad enough to have the company go on the rocks without personally suffering the same fate. Although a home equity loan can certainly be used to raise additional cash, in most cases it carries far too much risk.

Pressed to the wall, it's easy to come up with other ways to borrow personally. Perhaps another car loan. Or a loan against personal savings and investment accounts. IRAs and Keogh accounts can serve as collateral. Stamp and coin collections, antiques, paintings, and so on can also secure personal loans. But beware of the risk.

In closing, the following example clearly shows the danger of solving a company's cash shortage with personal debt. A close friend owned five hotels. Over the years he had made a substantial fortune by speculating on land and by building and selling hotels. Enjoying a lavish lifestyle, he invested heavily in antiques, paintings, other works of art, expensive sports cars, and stretch limousines, as well as a personal residence valued at well over $5 million.

As the financial markets collapsed, he found it increasingly difficult to raise construction loans. Cost overruns on his last four projects resulted in several defaults. Pressed by creditors and banks alike, he began borrowing against his wealth of personal assets. He also acquiesced to several personal guarantees to secure both business and personal loans.

As the recession deepened, room occupancy fell off dramatically and cash flows needed to meet the variety of debt service payments didn't materialize. Pushed to the wall, the entrepreneur considered putting his properties into Chapter 11, but his attorney warned him that all property loans and personal loans were cross-collateralized along with personal guarantees. If the business collapsed, so would he personally.

Eventually creditors forced a Chapter 7 against one of the hotels. The house of cards collapsed. In less than six months, everything was lost: hotels, house, and all personal treasures.

No magic formula raises the yoke of overleverage. No consultant, loan officer, government agency, or financial guru can make the pain of cash shortages go away. When all is said and done, business owners must solve their own problems in the best way they can in order to make a new beginning toward long-term growth. It has always been thus, and probably always will be.

Part 3

Strategies for Buying a Business or Product Line

Chapter 10

Preliminary Steps

Buying a going business or a self-contained product line has several benefits to long-term growth strategies:

- It abruptly adds a new range of products, production assets, customers, suppliers, and skilled personnel, which can be a big help in jump-starting a company that has been slumbering in a stable or declining market.
- It diversifies the business base, thereby offsetting a downward trending business cycle in one industry or market with a rising cycle in another.
- It ensures immediate access to new markets that might take years to develop from scratch.
- It increases market share, assuming that the target company is a competitor.
- It enables a company to finance a major expansion more easily and on better terms and conditions than one-at-a-time additions of machines, offices, or new products.

On the downside, a business or product line acquisition brings a variety of challenges not present in slower expansion strategies. Perhaps the biggest detriments are the substantial cost and high risk attendant in nearly every acquisition. Such costs and risk derive from:

- The extensive planning that goes into determining (1) which markets and product lines to go after, (2) the size of an acceptable target company, and (3) the timing of the acquisition. (It may also be necessary to restructure or reorganize the parent company prior to the addition of a new business unit.)
- The highly complex tasks of identifying a target company, valuing it, negotiating a purchase price, raising the financing, and drafting a limited-liability purchase contract.
- The intricacy of integrating the acquired company's personnel, distribution channels, accounting systems, and supplier network with the parent company.
- The magnitude of the financial commitment, both for the acquisition and for ongoing working capital.
- The inevitable drain on the acquiring (parent) company's resources.

This chapter and the following chapters in Part 3 examine the process of acquiring an entire business or product line and the strategies and tactics for making such an acquisition that will be least disruptive for employees, customers, and suppliers.

PRELIMINARY PLANNING

Just as it's a good idea to know the destination of a plane before boarding, it makes sense to know what type of acquisition you're going after before spending money and time searching one out. Although strategies that call for the acquisition of completely different businesses make sense under certain circumstances, the most prudent approach is to look for target companies with complementary product lines and/or markets. Synergies usually enable a smoother transition after the closing and faster integration into a parent company's operating procedures.

Diversification may be a key strategic objective of the acquisition, but diversification doesn't mean a completely different group of products. Complementary products sold to dissimilar markets or variations of products sold to similar markets could offset business cycles as readily as a totally different business.

In some instances, however, it does make sense to bring in completely new products or markets. A good example occurred with a company that manufactured small marine generators, used primarily in pleasure boats. When the bottom fell out of the pleasure boat market in the late 1980s (originally because of the recession, then because of onerous luxury tax laws, and finally because of several devastating hurricanes), Electro-Marine opted to diversify completely out of this market. Its strategy was to acquire a company that manufactured housings for diesel generators used in heavy road and off-road equipment, but not the complete generator. The strategy paid off; today, E-M-C (formerly Electro-Marine) is a major force in its new market niche.

However, buying a company that produces a product or service about which you have little or no knowledge is usually a big mistake. Time and again, such businesses fail, not because of undercapitalization (although inadequate financing remains a major contributor), but because the acquiring company doesn't have corollary product or market experience. It hardly seems wise to buy a car if you can't drive, to purchase an airplane without a pilot's license, or to buy a bookkeeping practice without a thorough knowledge of debits and credits.

Yet, time and again, we become enamored with the opportunities offered by diverse markets or product lines (the "grass is always greener" syndrome) and plunge ahead with only the barest knowledge of a target's technology, production requirements, or markets. Once the acquisition bug has bitten, it's difficult to hold back and wait for a target in a familiar industry or market; however, if you do not do so, the odds of failure escalate rapidly. So even when growth strategies call for diversification, it pays to go after businesses that have at least some complementary characteristics.

Location

The location of a target candidate can also be a key strategic consideration, especially when it comes to managing the new company after closing. Small retail or service businesses that draw customers from a narrow radius should obviously stay away from buying a business in an area already loaded with competitors. Conversely, the general shortage of professionals in rural areas might make this an ideal location in which to purchase a professional practice.

A business that requires substantial skilled labor would probably face difficulties in an area with low unemployment or in one without adequate technical and vocational schools. And sole proprietors without a complement of qualified managers would be likely to have difficulty managing acquisitions located great distances from their current businesses.

Size

The optimum size of a potential acquisition must also be carefully scrutinized. Although the maximum size is usually limited by the purchase price (the bigger the target, the higher the price) and the amount of acquisition capital that can be raised, the size of the parent company also bears heavily on the decision. Although exceptions certainly exist, a general rule of thumb states that a target company should be smaller or equal in size to the acquiring company, not larger. And there are logical reasons for this.

In the first place, a company currently doing $5 million in sales probably won't have enough skilled managers to integrate a company doing $15 million. Second, a small parent company most likely doesn't have the financial clout to swing a deal for a significantly larger company. Third, although a specific target company may be desirable because of its marketing organization or distribution system, merging it with a smaller parent's organization may not enhance the parent company's market position.

Although occasionally small groups of professional managers have made acquisitions of relatively large companies and successfully managed them through the initial high-debt service period, the exorbitant risk makes large, highly leveraged buyouts a tricky business. It is definitely not a recommended approach, assuming that you already have a successful business.

Timing

Timing can easily make the difference between a smooth, easily managed acquisition and one that causes severe hardship for the parent company. The difference lies in the price paid, the cash flow of the target company, the availability of financing for the deal and its cost, and the relative strength of market competition. All these factors are largely influenced by industry business cycles, national economic conditions, and capital market trends.

When industry and economic cycles are favorable, a company's profitability and future outlook will normally be stronger than if either or both cycles are trending downward. This pushes up the asking price and tightens payment terms.

At the same time, capital markets in a thriving economy are generally in full swing, making financing the deal easier and less costly.

Conversely, when either the industry or the national business cycle is unfavorable, more advantageous acquisition prices and terms can be negotiated. However, the target company's sales growth and profitability will also probably be less. Capital will be tighter and generally more costly. Competition will probably be stronger, with price cutting and sales promotions eating away at profits.

Like so many other business choices, the timing of an acquisition requires trade-offs—a higher price versus easier financing and less impact from competition; a lower price versus tighter capital markets and more intense competition. If possible, the best time to make an acquisition is when industry cycles and economic indicators have bottomed out and just begun their upward curve, but before competitive buyers saturate the market.

The Right Structure

In addition to evaluating the compatibility, location, and size of target companies and determining the most advantageous timing, the preliminary planning process should include an assessment of the form and structure of the entity that will make the acquisition. Although using an operating parent company as the purchaser is certainly the most straightforward method, it may be more desirable to hold the shares of the acquired business in a separate entity.

Several strategic considerations may enter into such a decision, although in most private businesses, two have an overriding priority: tax/legal ramifications and financing requirements. Current tax and liability laws usually influence the choice between a corporation and a partnership—either with family members or outsiders—as a separate acquisition entity. A corporation certainly provides greater personal protection from legal liability than either a proprietorship or a partnership. On the other hand, double taxation can easily arise with the corporate form. Estate tax considerations can also affect the choice of ownership structure. From an estate valuation perspective, it might be preferable to separate the ownership of the acquired company from that of the parent.

Financing arrangements also affect the form and structure of the acquiring entity. Bank financing is much easier to arrange with corporate ownership than with individual proprietorships or partnerships. Private equity investors and venture capital firms frequently require the corporate form, or perhaps a limited partnership. And multiple corporations with shares held by an "apex" holding company can very often bring the greatest advantage.

Although the complexities of forming and maintaining a separate acquisition entity tend to dissuade many first-time business buyers, effective growth strategies can usually be enhanced by doing so. Moreover, the proper ownership structure very often influences whether a deal can be financed at a reasonable cost (or financed at all). Obviously, most of us don't have the legal, tax, and financing expertise to weigh all the consequences of alternative structures, making the use of professional advisors a necessity.

Taxes

In addition to affecting the form and structure of the buying entity, current and anticipated tax laws play a major role in financing a deal. They also affect specific clauses in buy/sell agreements and other closing documents. Alternative options such as deferred payments or cash at closing, interest income or dividends, capital gains or ordinary income, and deductible or capitalized expenses all influence how to structure a deal. And the type of financing package, classification of acquisition costs, and negotiated contract clauses are all influenced by tax laws.

Regardless of the financial and tax expertise of company management, business or product line acquisitions should never be attempted without consulting professional tax advisors. Doing so can only prevent costly errors and omissions.

Timing, location, industry, structure, and taxes are all critical topics to investigate before starting out. In-depth planning to manage these issues will save an enormous amount of time and energy later on. There's nothing more frustrating than realizing halfway through the acquisition process that the timing is all wrong, or that you've set up a corporation when a limited partnership should have been used, or that you forgot to consider the tax consequences of future cash distributions. Once the acquisition process begins, slipping, sliding, and backtracking can be extremely costly. The costs involved in buying a business or product line are high enough. Repeating steps a second or third time can escalate costs beyond reason.

The three biggest mistakes made by inexperienced buyers are:

1. Ignoring preliminary planning
2. Neglecting the acquisition plan once it has been perfected
3. Underestimating the length of time it takes to make an acquisition

Time is money, and without an acquisition plan (described later in this chapter as part of a case study) containing milestones and budgeted costs, the acquisition process is likely to cost more than the target company is worth.

GETTING STARTED

Whether an acquisition involves an entire business or a single product line, adhering to a proven seven-step acquisition process ensures that minimum costs will be expended and that all matters will be attended to in an expeditious manner. The size of the acquisition or its industry makes little difference: The same steps are required whether the target is a neighborhood deli or a $50 million manufacturer. Although some costs and a little time might be saved by short-cutting the process, it generally isn't worth the gamble. In the end, brushing over a step or skipping one altogether will generally result in higher overall acquisition costs and more time to close than originally budgeted.

The following seven-step acquisition process has been successfully used by countless private businesses:

1. Choose the most appropriate target candidate and determine its market value

2. Perform a "due diligence" investigation of the target's affairs

3. Prepare a financing plan to attract appropriate capital for financing the purchase price and for subsequent working capital

4. Negotiate price and terms with sellers

5. Develop a schedule for integrating the target's operating procedures and personnel into those of the parent company

6. Draft the closing documents

7. Manage the transition and integration

Before companies embark on the acquisition trail, it makes sense to be certain that the addition of a new company or product line is the best way to go, that there are no other viable routes to reach the company's growth objectives, and that company personnel are fully capable of taking on additional tasks during the acquisition process, the transition, and the integration period.

The high level of unidentifiable overhead costs as well as actual out-of-pocket costs that will be incurred during the acquisition process (which may last from six months to a year) can cause a harmful drain on company cash. If the acquisition falls through (and many do), this cash drain and the accompanying impact on company earnings can easily put a damper on subsequent strategies. Also, the time devoted to administering the acquisition process, along with that involved in integrating a new business, drains valuable personnel resources. If key managers do not have this extra time to spend, their current duties will obviously be shortchanged.

The following factors need to be addressed and evaluated prior to beginning the search for a new business:

- The parent company should be profitable and should be generating a positive cash flow.

- Management personnel must be able to run their various functional activities with minimal supervision.

- If the company has made a previous business acquisition, avoid further acquisitions for at least three years. It normally takes that long to thoroughly integrate the first deal and establish a reputation in the financial community.

- Avoid targets whose locations are so far removed from the parent company that efficient controls are difficult to achieve.

- If possible, use equity capital for a reasonable portion of the purchase price—either internal cash reserves or capital raised through private equity sales and/or an initial public offering (IPO).

- When using debt capital to finance the acquisition, be sure its repayment schedule extends for several years and that the debt-to-equity ratios of the combined businesses meet current lender requirements.

- Search out a business that has at least one major synergism with the parent company (products, markets, technology, facilities, and so on) or that will reduce competition in the parent's markets.

- Establish a corporate office function to handle the administration of both the parent company and the acquisition.

- Implement daily, weekly, and monthly financial reports before bringing in another business.

- Do not attempt to manage the day-to-day affairs of the parent company while going through the acquisition process. Train or hire a general manager for the parent company and, after closing, install a general manager in the acquired business (if it is in a different location).

- Budget all acquisition overhead costs out of the parent company's cash reserves. Since the acquisition may never go through, borrowing new short-term funds to cover these costs is much too risky.

Once the decision has been made to grow a company through acquisition, it is easy to overlook the advantages to be gained by restructuring the parent company's organization to handle the management and administration of an expanded business base. Such restructuring requires two major actions. First, the day-to-day management of the parent company must be delegated to a general manager other than the business owner or owners. This is an important step because the acquisition process and the subsequent integration of two businesses usually require the undivided attention of the person or persons with the absolute authority to make hard and fast decisions, and that can only be the owner or owners of the business. One person can't be in two places at the same time. Unless you delegate authority to run the parent company, at least through the integration stage, the chances are good that either the acquisition will fail to close or the integration of the new business will turn into a nightmare.

Second, a corporate office, physically separated from the management activities of the parent company, should be established. The reason for such a separation is relatively simple: The person assigned the responsibility for running the day-to-day activities must have the appearance of being in charge as well as the de facto authority. When a business owner's office is located in close proximity to the general manager's, it's far too easy for employees to turn to the owner for opinions and decisions, thereby undermining the ability of the general manager to carry out assigned duties. The greater the distance between the corporate office and operating activities, the more effective both headquarters and operating personnel will be.

Although a corporate office is merely a luxury in a one-business company, as soon as a second company or product line in a new location is added, a distinct need to control and coordinate the two companies arises. This can only be done by a central authority, namely the business owner. Moreover, it can most easily be accomplished through centralized cash controls, regular financial reports, and perhaps the administration of joint overhead policies, such as business insurance, employee benefit programs, or the coordination of legal and auditing activities. A small corporate office, independent of day-to-day operating decisions, provides a framework within which such policies can be administered and monitored.

A corporate financial manager (or a business owner) should also monitor the operating results of both businesses. Of course, this requires the setting up of a financial reporting system to provide daily, weekly, and/or monthly performance information, but that is a relatively simple task once daily administrative chores abate.

Such restructuring costs money, above and beyond the out-of-pocket costs of conducting an acquisition search. Since it makes little sense to incur extra debt obligations at this stage, corporate office operating funds must be provided by the parent company, and a realistic budget of these expenses should be formulated before you make the final decision to proceed with an acquisition.

FILTCO, INC.: A CASE STUDY

Certain steps in the acquisition process are difficult to describe without concrete examples. An actual business acquisition case study demonstrating how these steps affect the total acquisition process is often easier to follow than mere generalizations. Therefore, we will recount the experiences of one company (a manufacturer of filtration equipment) to demonstrate those steps that normally cause the greatest confusion.

Prior to its acquisition by a Fortune 500 corporation, Filtco, Inc., was owned by a single entrepreneur who had started the company from scratch in 1972. For seventeen years Filtco had prospered along with most other companies in the filtration industry. As new and bigger competitors began to enter the market, however, Filtco's market share had begun to slip. A five-year strategic plan was developed to help the company reach its growth objectives. The plan included the acquisition of one or two of the more than twenty small suppliers of Filtco filter components. A task force comprising Filtco's president, controller, and marketing manager was set up to manage the acquisition process. As the first step, the task force put together an acquisition plan, including a budget of out-of-pocket expenses.

The Acquisition Plan

A typical acquisition plan outlines a sequence of major actions with go/no-go decision points and budgeted out-of-pocket expenses necessary to achieve each milestone. The actual search, investigation, legal, and transition costs can then be controlled to the progression of the plan. The Filtco plan is shown in Figure 10-1.

The total time allotted for the acquisition process was twelve months from start to finish, and out-of-pocket costs were capped at $55,000. Although $55,000 is probably a minimum budget for a small acquisition, it should be adequate, provided that sufficient preparation is done in the beginning. It is during the target

Figure 10-1
Filtco Acquisition Plan

Action	Start Date	Finish Date	Estimated Cost
A. Survey industry/product/market	10/31	1/1	$2,000
1. Economic growth curves—historical and future			
2. Market dominance—competition and pricing			
3. Foreign competition			
4. Economics of user applications			
5. List of companies			
6. Sales literature and financial data of companies in industry			
7. Trade association interviews			
B. Target search	1/1	4/1	3,000
1. Brokers, consultants, lawyers, accountants			
2. Investment bankers, venture capital firms, commercial banks			
3. Newspapers, investment journals, trade magazines			
4. Unsolicited mailings			
5. Personal contacts			
C. Preliminary due diligence			
1. Target 1	4/1	4/15	3,000
a. Meet with seller			
b. Facilities tour			
c. Obtain financials and sales literature			
2. Target 2	4/15	5/1	3,000
a. Same sequence as 1			
3. Target 3	5/1	5/15	3,000
a. Same sequence as 2			
D. Negotiate price and payment terms for the best of the three targets	5/15	6/15	3,000
1. Valuation of the business			
2. Earn-outs, contingencies, hold-backs			
3. Buyer paper			
E. Perform detailed due diligence	6/15	8/15	6,000
1. Financial—three years historical audit reports and monthly internal reports			
2. Prepare pro forma statements			
3. Organization chart			
4. Meet management and second facilities tour			
5. Customer data—competitors, pricing, market size and share			
6. Outstanding lawsuits or claims—government, employees, customers, etc.			
7. Contracts in force—union, vendor, customer, employee, leases			

Action	Start Date	Finish Date	Estimated Cost
F. Arrange financing	6/15	9/15	5,000
1. Prepare comprehensive business plan			
2. Commercial banks			
3. Finance companies—commercial and asset-based lenders			
4. Investment banks and venture capital firms			
5. Others			
G. Final due diligence	9/1	9/25	20,000
1. Update pro forma statements			
2. Appraisal of equipment and real estate			
3. Audit review by CPA firm			
H. Write buy/sell agreement and other closing documents	9/15	10/15	7,000
1. Engage legal counsel			
2. Negotiate final language and terms of sale			
3. Coordinate with financing parties			
I. Closing	10/31		
J. Transition integration	11/1	5/1	N/A
1. Meet with key managers			
2. Meet with entire work force			
3. Establish cash controls			
4. Set up operating budgets			
5. Develop performance incentives			
6. Implement financial reporting system			

search that budget overruns usually occur. To prevent the search from becoming an ongoing exercise, the time schedule established for each step must be closely adhered to.

One word of caution about acquisition planning: The only thing certain about it is that the timing and budgeted amounts will be missed. An acquisition plan should be used as a guideline and only a guideline. Its main function is to provide a framework within which decisions and actions can be directed and monitored. As long as you come within a reasonable margin of error (say sixty days and 10 percent of the cost), the plan has served its purpose.

Setting Financial Limits

Upon completion of the acquisition plan, the Filtco task force decided that before proceeding, it would be a good idea to set financial limits to determine how much the company could afford to pay for an acquisition. Prudent financial management was a byword of Filtco's owner, and any acquisition would have to fit the company's financial capabilities.

As can be seen from Filtco's financial statements in Figure 10-2 (pages 171 and 172), the company was turning a handsome profit of 8.6 percent after taxes on sales of just over $7 million. It also must have been generating a reasonable cash flow for the owner to draw annual dividends of $300,000. A total debt-to-equity ratio of 1.0 indicates that the company should be able to offer a financial institution at least some collateral assets as added security for a leveraged buyout (LBO).

Figure 10-2
Filtco, Inc.

STATEMENT OF INCOME
For the Year 1992
($000)

Sales	7,275
Cost of sales	
Material	3,698
Labor	436
Overhead	445
Total cost of sales	4,579
Gross profit	2,696
% of sales	37.1%
Operating expenses	
Selling expenses	509
Administrative expenses	542
Other expenses	20
Depreciation	350
Total	1,421
Net income before interest and taxes	1,275
% of sales	17.5%
Interest	267
Net income before tax	1,008
Taxes	383
Net income	625
% of sales	8.6%

BALANCE SHEET
As of December 31, 1992
($000)

Cash	125
Accounts receivable	909
Inventory	1,352
Prepaid expenses	5
Total current assets	2,391
Buildings	2,000
Machinery & equipment	3,000
Vehicles	50
Total	5,050
Less: Accumulated depreciation	(1,520)
Net fixed assets	3,530
Other assets	100
Total assets	6,021
Bank note payable	200
Accounts payable	487
Accrued expenses	200
Other current liabilities	50
Total current liabilities	937
Long-term debt	1,500
Mortgage loan	1,000
Total liabilities	3,437
Common stock	100
Retained earnings—beginning	2,305
Profit/(loss)	479
Dividends	(300)
Retained earnings—ending	2,484
Total net worth	2,584
Total liabilities and net worth	6,021

Filtco's current financial condition should enable it to integrate an acquisition in a size range of $4 to $6 million annual sales. To get a feel for the maximum purchase price that Filtco could handle, we need to look at the company's pro forma forecast prepared without the addition of a second business, as shown in Figure 10-3 (pages 173 and 174).

Figure 10-3
Filtco, Inc.

PRO FORMA STATEMENT OF INCOME
For the Years 1993 through 1997
(in dollars)

	Actual	Forecast				
	1992	1993	1994	1995	1996	1997
Sales	7,275,000	7,491,170	7,714,440	7,945,062	8,062,037	8,160,024
Cost of sales						
Material	3,697,500	3,815,704	3,938,027	4,064,622	4,120,278	4,168,427
Labor	436,305	450,253	464,687	479,625	486,193	491,874
Overhead	444,780	458,123	471,867	554,923	571,571	588,718
Total standard cost of sales	4,578,585	4,724,081	4,874,582	5,099,170	5,178,042	5,249,020
Gross profit	2,696,415	2,767,089	2,839,858	2,845,891	2,883,995	2,911,004
% of sales	37.1%	36.9%	36.8%	35.8%	35.8%	35.7%
Operating expenses						
Selling expenses	509,525	524,759	540,465	606,659	684,324	701,257
Administrative expenses	541,750	556,963	571,601	586,679	605,660	621,656
Other expenses	20,000	20,000	20,000	20,000	20,000	20,000
Depreciation	350,000	350,000	350,000	350,000	350,000	350,000
Total	1,421,275	1,451,721	1,482,066	1,563,338	1,659,984	1,692,913
Net income before interest and taxes	1,275,140	1,315,368	1,357,792	1,282,553	1,224,012	1,218,091
% of sales	17.5%	17.6%	17.6%	16.1%	15.2%	14.9%
Interest	267,000	239,500	212,000	184,500	157,000	129,500
Net income before tax	1,008,140	1,075,868	1,145,792	1,098,053	1,067,012	1,088,591
Taxes	383,093	408,830	435,401	417,260	405,464	413,665
Net income	625,047	667,038	710,391	680,793	661,547	674,927
% of sales	8.6%	8.9%	9.2%	8.6%	8.2%	8.3%

PRO FORMA BALANCE SHEETS
For the Years 1993 through 1997 (in dollars)

	Actual	Forecast				
	1992	1993	1994	1995	1996	1997
Cash	125,000	271,713	304,203	290,401	302,341	279,553
Accounts receivable	909,375	936,396	964,305	993,133	1,007,755	1,020,003
Inventory	1,351,932	1,585,904	1,827,111	1,971,650	2,083,426	2,256,311
Prepaid expenses	5,000	5,000	5,000	5,000	5,000	5,000
Total current assets	2,391,307	2,799,013	3,100,620	3,260,184	3,398,522	3,560,867
Buildings	2,000,000	2,000,000	2,000,000	2,000,000	2,000,000	2,000,000
Machinery & equipment	3,000,000	3,000,000	3,000,000	3,000,000	3,000,000	3,000,000
Vehicles	50,000	50,000	50,000	50,000	50,000	50,000
Total	5,050,000	5,050,000	5,050,000	5,050,000	5,050,000	5,050,000
Less: Accumulated depreciation	(1,520,000)	(1,870,000)	(2,220,000)	(2,570,000)	(2,920,000)	(3,270,000)
Net fixed assets	3,530,000	3,180,000	2,830,000	2,480,000	2,130,000	1,780,000
Other assets	100,000	100,000	100,000	100,000	100,000	100,000
Total assets	6,021,307	6,079,013	6,030,620	5,840,184	5,628,522	5,440,867
Bank note payable	200,000	200,000	200,000	200,000	200,000	200,000
New bank note	0	0	0	0	0	0
Accounts payable	487,380	503,047	519,263	523,034	524,825	537,244
Accrued expenses	200,000	200,000	200,000	200,000	200,000	200,000
Other current liabilities	50,000	50,000	50,000	50,000	50,000	50,000
Total current liabilities	937,380	953,047	969,263	973,034	974,825	987,244
Long-term debt	1,500,000	1,300,000	1,100,000	900,000	700,000	500,000
Mortgage loan	1,000,000	925,000	850,000	775,000	700,000	625,000
Total liabilities	3,437,380	3,178,047	2,919,263	2,648,034	2,374,825	2,112,244
Common stock	100,000	100,000	100,000	100,000	100,000	100,000
Retained earnings— beginning		2,483,927	2,800,966	3,011,357	3,092,150	3,153,697
Profit/(loss)		667,038	710,391	680,793	661,547	674,927
Dividends		(350,000)	(500,000)	(600,000)	(600,000)	(600,000)
Retained earnings— ending	2,483,927	2,800,966	3,011,357	3,092,150	3,153,697	3,228,623
Total net worth	2,583,927	2,900,966	3,111,357	3,192,150	3,253,697	3,328,623
Total liabilities and net worth	6,021,307	6,079,013	6,030,620	5,840,184	5,628,522	5,440,867

Although a modest improvement in sales will occur over the next five years, the annual increases are probably caused by the impact of inflation on prices rather than by higher unit volumes. The steady deterioration in gross margin (from 37.1 percent to 35.7 percent) and the drop in the ratio of net income to sales during the final three years (from 9.2 percent in 1994 to 8.3 percent in 1997) confirm that Filtco's sales volume is at best constant; more likely it will suffer from increased competitive pressures in the later years.

The company's pro forma balance sheet remains very strong over the five-year period: Long-term debt continues to decline; the current ratio and quick ratio improve from 2.6 and 1.1 to 3.6 and 1.3, respectively; and asset turnover jumps from a healthy 1.2 times to 1.5 times. Furthermore, Filtco's current business base obviously generates substantial cash flow, enabling the owner to withdraw dividends of $350,000 in 1993, $500,000 in 1994, and $600,000 in each of the later three years.

Nevertheless, without the addition of new markets or products, it appears that the company's long-term future may be in danger. Inventory builds at an alarming clip, from 119 days' sales in 1992 to nearly 177 days' sales in 1997. The high cash throw-off indicates an underutilization of leveraging and assets. Based on this analysis, Filtco should be able to handle a purchase price for a new business in the range of $2 million (with debt and equity capital from the parent) to $4 million (assuming that the target company can carry sufficient new debt).

Corporate Office

Like many entrepreneurs, the owner of Filtco had always directed the day-to-day operations of the company. Although over the years several key managers had been added, the ultimate authority for practically all decisions had rested with the owner. Following the advice of a consultant hired to assist in the acquisition process, the acquisition task force rented a small office two blocks from the Filtco plant.

They hired a secretary and installed telephones, fax machines, a personal computer, and other minor office equipment needed during the acquisition period. The controller also established a new set of financial reports to be filed weekly by key Filtco managers. The owner's from Filtco's day-to-day operation necessitated the promotion of the production manager to a new role as general manager of the Filtco plant.

The strategy was to run the Filtco plant and the new acquisition as autonomous business units, with general managers responsible for each unit's profitability and cash flow goals. At the corporate office, the marketing manager would coordinate all marketing efforts for both business units, the controller would implement and manage a centralized cash management function, and the business owner would oversee the entire operation. Once these new reporting lines were established, the task force moved to the next step of searching out an appropriate acquisition candidate.

GETTING PROFESSIONAL HELP

The myriad details involved in acquiring a business or product line take an inordinate amount of time and effort away from the management of current operations. To alleviate some of this pressure, and in many cases to hasten the acquisition process, professional advisors should be engaged early in the game. Such advisors can do much of the legwork required to search out potential candidates and qualify those that appear to offer the best possibilities. They should also be capable of assisting in the sourcing of new capital providers, helping in the valuation of target companies, and directing the negotiation of contract language in buy/sell agreements.

Not all acquisition advisors are qualified to handle all these chores, and in many cases, a buying company doesn't need help in all areas. In the Filtco case, for example, the task force decided to engage a merger and acquisition (M&A) consultant early in the game to work primarily on identifying viable candidates. It was also presumed that later in the process, this consultant could be of service in locating appropriate debt and/or equity investors, if needed.

An expensive consultant may not be needed if a company's management has sufficient time and expertise. In that case, brokers can be used to locate target candidates and, in rare cases, help with financing leads. For smaller acquisitions, business brokers (or, in rural areas, certain real estate agencies) do an adequate job of identifying local businesses for sale and accumulating appropriate financial statements—but don't count on them to know much about capital sources.

There are several highly qualified financial brokers that maintain contacts with financial institutions and private investors throughout the country. These brokers can be engaged to round up debt or equity capital. Don't expect any management-oriented help from them, however. Few are qualified in management disciplines, and if they are looked upon as professional advisors, they can do more harm than good.

There is one cautionary note. State licensing presumably verifies the expertise of real estate agents and to a lesser extent controls their compliance with rules of conduct and business ethics. However, since no licensing is required for business brokers or consultants, anyone may claim either title and the assumed expertise that accompanies it. This leaves the door open to many unqualified brokers and consultants who have a nasty habit of taking your money without providing any meaningful service in return or, worse, giving bad advice.

When selecting a broker or consultant to help in acquisition work, it's a good idea to interview at least three before signing any contract. The guidelines in Figure 10-4 can be helpful as a reference during interviews.

Business brokers do exactly what the name implies: They list businesses for sale and advertise for buyers. Fees are nearly always contingent on closing the deal and are usually, but not always, paid by the seller, not the buyer. The amount ranges from 10 percent of the purchase price to a modified Lehman scale formula (described later in this chapter).

Figure 10-4
Guidelines for Interviewing M&A Consultants and Brokers

1. Is the firm listed in the telephone directory? (It's amazing how many are not!)
2. Have the Better Business Bureau and the Chamber of Commerce ever heard of the firm?
3. Does the company belong to any professional organizations? Which ones?
4. How many deals were closed in the past twelve months? (If less than three, go elsewhere.)
5. Get the names of these sellers for references.
6. Get the names of the buyers for references.
7. Get at least two references from banks that financed the deals.
8. Have any of the closed deals involved a company of similar size and in the same industry as yours?
9. How does the broker or consultant plan to locate a target? Networking? Advertising? Personal contacts?
10. How long will take to find a viable target? To close the deal? If the estimate is less than 180 days, go elsewhere.
11. Does the broker or consultant insist on an exclusive listing? They should.
12. What information do you have to provide? Bank and trade references should be the minimum.
13. What is the fee arrangement? Compare this with the others. Brokers should all charge about the same. M&A consultants may vary, but never pay more than the Lehman scale (discussed later in the chapter).
14. What type of contract is involved? It should be inclusive and should guarantee the amount of time the broker or consultant will spend on your deal—five days per month, one week, four months, or whatever. If the firm will not make specific time commitments, go somewhere else.

A business broker does little to investigate listed businesses. Usually, however, buyers are provided with one or two sheets of financial and other data about the business. Business brokers generally handle only small local retailing and wholesaling businesses, restaurants and bars, small hotels and inns, service firms, and some small manufacturing and assembly companies. They are listed in the Yellow Pages of any city telephone directory.

For larger acquisitions (in excess of $2 million sales), M&A consultants can be a valuable source of target companies. M&A consultants do more than merely list businesses for sale. They offer advice to either buyers or sellers about how to structure a sale and where to get the financing. They also assist in negotiations and business valuations and, of course, try to locate the right target company. They usually have a broad knowledge of the acquisition market.

Some consultants specialize in a particular industry, such as larger hotels, plastics manufacturing, metalworking companies, or health care. They keep track of parent companies considering a corporate restructuring that could result in divestitures of divisions and subsidiaries. Many consultants specialize in smaller companies in specific industries and maintain a network of owners throughout the country who are currently interested in selling. Others are regionalized, however, and are familiar only with the markets in their areas.

Some M&A consultants work on a contingency basis, which means that no fee is paid unless a deal closes. Speaking of fees, most M&A consultants base their fees on the so-called Lehman scale:

5 percent for the first $1 million of sales price

4 percent for the second $1 million

3 percent for the third $1 million

2 percent for the fourth $1 million

1 percent for the fifth $1 million

1/2 percent for the excess over $5 million

The recent acceleration in the M&A market has led consultants to charge multiples of the Lehman scale, such as 1.5 or 2 times these percentages. Most of these consultants also charge an up-front retainer, frequently offset against the contingency fee at closing.

If you're going after a smaller acquisition, don't waste money on an M&A consultant. A good business broker knows more about local markets and can provide a much greater variety of candidates. But for anything over $2 million in sales, M&A consultants are the way to go. When engaging either a broker or a consultant, be sure to clarify which specific steps in the acquisition process the company will perform and which the consultant or broker is expected to do.

Banks, professional accountants, and occasionally lawyers can also help during the search stage. However, the fastest way to locate a good target is still through a broker or M&A consultant.

Unsolicited Mailings

Many companies have also been extremely successful in uncovering privately owned businesses or divisions of large corporations that are not for sale openly in the marketplace by implementing an unsolicited mailing campaign. Several national and regional databases can be purchased that produce practically any data sort a customer may want: by industry, location, sales, product line, and so on. Either hard copy or downloaded listings come complete with names of officers, mailing addresses, and telephone numbers.

Some of the best acquisition databases are sold by computer on-line companies such as Dialog Business Connection, 3460 Hillview Avenue, Palo Alto, California 94304, 800-334-2564 and Dun & Bradstreet (through various offices). These databases can be downloaded directly to your computer, and this will save substantial amounts of time. Additionally, any reputable mailing list company (such as Ed Burnett Consultants of Englewood, New Jersey) will provide hard copy lists customized to your specifications. These purchased databases vary in cost from a few hundred dollars to several thousand dollars depending on the number of companies listed, the number of sorts required, and special services such as mailing labels or computer disks. Be sure to specify the selection criteria and the different data sorts you need, and get quantity price quotes to judge how far you can afford to go.

With a mailing list in hand, compose an eye-catching, sales-oriented letter, designed to attract the attention of even the most jaundiced financial executive. By the way, it's best to address such mailings to the chief financial officer for listed companies and the chairman or president of privately held companies. It's important to use the person's name in the address, not just a title; this seems to compel an answer. If you wish to keep the name of your company confidential, many M&A consultants will use their letterhead for such a mailing.

Once two or three potential targets have been identified, the next step in the acquisition process is to begin the investigation stage, which will lead to a valuation of the target company, further due diligence analyses, and the negotiation of a purchase price and terms.

Chapter 11

Evaluating Acquisition Candidates

It goes without saying that every company has its own set of standards for judging acquisition candidates. Primary criteria may involve the target company's management expertise, its potential for rapid sales growth, the compatibility of product lines, the capture of major market shares, or the elimination of competition. What looks like an ideal candidate to one buyer may look dismal to another.

Yet, certain criteria seem to characterize those small business acquisitions that over the long run make the greatest contribution to overall growth plans. Although the following qualities vary somewhat by industry and market, they provide fairly reasonable guidelines for making at least an initial cut in the search process. The acquisition target should:

- Be unique (There should be something different or unusual about the company that gives it an advantage in the marketplace—perhaps proprietary products with extraordinarily high quality, or incomparable customer service, or unusual distribution systems and delivery methods, or a prime location.)
- Show increasing profits for the past three years
- Be capable of consistent returns on investment in the 15 to 20 percent range (The average return on New York Stock Exchange companies in 1992 was 10 to 20 percent, and venture capital funds look for returns of 30 to 40 percent.)
- Have a broad customer base, with no single customer accounting for more than 10 percent of total sales
- Employ competent, motivated people, with key employees willing to stay after the deal closes
- Be free of outstanding lawsuits or claims

Returning to the Filtco case study introduced in Chapter 10, as the acquisition task force used the criteria to analyze alternative choices, it became clear that three candidates stood out from the rest:

- Candidate 1 was a company with $3.5 million annual sales that manufactured in-line water filters for residential markets.

- Candidate 2 was a company generating sales of $4 million that distributed mostly imported disposable filters for use in the chemical industry.
- Candidate 3 was a company with $5.2 million in sales that designed, manufactured, and installed electronically monitored air filters, primarily for export markets.

PRELIMINARY INVESTIGATION

Filtco's candidate 1, the water filter company, manufactured filters to remove impurities from well water. These filters were installed directly into the water line between the well and the tap, mainly for residential customers, and were mostly used for filtering well water for single-family dwellings. However, filters were also installed in well water lines to apartment complexes and condominiums. In addition, the company sold a small selection of products to industrial customers. Upon investigating these market niches, the Filtco task force determined that this candidate probably controlled about 20 percent of the single-family residence filter market and significantly lesser shares of the other market niches.

Independent distributors made up the company's main distribution channel, although on request, the company sold direct from the factory. The company had showed steadily increasing profits for the past four years. A single shareholder owned all the company's shares, for which an asking price of $3 million had been established. The building that housed the factory and offices was owned separately by the same shareholder, but could be included in the deal for an extra $1 million.

Since this candidate met many of the Filtco criteria, the next step was to determine a preliminary value by analyzing the company's financial statements. However, the sole shareholder of candidate 1 balked at releasing complete financial statements without a firm commitment to purchase from Filtco. With intermediary help from Filtco's consultant, the seller finally agreed to accept a letter of intent from Filtco in lieu of a purchase commitment, provided the company would also furnish current financial statements to prove its financial viability as a legitimate buyer.

Level of Interest Letter

In many cases, the best way to deal with recalcitrant sellers is with a nonbinding *level of interest* letter (also called a *letter of intent*) indicating a desire to proceed with negotiations for the acquisition contingent on the satisfactory completion of a due diligence investigation. The following sample is typical of such a letter of intent.

Filtco Corporation
Letter of Intent to Purchase ACE Company

This letter will confirm the intention of Filtco Corporation ("Buyer") to proceed to draft an Offer to Purchase all of the assets and/or common stock of ACE Company ("Company") as soon as negotiations concerning the aggregate purchase price and terms of sale have been negotiated.

Buyer is prepared to proceed promptly to negotiate such price and terms, to draft and present such an Offer to Purchase, to perform the formal investigations and "due diligence," and to negotiate and draft as rapidly as possible a definitive purchase agreement acceptable to both parties. It is understood by both parties that Buyer will make a detailed review and analysis of the business, financial conditions, and prospects of the Company and that Buyer must be satisfied in all respects with the results of its review and analysis prior to the execution of any definitive purchase agreement.

Upon acceptance of this letter, Mr. Joe C. Lead ("Seller") agrees to furnish Buyer with sufficient information regarding the condition and affairs of the Company to enable Buyer to proceed with the above mentioned Offer to Purchase and to negotiate to conclusion such price and terms as will be mutually acceptable. Seller further agrees that until such time as negotiations are terminated by either party, Seller will not continue nor begin any negotiations or make any business disclosures with or to any potential buyer other than the Buyer, as defined herein.

Neither party shall have any legal obligation to the other with respect to the transaction contemplated herein unless and until the parties have executed and delivered a definitive purchase agreement, at which point all obligations and rights of the parties hereto shall be governed by such agreement.

_____   Filtco Corporation
      Joe C. Lead

Date_____   Date_____

Confidentiality Agreement

It's also a good idea to execute a *confidentiality agreement* at this time. This binding contract specifies that the potential buyer will not reveal any of the target company's confidential information to third parties. The execution of such an agreement is usually accepted as an indication that the buyer has a genuine interest in proceeding with the transaction. The execution of a confidentiality agreement as well as a letter of intent normally pries loose financial information from recalcitrant sellers. The following is an example of a commonly used confidentiality agreement.

Confidentiality Agreement

Dear_____:

This letter is written with respect to the furnishing of certain information to _____ ("Buyer") regarding Buyer's possible acquisition of _____ ("Company") from _____ ("Seller").

In consideration of Seller furnishing to Buyer certain information, all of which Seller regards as confidential ("the Confidential Information"), relating to the

Company's business, assets, rights, liabilities, and obligations, Buyer hereby agrees as follows:

1. The Confidential Information will be used solely for the purpose of evaluating a possible transaction between Buyer and Seller, and such information will be kept confidential by Buyer and its advisors; provided, however, that (i) any of such information may be disclosed to Buyer's employees and representatives who need to know such information for the purpose of evaluating any such possible transaction between Buyer and Seller (it being understood that such employees and representatives shall be informed by Buyer of the confidential nature of such information and shall be directed by Buyer to treat such information confidentially), and (ii) any disclosure of such information may be made to which Seller consents in writing.

2. The restrictions set forth in paragraph 1 shall not apply to any part of the Confidential Information that:

   (a) was at the time of disclosure or thereafter becomes generally available to the public other than as a result of a disclosure by Buyer; or

   (b) was at the time of the disclosure, as shown by Buyer's records, already in Buyer's possession on a lawful basis; or

   (c) is lawfully acquired after the time of the disclosure by Buyer through a third party under no obligation of confidence to Seller.

3. Buyer will not disclose to any person either the fact that discussions or negotiations are taking place concerning a possible transaction relating to the Confidential Information or any of the terms, conditions, or other facts with respect to any such possible transaction, including the status thereof.

4. At any time, upon the request of Seller, Buyer shall return the Confidential Information to Seller and shall not retain any copies or other reproductions or extracts thereof. At such time all documents, memoranda, notes, and other writings whatsoever prepared by Buyer relating to the Confidential Information shall be destroyed.

Sincerely,

_____

President

Facilities Tour

In some cases, overly suspicious sellers continue to hold back full financial statements even when buyers execute letters of intent and confidentiality agreements. Since it is impossible to move forward in assessing the future potential of a company without having financial statements as a starting point, a visit to the target company's facility may be necessary to pry them loose. Even with financial statements in hand, it's a good idea to get a look at the operation early in the game. Many matters may come to light during an initial facility tour that could keep you from spending unnecessary time analyzing financial statements.

A case in point occurred when a client zeroed in on a target acquisition whose owner willingly forwarded financial statements for three years at the first request. The controller analyzed the statements and saw that the asking price was in the right range and that the cash flow promised to repay the investment within five years. The marketing organization was enthusiastic about adding the new product lines, and the target's key employees presented excellent credentials on their résumés.

Bypassing a facilities tour and interviews with key employees in his eagerness to reach a quick close, the owner of the parent company forwarded an offer to purchase contingent only on arranging satisfactory financing. A good faith deposit of $200,000 took the target company off the market. After spending another $100,000 on legal fees, my client finally decided to take a look at the soon-to-be-acquired company's facility.

As I accompanied him on this first tour, I pointed out that the machinery seemed to be in disrepair, that much of the inventory was gathering dust, and that the factory workers appeared to be spending more time at the coffee machines than at their work stations. After one day at the facility, it became clear that this was a decrepit company that could easily take another half million dollars to clean up—on top of the purchase price. My client backed off and forfeited the $200,000 deposit.

When touring a target company's facility, pay special attention to its cleanliness and orderliness. Even in the messiest manufacturing processes, a well-maintained and organized shop, with trash in trash containers and work areas swept clean at the end of a work shift, indicates the workers care about and have pride in their operation. Also take a close look at the condition of the company's hard assets—equipment, machinery, inventory, and real estate (if it is included in the deal). The cost of upgrading or repairing facilities or disposing of obsolete inventory must be deducted from forecasted cash flow to establish a market value for the business.

Also take a close look at the workers in the production area. Do they appear to be busy and at their work stations? Can you count roughly the same number of employees as reported on the payroll? You can tell a great deal about the efficiency and productivity of a business simply by being observant. If the number of employees seems to be at odds with the company's records, chances are good that something is seriously wrong with management controls and that additional investigation will be necessary before you commit to further expenditures.

Assuming that the facility looks acceptable, during this visit you should be able to convince the seller to release the company's financial statements. Try to get them for the most recent three years, audited if possible. Also, pick up sales and product literature. This can be very helpful in evaluating the company's market potential and competitive positioning.

MANAGEMENT CAPABILITY

Filtco's candidate 2, a distribution company with $4 million in sales, sold disposable filters to industrial customers in the chemical industry. Although most of its products were imported from Europe and East Asia, the company also handled a limited line of filters from domestic manufacturers. Markets were concentrated in the southeastern United States, excluding Florida. Most of the company's major customers were chemical divisions and subsidiaries of Fortune 1000 companies. These products were uniquely designed to capture impurities in the raw materials used in processing chemicals as well as impurities in recyclable waste products. This market niche was small, but relatively free of serious competition.

This could easily be the right acquisition for Filtco. Market demand should be accelerating for several years, and the company's distribution system complemented Filtco's. Moreover, with such a small market niche, there was little likelihood that large competitors would enter.

The first meeting between the Filtco task force and the entrepreneurial seller went smoothly. The team collected summary financial statistics for the past ten years and toured the facilities. The seller openly discussed the complementary nature of products from this business and Filtco products. The acquisition team was unable to meet key management personnel individually, but were told by the owner that the quality control manager and the plant manager (who was the owner's brother) planned to retire as soon as the business was sold. It also came out that the company's controller was in over her head and should be replaced. Despite the perfect product fit, the company's excellent market position, and its modern facility, the Filtco team saw problems down the road if, in fact, three key managers had to be replaced.

Recruiting key management personnel can be one of the most time-consuming and difficult jobs faced by a new owner, especially when the target is located some distance from the parent company. Integrating a new business is hard enough; attempting this feat while simultaneously recruiting for key positions can be nearly impossible.

The evaluation of management capability and the status of key personnel brings up another important element to be addressed during the preliminary investigations: the need to obtain (or construct) an organization chart of target company personnel. Despite the array of business literature proclaiming that a clearly defined organization structure ensures that the right people are in the right jobs, the majority of privately held businesses tend to ignore this sound advice. "Organization planning" has a ring to it that smacks of exorbitant consulting fees. The short shrift given by many of our nation's business schools to developing organization charts seems to relegate this art to the outdated management practices of forty years ago. So seldom are organization charts formally prepared and regularly updated that many younger managers have never seen one.

Yet nothing has adequately taken the place of organization charts as a means of portraying the lines of responsibility, authority, and communication present in every company, large or small. The chances are good that you will not find an organization chart during your acquisition search and evaluation. In that case, get one prepared. As a minimum, be sure that it identifies the individuals responsible for making decisions in each functional area. Even if a full organization chart for the entire company isn't practical, one showing how key personnel relate to one another can be a big help in assessing management capability.

Not only does such a picture help in evaluating the advisability of proceeding with an acquisition analysis, it becomes crucial if the target company is actually acquired. Without a thorough understanding of the current lines of responsibility and the type of people who fill the key slots, it is practically impossible to efficiently integrate a new business with the parent.

One cautionary note regarding acquisitions of mature businesses with older, long-tenured management personnel: Over the years, privately held companies tend to become inbred. Nepotism can create unimaginable difficulties, especially when relatives of the selling shareholder hold key positions. The protection of long-term employees is also a prevalent practice in smaller private companies. Both of these conditions can make the smooth integration of a new business virtually impossible. Fortunately, asking pertinent questions when preparing an organization chart usually ferrets out such relationships and practices.

OWNERSHIP HURDLES

Filtco's candidate 3, a high-tech company with $5.2 million in sales, designed, manufactured, and installed electronically monitored air filters used by large apartment complexes, hotels, resorts, and shopping malls to measure impurities in private wells and swimming pools. Since it has major customers in Europe and East Asia, this company could give Filtco an entree into foreign markets that it did not presently enjoy. By integrating the target company's customer base and foreign distribution system with Filtco's product lines, Filtco would have whole new markets available that otherwise could take it years to develop. As an important part of the company's long-term growth strategy, this candidate seemed to offer the greatest opportunity of the three.

However, Filtco's acquisition team was apprehensive about striking a reasonable deal with the target company's multinational New York Stock Exchange parent. The asking price of $8.5 million seemed high, but since the multinational's restructuring plans called for disposing of this subsidiary, the team surmised that there might be negotiating room. They were also assured that the target's management team would remain after the close.

Although arranging facility tours and getting financial statements for the acquisition of a division or subsidiary of a large corporation are usually very straightforward, negotiating a purchase price and terms can be a real challenge. Large corporations tend to be much less flexible than entrepreneurial sellers and frequently believe that their sheer size and resources intimidate buyers.

A case in point was related in my book about buying small businesses, *Buying In: A Complete Guide to Acquiring a Business or Professional Practice* (McGraw-Hill, Inc., TAB Books, 1990). Near the peak of the last business cycle, a major American Stock Exchange company offered one of its high-tech divisions for sale—a real glamour candidate. My client was so excited about the opportunity to buy this business that the extraordinarily high asking price of twenty-two times earnings was ignored. We went through the complete due diligence phase before trying to negotiate a more reasonable figure. When it became clear that the high price could not be supported by projected cash flows, the president of my client company tried to get the CFO of the parent to negotiate something lower. The two parties met several times but could not reach a conclusion. The CFO kept deferring decisions to the parent company's chief executive officer, who was seldom available. When the CEO and my client finally did meet, the CEO deferred all pricing decisions to the company's board of directors—which met only every other month.

Needless to say, my client was frustrated. Thousands of dollars and several months of time had been spent on this candidate, and now it seemed impossible to even begin negotiations—nobody could or would make a decision. Undaunted, we continued to be patient, waiting two months for the board's decision. After the board meeting, the CFO politely announced that the answer was no, the board would not reduce the price, but if the stock market began to slip, it might reconsider. In a couple of months the market did turn down, and my client called the CEO (by this time he had learned to bypass the chief financial officer). The board voted to reduce the offering price to twenty times earnings, but that was as far as they would go.

That was the end. My client finally realized that valuable time and funds had been wasted on an acquisition that could never happen. This target was dumped, and we went on to less glamorous but more reasonably priced candidates.

Dealing with the divestiture of a public company requires different tactics than dealing with a private seller. Even though a meaningful valuation (to support a price) can easily be determined from freely accessible annual reports and SEC filings, if the asking price isn't in line, it would probably be advisable to drop the candidate. Meaningful price negotiations between an entrepreneur buyer with little or no leverage and a large corporate seller can be a frustrating and often fruitless exercise that often is not worth the time and expense.

PRELIMINARY VALUATION INVESTIGATION

Once potential target candidates have been identified, facilities tours completed, and financial statements obtained, preliminary investigations to determine how much the business is worth and whether the asking price is within a reasonably negotiable range can begin. The balance of this chapter and the next chapter take a brief look at the procedures involved in performing such an investigation and the methodology for building a cash flow forecast to serve as the foundation for determining market value. Be aware, however, that this is a *brief* review of *one* approach to establishing business value. For those readers who require a more in-depth explanation of this and other valuation approaches, my companion book in this series, *The Small Business Valuation Book*, is highly recommended.

Before a meaningful cash flow forecast can be constructed, it is necessary to accumulate a great deal of data about the target company. Some of this data involves product specifications and market intelligence. Some involves administrative matters, such as unresolved lawsuits, leasing arrangements, and outstanding contracts. Data about employees, customer bases, and supplier relationships is also desirable. When buying the stock of a company (as opposed to its assets), it's essential to gather all information related to outstanding debt obligations, including loan documentation, payment history, lender relationships, and collateral pledged.

The data gathered during this investigation is important input for adjusting the target company's financial statements, preparing pro forma statements and cash flow forecasts, and comparing the target company's financial performance with that of competitors and other companies in the industry. Figure 11-1 provides a convenient checklist of data to be gathered during the investigative or due diligence phase, in addition to financial statements for the previous three years.

Figure 11-1
Due Diligence Checklist

A. General

   1. Brief history of the company

   2. Company ownership structure

   3. Unique characteristics of the company

   4. Strategic plan (if available)

   5. Description of export program (if any)

B. Marketing

   1. Listing of products or services offered for sale

   2. Position of the company in the market (i.e., market share)

   3. Description of distribution channels

   4. Listing of competitors

   5. Size of markets

   6. Customer order backlog reports by customer and product line as of the end of each quarter for the past three years and the current year to date.

   7. Listing of orders received by customer and product line for each month for the past three years and the current year to date.

   8. Listing of shipments by customer and product line for each month for the past three years and the current year to date.

   9. Listing of outstanding customer contracts and outstanding customer bids: domestic, export, and international.

  10. Listing and description of all manufacturer's rep organizations, agreements, and commission schedules.

  11. Listing of buying sources: export and international.

C. Financial
1. Detailed income statements and balance sheets by quarter (including annual reports) for the past three years and for each quarter of the current year to date.
2. All supporting schedules to the above financial statements for the periods listed (e.g., manufacturing overhead detail accounts, selling, general, and administrative accounts, and detailed cost of sales). These schedules should be by major product line, if available, but at a minimum, there should be separate schedules for export and international.
3. Aged accounts receivable by customer as of each quarter for the past three years and for each quarter of the current year to date.
4. Physical inventory summary (if any) or detailed breakdown of inventory (raw materials; work in process: material, labor, overhead: and finished goods: material, labor, overhead) as of each year-end for the past three years.
5. Aged accounts payable by vendor as of each quarter for the past three years and for each quarter of the current year to date.
6. Listing of accrued expenses as of each year-end for the past three years.
7. Federal and state tax returns for the past three years.
8. Last year audited by IRS.
9. Financial forecasts for five years (if available).

D. Personnel
1. Personal résumés of key employees.
2. All employment contracts or agreements, oral or written, including any severance or termination compensation arrangements, with salaried, hourly, or collective bargaining unit employees.
3. All bonus, deferred compensation, stock option, profit sharing, or retirement programs or plans covering salaried, hourly, or collective bargaining unit employees.
4. If there is a pension plan, all documentation, including actuarial reports, tax returns, trustee reports, population census reports, funding requirements, unfunded liabilities, and so on, for the past three years.
5. Schedule of hourly wage rates and number of personnel at each rate, by work center, department, and geographic location.
6. Organization chart of salaried personnel, by location, showing function responsibility, tenure, age, salary, name, and title.
7. All documentation relating to employee insurance coverages—health, life, AD&D, dental, etc.

E. Contracts, Agreements, Appraisals, Insurance, and Litigation
1. Addresses of facility locations, including warehouses and sales offices.
2. All contracts or agreements with vendors and customers.
3. All contracts or agreements with employees.
4. All contracts or agreements with collective bargaining
5. All contracts or agreements with other third parties.
6. All recent (within three years) appraisals of real estate or machinery and equipment.
7. Listing of machinery and equipment.
8. All insurance claims outstanding.
9. All patents, copyrights, or license agreements.
10. All noncompete covenant agreements.
11. All lease or purchase agreements for machinery and equipment, autos, or real estate.
12. Legal descriptions of all real estate, including deeds, title reports, and title insurance documentation, together with documentation of any lien thereon.
13. Listing and description of all outstanding litigation or anticipated litigation.
14. Is the union contract transferable? If yes, then description of mechanics of making transfer, such as required approvals.

Although several of these matters may not be relevant for smaller companies, it doesn't hurt to at least ask the question. Information may come out that you may think doesn't apply but that in reality will become a key factor in making the valuation. It's important to gather as much data as possible so that the valuation calculation will portray the true market worth of the company.

RECONSTRUCTING FINANCIAL STATEMENTS

Regardless of whether a target company is privately owned or a division or subsidiary of a public corporation, the odds are very high that its financial statements will have to be reconstructed before they can be used for cash flow projections. Adjustments will probably be necessary to reflect any or all of three situations:

1. Adaptations to the way a company has elected to keep its accounts in order to bring them as much as possible into line with generally accepted accounting principles

2. Eliminations of certain unusual or discretionary expenses (such as owners' draws, extraordinarily high management bonuses, or the use of company funds to pay owners' personal expenses) or such nonrecurring income as tax rebates from the carryover of prior years' losses, gains from the sale of hard assets, or one-time contract progress payments

3. Provisions to reflect expected future events that materially differ from past experience, such as the projected closing of a branch plant, or the discontinuance of a product line, or the gain or loss of a major customer or order

Such adjustments may affect either the income statement or the balance sheet, or they may affect both. Typically, those transactions that lead to adjustments and that cause the most difficulty include:

- Overdue receivables
- Revenue recognition on long-term contracts
- Inventory valuations
- Leases
- Recording and writing off of intangible assets
- Unrecorded or unfunded pension liabilities
- Sales with contingent liabilities attached
- Intracompany pricing and borrowing
- Investments in affiliated companies
- Nonrecurring losses
- Owner/manager's expenses and compensation
- Conversion from a C corporation to an S corporation

Receivables and Revenues

As a matter of policy, many companies do not write off overdue receivables unless a customer has actually gone out of business. Even accounts from companies in Chapter 11 bankruptcy may be carried at full value in the hope that at some indeterminable date they can be collected. If you cannot determine that accounts will be collected according to the company's normal terms of sale, make an adjustment to write them off, or at least set up a reserve for uncollectible accounts.

An aged receivables listing (also called an aged trial balance of receivables) is the quickest way to identify potentially bad accounts. In most cases, a review of payment histories should be sufficient to determine collectibility, but on occasion, especially for large open balances, it may be desirable to confirm balances directly with customers (provided the seller grants permission). If the company has recently been audited, a quick check with its audit firm could also reveal any questionable accounts.

Companies that receive advance payments or progress payments, as on government or construction contracts, frequently record progress billings as a liability against an offsetting receivable. Advance payments can also distort revenue recognition, causing sales to be recorded in periods other than those in which related costs are incurred. In these cases, it may be necessary to adjust for or reserve against unrealized sales that may never come to fruition, or to shift sales from one period to another.

In those cases where it appears that accounting practices may in fact shift receivables or costs, but especially sales, between periods, several questions must be addressed, such as the following:

- When should the company recognize sales in its income statement?
- How should the company record inventory?
- What will be the impact on the cash flow forecast of customer payments received a year or more in advance of shipping products?
- How should you forecast cash flow for new contracts whose terms may be different?

Accurate adjustments for variations in revenue recognition can be a nightmare, usually requiring "best guess" estimates. It is not uncommon to forecast future cash flow based on historical averages of progress payments and expenditures for materials and labor, rather than aiming futilely for precision.

Inventory Valuation

The *last-in, first-out*, or *LIFO*, inventory method permits companies to defer gains that result from increases in the cost of material during inflationary periods by recording cost of sales at the most recent inventory acquisition prices. Ending inventory is then understated by the same amount that earnings are understated. The IRS accepts LIFO as a valid inventory valuation technique for tax purposes, and many companies now use it in their financial statements as well.

The distortion that the LIFO method brings to cash flow projections is even more important than the misstatement of earnings and inventory. Since both cost of sales and inventory are reported at fictitious prices that do not match the flow of actual costs, appropriate adjustments must be made to bring both in line with actual expenditures.

Leases

The Financial Accounting Standards Board (FASB) Statement No. 13, *Accounting for Leases*, holds that capital leases must be capitalized as an asset with an offsetting liability for future rental payments. Typically, a capital lease runs for the entire useful life of the asset, and the lessee has responsibility for asset maintenance, insurance, property taxes, and other costs of keeping the asset in good working condition.

According to FASB No. 13, a lease must be treated as a capital lease if, at its inception, it meets one or more of the following criteria:

- Ownership of the asset will be transferred to the lessee at the end of the lease period.
- The lessee has a right to buy the asset at a price significantly below its fair market value.
- The lease term is equal to or greater than 75 percent of the asset's useful life.
- The present value of the "minimum lease payments" at the lease's inception is equal to or greater than 90 percent of the excess of the fair market value of the leased property over any investment tax credit claimed and expected to be realized by the lessor (assuming that the IRS allows investment tax credits). The present value is arrived at by discounting the lease payments at the lower of the lessor's implicit lease interest rate or the rate the lessee would have to pay for a loan of a comparable term (the lessee's "incremental borrowing rate"). Minimum lease payments are defined as those payments that the lessee must make or can be required to make, including rent payments, residual value guarantees, and payments for failing to renew or extend the lease term.

Any lease that does not meet one of these criteria is considered an operating lease. Operating leases are relatively short term, with the lessor retaining responsibility for the asset's maintenance, insurance, and taxes. Operating leases are not recorded on the balance sheet, and rental payments are written off as expenses when paid.

These rules are straightforward, but applying FASB No. 13 to cash flow projections can be confusing, for three reasons:

1. The asset and the obligation must both be recorded on the balance sheet at an amount equal to the present value of the minimum lease payments.

2. If the present value turns out to be greater than the asset's "fair value," which is generally the asset's purchase cost, then the fair value is recorded in place of present value.

3. The capitalized lease must be amortized at a rate designated in FASB No. 13; the specific rate depends upon which of the categories the lease falls into. This may or may not be consistent with a company's depreciation policy.

Since minimum lease payments include noncash contingent items, such as residual value guarantees and penalties for failure to renew or extend the lease term, the annual reduction in the obligation cannot be considered as a cash outlay. Two adjustments must be made: (1) The present value of the minimum lease payments liability should be replaced with an obligation equal to the sum of the total rental payments over the lease term, and (2) the annual reduction in this liability should be adjusted to reflect actual cash payments. Of course, the same adjustments must be made if the asset and obligation are recorded at fair value rather than at discounted minimum lease payments.

If capitalized leases are incidental to the target company's overall financial statements, it's usually easier to adjust them out of the balance sheet entirely and treat them as operating leases. That way cash expenditures for rental payments can be treated as expense items in cash flow projections.

Intangibles

In many small businesses, intangible assets contribute more toward earnings, and hence cash flow, than tangible assets. Yet the rules of both the accounting fraternity and the IRS do not always permit these assets to be recorded on balance sheets. Examples of intangible assets include:

- Goodwill
- Patents
- Copyrights
- Trademarks
- Customer/client lists
- Client files
- Noncompete covenants
- Employment contracts for key employees
- Licenses
- Franchises
- Organization costs for new branches, divisions, or subsidiaries
- Unpatented technical know-how

Companies are allowed to capitalize some of these assets—such as patents, copyrights, noncompete covenants, and organization costs—and then amortize them over their useful lives. In those cases where intangible assets have been developed internally rather than purchased and have a significant bearing on earning power, the exclusion of these assets would result in substantial undervaluation. When companies rely heavily on unrecorded or fully written off intangibles, adjustments for the estimated value of these assets should be made in the company's balance sheet as well as its income statement.

Pension Liability

Two types of unrecorded or underrecorded pension liabilities must be guarded against:

1. A liability that reflects the amount of pensions that will have to be paid to employees for past service to the company
2. A liability that reflects the amounts that employees earn for future service to the company.

The former is called *past service costs*; the latter, *future service costs*. Although accounting rules have for decades specifically required the partial funding of past service costs, only in 1993 did such requirements extend to full funding of past as well as future service costs. To the extent that the target company has not yet complied with the new FASB regulations, an adjustment should be made to record the liability.

Another type of discrepancy frequently arises in very small businesses with few employees. In most cases, if those companies do have pension plans, they use one of the defined benefit plans sanctioned by the IRS as individual retirement plans. Both Simplified Employee Plans (SEPs) and the more complex 401(k) plans are popular. Some are managed through trustees, others by the company. When analyzing a company's financial statements, it's important to ascertain that payments required by law have in fact been made. If not, balance sheets must be adjusted to reflect the proper liability.

Intercompany Transactions and Investments

A target company may have divisions and subsidiaries with which it conducts business, thereby creating intercompany transactions. Accounting for such transactions and for investments in affiliated companies often causes more confusion in estimating future earnings and potential cash flow than it should. Transactions between affiliated companies should, of course, be priced at arms length. In practice, however, this seldom occurs in smaller companies.

Assume, for example, that a separate entity holds title to the real estate that houses the operating business. It could be a partnership, a limited partnership, or an S corporation. This holding company charges rents calculated to minimize taxes, not necessarily to reflect an arms-length arrangement. The same holds true for intercompany charges for management fees. Pricing of intercompany sales and purchases tends to more accurately reflect market prices, but even here, tax considerations dominate.

The recording of investments in affiliates may create a different type of inconsistency. If you are looking at a branch operation, it doesn't make much difference how the parent handles its investment in the branch. It makes a big difference, however, when valuing the parent. The greatest distortion arises when the cost method (as opposed to the equity method) is used to record investment in affiliates.

Accounting rules permit parent companies to use the cost method when investments in affiliates represent less than 50 percent of total ownership. Above 50 percent, the equity method should be used. The equity method reflects a share of the subsidiary's earnings in the parent company's income statement, whereas the cost method does not. If the cost method is used, it may be necessary to adjust both balance sheet and income statement accounts to accurately reflect the value of investments in subsidiaries.

Nonrecurring Events

When analyzing historical financial statements, it's important to eliminate income or expense items, as well as assets and liabilities, that have arisen as a result of extraordinary or nonrecurring conditions. Accounting standards define extraordinary events or transactions as those meeting *both* of the following criteria:

- The underlying event or transaction must be *unusual;* that is, it must have a high degree of abnormality and not be related to the ongoing business of the company.
- The underlying event or transaction must be *infrequent;* that is, it would not be reasonable to expect it to occur again in the foreseeable future.

Clearly, a large insurance settlement for a major fire that destroyed an entire factory would be extraordinary. A labor strike that forced the closing of a branch plant would also be extraordinary. So would the sale of a division or subsidiary.

Profits or losses of a discontinued operation that arose prior to its discontinuance would not meet the accounting definition of extraordinary but should be eliminated from financial statements before pro forma projections are prepared. The same holds true for a raft of other nonrecurring items that may not fit the definition of extraordinary items but nonetheless do not affect future earnings. Examples of such items include:

- Proceeds or expenditures from the settlement of a lawsuit
- Life insurance settlements from the death of a key employee or owner
- Any gains or losses on the sale of operating assets
- One-time radical swings in the price of purchased materials, as with the price of oil during the embargo of the early 1970s

To the extent that it can be determined that these events are not likely to recur during the forecast period, their impact on historical balance sheet and income statement accounts should be eliminated before you prepare projections.

Owner's Compensation and Expenses

As most owners of small businesses know, tax laws make it difficult to withdraw significant amounts of cash from a business without risking the IRS treating them as dividends and thus paying taxes twice on the same income. (First, the dividends are not deductible to the corporation and therefore come from after-tax income, and second, dividend income is taxed to the recipient.) Business owners have found several ways around this obstacle:

- The corporation can elect to be taxed as an S corporation, so that all business income and losses are taxed to shareholders and cash distributions are essentially tax-free.
- The owner/manager can pay wages to relatives (spouse, children, and so on) for services performed.
- The business can pay certain personal expenses of the owner/manager from company cash and treat them as business expenses.
- The owner/manager can borrow cash from the business.

All such transactions should be adjusted out of the financial statements to reflect the company's true financial performance, untainted by the owner's peculiar needs.

In addition, small businesses that elect to be treated as S corporations for tax purposes and that choose to keep their accounting records on the same basis present a peculiar set of problems. The major areas to be reconciled that require financial statement adjustments include:

- Distributions to shareholders in excess of proportionate profit shares, treated as a return of capital (reducing the company's net worth), loans to shareholders, dividends, or gains from the sale of property
- Retained earnings prior to the S election
- Corporate tax liability if the company was originally a C corporation
- Accumulated adjustments account and retained earnings when the accumulated adjustments account (which is treated like to partnership capital accounts) may not accurately reflect retained earnings.
- Built-in gains tax to the corporation (applies only for C corporations that switch to S corporations after 1986)

In addition to adjustments that reconcile S corporation bookkeeping to generally acceptable accounting principles, and reconstructions that result from owner/manager draws and company-paid expenses, adjustments may be required to reconcile the classes of stock permitted under the S election. Be aware that under certain conditions, the IRS treats S-corporation stock warrants, rights, and call options as outstanding stock even though they have not been exercised. To the extent that the company keeps its books in compliance with IRS rules, the value of these near-stock obligations will have to be dealt with.

Impact of Inflation

Even though the current economic outlook does not indicate the type of skyrocketing inflation we experienced in the 1970s, it would be foolhardy not to consider the impact of price inflation on the value of a business. The major difficulty arises because sales (or revenues) and expenses are almost always stated in current dollars, whereas many of the assets used to generate income (specifically plant and equipment and inventory) may have been purchased at significantly lower price levels. Thus, an upward trend in profits may be more a function of the inflationary pressure on prices than of managerial ability.

Although the Financial Accounting Standards Board did issue rulings requiring approximately 1,300 large corporations to disclose inflation-adjusted accounting in their financial statements, few continue to do so now that inflation has ebbed. Very few closely held businesses ever revealed such adjustments.

When looking at a stream of cash flows from a closely held company, one must be constantly alert to the need to adjust for inflationary profits. Without such adjustments, inflation-driven profits feed on themselves, and when volume tapers off or prices stabilize, the company could suddenly be faced with selling higher-cost inventory at lower prices.

Chapter 12

Pricing and Financing

Determining the market value, and hence a reasonable purchase price, for a privately held business can be (and usually is) the most divisive and misunderstood step in the acquisition process. Owners of small businesses invariably overvalue their companies, just as homeowners overvalue their homes. It is the intangibles that in our eyes add significant value to these assets: The loving care and attention to detail that make these assets unique, the little things that have been added over the years, the fashioning of these assets as an extension of our dreams—all make our business or home an integral part of our being. Certainly, buyers must recognize, as we do, that such assets are unique, one of a kind, and therefore worth significantly more than other apparently comparable ones.

Unfortunately, the market never sees these hidden values. There is no way to quantify them, to measure them, to weigh them against alternatives. Business buyers value the worth of business assets by the cash flows that they generate; home buyers value the worth of dwellings by the prices that similar dwellings have already brought in the market.

To the extent that business buyers and sellers will compromise and negotiate a purchase price based on quantifiable valuations tempered by goodwill or other intangibles, transactions can be consummated. When compromise is not possible, deals usually fall through. In the end, of course, the worth of a going business (or a dwelling, for that matter) is in the eye of the beholder. Nevertheless, except in very unusual circumstances, acceptable prices must be based on quantifiable evidence, not "blue sky" dreams.

This chapter reviews the basic procedures involved in establishing quantifiable market values that serve as a base for negotiating purchase prices of privately held businesses. In addition, we will look at the mechanics of raising equity capital to finance business acquisitions through the sale of partial interests in partnerships.

As mentioned in Chapter 11, discussions in this book related to business valuations are, of necessity, very abbreviated. *The Small Business Valuation Book* offers a complete discussion of various valuation methods applicable to a wide range of circumstances. I strongly recommend that book to readers who are in the process of making an acquisition or who have incorporated such an objective into their strategic plans.

Although financial analysts and appraisers use a plethora of valuation techniques for a variety of purposes, those applicable to the determination of purchase prices for going businesses or major product lines are limited. They focus almost exclusively on a straightforward forecasted stream of benefits (specifically cash flows) discounted to reflect perceived risk.

Such a forecasted stream of cash benefits should be based on pro forma financial statements, derived from historical cost/sales/asset relationships. The data gathered during the due diligence process (described in Chapter 11) and an evaluation of relevant economic and industry indicators provide the underpinnings for translating these functional relationships into a forecast.

Once financial statement and cash flow projections have been prepared, we can apply a relatively standard set of financial ratios to help us measure the risk that we will not attain the forecasted results. This, in turn, serves as the basis for developing discount factors that convert future cash flows to present values.

Probably the clearest way to demonstrate the practical application of these valuation steps is to return to the Filtco case study introduced in Chapter 10. It should be recognized, however, that although this case study involves manufacturing companies, the same valuation principles and procedures apply to target companies in any industry and of any size, other than very small micro businesses.

VALUING THE PRIME CANDIDATE

Of the three target candidates—the $3.5 million water filter manufacturer, the $4 million disposable filter distributor, and the $5.2 million multinational subsidiary that designed, manufactured, and installed electronic monitoring devices—the Filtco acquisition task force chose the water filter company, Purco, Inc., as the best target to go after. The first step in arriving at a reasonable offering price was to analyze the cost/sales/asset relationships derived from the Purco historical financial statements, which are shown in Figure 12-1 (pages 200 and 201).

Here is a company in a stable but steadily growing industry. Sales growth of 8.5 percent in 1991 reflected unusually large orders from three housing developments in Texas. The 1992 growth of just over 1 percent is more realistic, considering that the nation was in a recession and housing starts (along with new well drillings) were severely depressed. The company's ability to maintain its high gross margin, however, was encouraging. Even in a slow year such as 1990, net income as a percent of sales was a respectable 5 percent, and it reached a very satisfactory 11 percent in 1992, a flat sales year.

The spurt in sales during 1991 enabled Purco to completely pay off the balance of its long-term note, and the excess cash generated in 1991 and 1992 provided a welcome dividend to the owner. Clearly, this company is underleveraged, without short- or long-term debt on its books. It could be that its lack of aggressiveness in the marketplace, especially during 1992, was a result of excessive financial conservatism on the part of Purco's owner.

Figure 12-1
Purco, Inc.

STATEMENT OF INCOME
For the Year Ended December, 31
(in dollars)

	Actual		
	1990	1991	1992
Sales	3,200,000	3,475,000	3,525,000
Cost of sales	1,980,750	1,946,000	1,938,750
Gross profit	1,219,250	1,529,000	1,586,250
% of sales	38%	44%	45%
Selling expenses	386,464	398,058	410,000
Commissions	160,000	173,750	176,250
Administrative expenses	360,000	365,250	364,000
Other expenses	5,000	5,000	5,000
Depreciation	17,500	17,500	17,500
Total expenses	928,964	959,558	972,750
Net income before interest and taxes	290,286	569,442	613,500
% of sales	9%	16%	17%
Interest expense	15,000	0	0
Net income before taxes	275,286	569,442	613,500
Taxes	104,609	216,388	233,130
Net income	170,677	353,054	380,370
% of sales	5%	10%	11%

BALANCE SHEET
As of December 31
(in dollars)

| | Actual | | |
	1990	1991	1992
Cash	16,945	28,564	98,454
Receivables	533,333	579,167	587,500
Inventory	616,638	637,600	669,036
Total current assets	1,166,916	1,245,331	1,354,990
Building	100,000	100,000	100,000
Equipment & vehicles	120,000	120,000	120,000
Total	220,000	220,000	220,000
Less: Accumulated depreciation	(50,000)	(67,500)	(85,000)
Net fixed assets	170,000	152,500	135,000
Other assets	5,000	5,000	5,000
Total assets	1,341,916	1,402,831	1,494,990
Accounts payables	184,991	191,280	200,711
Accrued expenses	46,248	47,820	50,178
Total current liabilities	231,239	239,100	250,888
Long-term note	150,000	0	0
Total liabilities	381,239	239,100	250,888
Common stock	100,000	100,000	100,000
Retained earnings—beginning	690,000	860,677	1,063,731
Profit	170,677	353,054	380,370
Dividends	0	(150,000)	(300,000)
Retained earnings—ending	860,677	1,063,731	1,144,101
Total equity	960,677	1,163,731	1,244,101
Total liabilities and equity	1,341,916	1,402,831	1,494,989

On the other hand, the acquisition of such a cash-rich company that also has a respectable market position looks like an excellent expansion opportunity for Filtco. With modest injections of fresh capital, additional markets could probably be opened and new products introduced. Moreover, the company's strong cash flow should make Purco an ideal candidate for a leveraged buyout.

With this brief analysis behind it, the acquisition team turned to the task of calculating the return on investment that Filtco could expect. This required the preparation of pro forma financial statements and cash flow forecasts covering the next five years. These projections would also be used to determine the amount of acquisition debt Purco can carry and how much of the purchase price will have to be contributed out of Filtco's earnings.

Figure 12-2 (pages 202-204) shows the Purco pro forma financial statements and supporting cash flow forecast prepared by the Filtco team.

Figure 12-2
Purco, Inc.

PRO FORMA STATEMENT OF INCOME
For the Year Ended December, 31
(in dollars)

	Actual	Forecast				
	1992	1993	1994	1995	1996	1997
Sales	3,525,000	3,595,500	3,703,365	3,777,432	3,928,530	4,046,385
Cost of sales	1,938,750	1,977,525	2,036,851	2,077,588	2,160,691	2,225,512
Gross profit	1,586,250	1,617,975	1,666,514	1,699,845	1,767,838	1,820,873
% of sales	45%	45%	45%	45%	45%	45%
Selling expenses	410,000	422,300	434,969	448,018	461,459	475,302
Commissions	176,250	179,775	185,168	188,872	196,426	202,319
Administrative expenses	364,000	374,920	386,168	397,753	409,685	421,976
Other expenses	5,000	5,000	5,000	5,000	5,000	5,000
Depreciation	17,500	17,500	17,500	17,500	17,500	17,500
Total expenses	972,750	999,495	1,028,805	1,057,142	1,090,070	1,122,097
Net income before interest and taxes	613,500	618,480	637,709	642,702	677,768	698,776
% of sales	17%	17%	17%	17%	17%	17%
Interest expense	0	0	0	0	0	0
Net income before taxes	613,500	618,480	637,709	642,702	677,768	698,776
Taxes	233,130	235,022	242,330	244,227	257,552	265,535
Net income	380,370	383,458	395,380	398,475	420,216	433,241
% of sales	11%	11%	11%	11%	11%	11%

PRO FORMA BALANCE SHEET
As of December 31
(in dollars)

	Actual	Forecast				
	1992	1993	1994	1995	1996	1997
Cash	98,454	465,607	837,793	1,216,117	1,604,532	2,010,788
Receivables	587,500	599,250	617,227	629,572	654,755	674,398
Inventory	669,036	704,323	740,669	781,160	819,750	859,497
Total current assets	1,354,990	1,769,180	2,195,690	2,626,849	3,079,037	3,544,683
Building	100,000	100,000	100,000	100,000	100,000	100,000
Equipment & vehicles	120,000	120,000	120,000	120,000	120,000	120,000
Total	220,000	220,000	220,000	220,000	220,000	220,000
Less: Accumulated depreciation	(85,000)	(102,500)	(120,000)	(137,500)	(155,000)	(172,500)
Net fixed assets	135,000	117,500	100,000	82,500	65,000	47,500
Other assets	5,000	5,000	5,000	5,000	5,000	5,000
Total assets	1,494,990	1,891,680	2,300,690	2,714,349	3,149,037	3,597,183
Accounts payables	200,711	211,297	222,201	234,348	245,925	257,849
Accrued expenses	50,178	52,824	55,550	58,587	61,481	64,462
Total current liabilities	250,888	264,121	277,751	292,935	307,406	322,311
Common stock	100,000	100,000	100,000	100,000	100,000	100,000
Retained earnings— beginning	1,063,731	1,144,101	1,527,559	1,922,938	2,321,414	2,741,630
Profit	380,370	383,458	395,380	398,475	420,216	433,241
Dividends	(300,000)					
Retained earnings— ending	1,144,101	1,527,559	1,922,938	2,321,414	2,741,630	3,174,871
Total equity	1,244,101	1,627,559	2,022,938	2,421,414	2,841,630	3,274,871
Total liabilities and equity	1,494,989	1,891,680	2,300,689	2,714,349	3,149,036	3,597,183

PRO FORMA STATEMENT OF CASH FLOW
For the Year Ended December, 31
(in dollars)

	1993	1994	1995	1996	1997	1998
Cash Receipts						
Receivables—						
beginning	587,500	599,250	617,227	629,572	654,755	674,398
Sales	3,595,500	3,703,365	3,777,432	3,928,530	4,046,385	4,167,777
Receivables—						
ending	(599,250)	(617,227)	(629,572)	(654,755)	(674,398)	(694,630)
Receipts from						
operations	3,583,750	3,685,388	3,765,088	3,903,347	4,026,743	4,147,545
Cash Expenditures						
Accounts payable—						
beginning	200,711	211,297	222,201	234,348	245,925	257,849
Purchases	1,680,896	1,731,323	1,765,950	1,836,588	1,891,685	1,948,436
Accounts payable—						
ending	(211,297)	(222,201)	(234,348)	(245,925)	(257,849)	(270,131)
Material						
expenditures	1,670,310	1,720,419	1,753,802	1,825,011	1,879,761	1,936,154
Accrued expenses—						
beginning	50,178	52,824	55,550	58,587	61,481	64,462
Labor	331,916	341,873	352,130	362,693	373,574	384,781
Selling expense	422,300	434,969	448,018	461,459	475,302	489,561
Commissions	179,775	185,168	188,872	196,426	202,319	208,389
Administrative						
expense	374,920	386,168	397,753	409,685	421,976	434,635
Other expense	5,000	5,000	5,000	5,000	5,000	5,000
Accrued expenses—						
ending	(52,824)	(55,550)	(58,587)	(61,481)	(64,462)	(67,533)
Total operating						
expenditures	1,311,264	1,350,452	1,388,735	1,432,369	1,475,191	1,519,296
Taxes	235,022	242,330	244,227	257,552	265,535	273,757
Total						
expenditures	3,216,597	3,313,201	3,386,764	3,514,932	3,620,486	3,729,208
Net Cash						
Generated	367,153	372,186	378,324	388,415	406,256	418,338
Cash in bank—						
beginning	98,454	465,607	837,793	1,216,117	1,604,532	2,010,788
Cash in bank—						
ending	465,607	837,793	1,216,117	1,604,532	2,010,788	2,429,126

The growth assumptions used in these projections were:

- *Sales*—a 2 percent increase in 1993, 3 percent in 1994, 2 percent in 1995, 4 percent in 1996, and 3 percent in 1997 and 1998
- *Gross margin*—the same 45 percent for the entire period
- *Selling expenses and administrative expenses*—a 3 percent increase each year
- *Taxes*—a 38 percent tax rate
- *Receivables*—the same sixty-day turnover as in the previous three years

- *Inventory*—a slight deterioration in turnover caused by advance stocking for sales increases

With these projections in hand, the following steps were performed to determine a quantifiable value for Purco:

1. Analysis of financial ratios for the forecasted period, highlighting those areas that may cause an increase in risk

2. Evaluation of the qualitative factors that could affect future performance

3. Development of a realistic capitalization rate to reflect the perceived risk of achieving projected cash flows

4. Estimation of a continuing cash flow stream beyond the forecast period and a corresponding capitalization factor

5. Discounting of the future cash flow stream to its present value

Financial Ratio Analysis

The slow growth in Purco's sales (barely equivalent to the estimated 3 percent annual inflation rate) was reflected in an approximately constant ratio of net income to sales (nearly 11 percent over the entire period). Although 11 percent after taxes is certainly acceptable for a business of this type and size, the absence of sales volume growth had a dampening effect on the return-on-equity ratio, which showed a steady decline from 26.6 percent in 1992 to 13.2 percent in 1997. This troubled the Filtco task force and, as we'll see later, caused the team to increase its estimated capitalization factor for discounting future cash flows.

It should be noted that in the Purco case, the return on equity ratio was calculated by averaging the equity at the beginning and end of each year after adjusting for the dividends paid in 1991 and 1992. Some analysts believe that this method does not produce a true return. They argue that net income should be compared to equity balances at the beginning of each year, since it is this base from which the current year's earnings are generated. This approach has merit, especially when the only factor changing the equity is the current year's net income, as in the Purco pro forma financial statements. Regardless of the method, however, the lack of unit sales growth has caused a steep slide in the ratio over the forecast period, as shown in the following table, which compares results from the two calculation methods.

	Return on equity	
	Filtco Calculation	Beginning Equity Only
1991	31.0%	36.8%
1992	26.6	32.7
1993	23.1	30.8
1994	19.3	24.3
1995	16.3	19.7
1996	14.7	17.4
1997	13.2	15.2

A quick look at the other pertinent ratios in Figure 12-3 verifies Purco's cash-generating ability. Even with little or no growth in sales volume, the company's cash reserves grow steadily throughout the period (as a result of the high gross profit margin and relatively low operating expenses), and this causes substantial improvements in both the current ratio and the quick ratio. As long as receivable turnover can be held to two months, more than enough cash is generated to support the buildup in inventory. On the other hand, one might ask, why should inventory days' sales be as high as 126 days supply in 1992, climbing to 141 days in 1997, when unit sales volume is relatively constant?

Several answers are possible. There may be:

- Increasing scarcities of critical materials, forcing advance buying to ensure supplies
- A deterioration in the company's internal control procedures, allowing unwarranted inventory buildups
- Production problems that cause increased scrap rates and/or quality rejects
- Material theft

Although further investigation should be attempted when such an anomaly is found, it is probably unlikely that an outsider could uncover the real reason. That being the case, the only alternative is to weight this risk very high in the capitalization rate.

Figure 12-3
Purco, Inc.

FINANCIAL RATIOS

	Actual			Forecast				
	1990	1991	1992	1993	1994	1995	1996	1997
Liquidity								
Current ratio	5.0	5.2	5.4	6.7	7.9	9.0	10.0	11.0
Quick ratio	2.4	2.5	2.7	4.0	5.2	6.3	7.3	8.3
Profitability								
Gross profit (%)	38.1	44.0	45.0	45.0	45.0	45.0	45.0	45.0
Net income (%)	5.3	10.2	10.8	10.7	10.7	10.5	10.7	10.7
Return on equity (%)	21.6	31.0	26.6	23.1	19.3	16.3	14.7	13.2
Asset Utilization								
Receivable turns (times)	6	6	6	6	6	6	6	6
Receivable days' sales	60	60	60	60	60	60	60	60
Inventory turns (times)	3.2	3.1	2.9	2.8	2.8	2.7	2.6	2.6
Inventory days' sales	113.6	119.6	126.0	130.0	132.7	137.2	138.5	141.0

Weighing Qualitative Factors

Qualitative data gathered during the due diligence process should include as much nonfinancial information as possible that might indicate uncertainty about receiving future returns. Such data may or may not be quantifiable and in most cases will add little to the market value of a business. It can, however, detract from a company's value or confirm suspicions of potential problems developed through more formal ratio analyses.

For instance, qualitative information may substantiate or disprove suspicions about Purco relative to the mismatch between stagnating sales volume and concurrent inventory buildups. Although the types of available qualitative data certainly vary with every company, most businesses have sufficient internal records to produce the following statistics.

For Manufacturing Companies:

- Sales per employee
- Percentage of total material cost accounted for as scrap
- Percentage of total labor hours spent on rework
- Percentage of units shipped returned by customers

For Both Manufacturing and Nonmanufacturing Companies:

- Trends showing an increase in sales allowances or discounts
- Employee turnover
- Average accounts payable balances as a percentage of average receivables
- Accounts payable turnover
- Aging of accounts receivable
- Aging of accounts payable

In addition to this data, the level of management capability has a great deal to do with business value. Unfortunately, no one has yet come up with a way to measure the ability of managers to manage or a universal measure of management technical capability. However, the fact that universal measures do not exist does not in any way detract from the importance of forming subjective judgments about management competence; it only makes the conclusions more susceptible to disagreement. The Filtco acquisition team determined early in the game that the key personnel at Purco were in fact highly competent and capable of managing much higher growth than the owner desired.

Choosing a Capitalization Rate

The next step in determining a reasonable market value is the selection of an appropriate capitalization rate to calculate the present value of Purco's forecasted cash flows. A capitalization rate (or discount rate) comprises two elements:

1. A risk-free rate
2. A added premium for the uncertainty of achieving the forecasted cash flows

The risk-free rate is the easiest to determine. The current rate for U.S. Treasury obligations with maturities comparable to the forecast period is about as risk-free as one can get.

The premium for perceived risk, however, depends on the acquiring company's confidence in its ability to improve the growth curve and profitability of the target candidate. High confidence translates to low risk: a lack of confidence means a much higher risk. Regardless of which of the many pseudoscientific business valuation approaches a person chooses—risk analyses, one of the many cost of capital theories, or ratio analyses—in the end, a buyer's personal judgment determines the capitalization rate. It is possible, however, to develop a quantifiable base from which to negotiate a rate should the seller accede to your judgment.

One method for developing such a base is to isolate and then weight the various levels of risk using ratio and risk analyses. This can be a complex undertaking, however, and unless financial analyses reveal interacting levels of risk, the assignment of different weights to each risk category can become very cumbersome. A much easier approach is to use a traditional valuation model. One of the easiest to use was advanced by James H. Schilt in "A Rational Approach to Capitalization Rates for Discounting the Future Income Stream of Closely Held Companies," *The Financial Planner*, January 1982, and supported by Shannon P. Pratt in *Valuing a Business*, 2nd Edition (Business One Irwin, 1989).

Schilt developed a set of simplistic guidelines for determining risk premium that incorporate the concept of discounting future earnings streams to present value. Closely held companies were grouped into five categories, each with a range of capitalization rates to be added to a risk-free rate. These categories are as follows:

- *Category 1*: Established businesses, good trade position, good management, stable past earnings, predictable future—6 to 10 percent
- *Category 2:* Same as category 1 except engaged in more competitive industries—11 to 15 percent
- *Category 3:* Companies in highly competitive industries, with little capital investment and no management depth, although with a good historical earnings record—16 to 20 percent
- *Category 4:* Small businesses that depend on the skill of one or two people, or large companies in highly cyclical industries with very low predictability—21 to 25 percent
- *Category 5:* Small personal services businesses with a single owner/manager—26 to 30 percent

An analysis of Purco's historical financial performance and its pro forma forecasts indicates that this target candidate would probably fall into Category 1, which carries a 6 to 10 percent risk factor. The Filtco team chose a midpoint rate of 8 percent to represent its assessment of the risk of achieving the Purco forecasted results. When added to a 7 percent U.S. Treasury long-term bond rate, a total capitalization factor of 15 percent was used to arrive at the present value of Purco's future cash flow.

Before using this capitalization rate, however, two additional steps are necessary: (1) an estimate must be made of the cash flow associated with continuing operations beyond the 1993–1997 forecast period, and (2) a capitalization rate must be assigned to this continuing value.

Calculation of Continuing Value

Filtco was looking at an acquisition not as a short-term strategy but as an integral part of the company's long-term growth program. Therefore, it must be assumed that Purco's stream of earnings (and hence cash flow) will continue for many years beyond the forecast period. Since the precise number of years a going concern will be in operation is unknown, an estimated life span should be used: fifty years, seventy-five years, one hundred years, or some other period. The longer the period, the greater will be the cash flow stream; however, the uncertainty of achieving it will also be greater. To quantify Purco's continuing value, an arbitrary period of fifty years was used.

You can use the same capitalization rate for the continuing value calculation that you used for the forecast period; or you can use the discount rate you applied in the final year of the forecast, or you might find it more reasonable to use an entirely different rate, determined independently to reflect changing conditions. For most closely held acquisitions, the last choice is probably the most sensible. The new rate should reflect the uncertainty of future events, such as the possibility that major new competitors might enter the market or the likelihood that important technological innovations will be developed, either of which could make the company's products noncompetitive or obsolete. With these possibilities in mind, a discount rate of 50 percent, or approximately 6 times the forecast period risk factor of 7.5 percent, seemed reasonable to apply to Purco's continuing cash flow.

Once the various discount rates have been determined, they can be applied to the forecasted stream of cash flows to arrive at a preliminary purchase price from which to negotiate the final terms and conditions of sale.

Calculating Market Value

Referring back to Figure 12-2 (pages 202-204), it can be seen that Purco's cash flow forecast resulted in the following net cash generated for each of the forecast years:

Year	Cash Flow
1993	$367,153
1994	372,186
1995	378,324
1996	388,415
1997	406,256
Total	$1,912,334

Based on this cash flow projection plus a continuing value estimate, the Filtco team used the following analyses to arrive at the present value of future cash flows that would serve as a basis for determining a reasonable purchase price:

- As a conservative estimate of continuing value, the team used the mean of the cash flows of the forecast period ($382,467) for each of the fifty years, rather than an extrapolation of the 1997 amount. Then it multiplied $382,367 by fifty to arrive at a total cash flow of $19,123,343 for the 50 years 1998 through 2047.

- Next, the team applied a capitalization rate of 15 percent to the stream of cash flows projected for the years 1993 through 1997. This yielded a present value of $1,273,503.

- Following its leader's conservative bent, the team then applied a capitalization rate of 50 percent to the continuing cash flow stream, giving it a present value of $764,934.

- As a final step, it added the two present values ($1,273,503 + $764,934) to get a total value for the business of $2,038,437.

It should be reiterated that a present value calculation is only a starting point for further negotiations. Given this calculated market value, additions and subtractions can be negotiated to reflect the myriad qualitative factors that defy numerical analysis. It goes without saying that the desire of each of the parties to reach an accord will have the strongest bearing on the final negotiated value. In the Filtco case, a calculated market value of $2 million was too far off the asking price to be acceptable. After several negotiating sessions, the parties finally agreed to a price of $2.4 million.

For the acquisition of small service businesses, the present value of future cash flows usually plays a minor role in determining the final price. Competitive bidders, the seller's continued participation in the business, guarantees, additional contracts (such as noncompete covenants), the composition of customer bases, and a variety of other nonquantifiable matters enter into the final decision. However, to bring some semblance of order to what could otherwise be a chaotic negotiation, it's usually a good idea to begin with numerical analyses. And the main purpose of the present value exercise is to lay a foundation for such analyses.

One final note on the determination of the market value of a privately held business: For companies that produce or sell products that are generically the same as those sold by competitors (as contrasted with proprietary products), one additional step may be necessary—a comparison of the calculated value with verifiable values or recent selling prices of similar businesses. In the Purco case, however, the company's proprietary products made such a comparison less relevant.

Determining an Affordable Price

One truism concerning the decision to achieve long-term growth through the acquisition of a business or product line is that regardless of a target candidate's market value, the deal makes sense only if the parent company can afford it. It is equally true that the reason more companies fail to achieve their goals after making an acquisition is that the purchase price was more than the two businesses combined could support.

To determine an affordable purchase price, three types of questions must be addressed:

1. Can the target company's cash flow support a fully leveraged price without help from the parent company?

2. If not, then how much capital must the parent contribute to make the deal viable?

3. Does the parent company have sufficient free assets to secure additional debt capital, or must all of the contribution be in equity; and if the contribution must be 100 percent equity, does the parent company have the necessary cash reserves?

The first test views the viability of the target company as a fully leveraged, stand-alone entity. Figure 12-4 (pages 212-214) shows fully leveraged pro forma financial statements and cash flow projections for Purco. Even after the elimination of redundant administrative expenses, as a stand-alone business, Purco can handle no more than $1.5 million in a five-year term loan (the standard amortization period for acquisition debt). Principal and interest payments on this amount of debt absorb practically all excess cash for the first four years, leaving very little as a return to Filtco. Furthermore, based on the minimum price acceptable to the seller ($2.4 million), Filtco would still have to raise an additional $900,000, either with debt secured by its own assets or with equity contributions.

Since Filtco is free of long-term debt and excess cash will be available to pay dividends of more than $2.6 million over this five-year period, it initially appears that either the debt or the equity route would be financially possible. The next step is to run two "what if" cash flow forecasts for the two companies combined:

- One showing the financial results of Purco carrying a full debt load of $1.5 million on a five-year note and Filtco financing the balance of the $2.4 million purchase price with a loan against its own assets—probably its building and/or equipment

- Another forecast showing Purco carrying the same $1.5 million debt, Filtco contributing $500,000 in equity and the balance of $400,000 needed to meet the $2.4 million purchase price coming from a new five-year note

As a footnote, consolidated financial statements should be prepared using the American Institute of Certified Public Accountants' *purchase accounting format*, which allocates as much as possible of the excess purchase price over book value to the hard assets of the target company. In the Filtco case, the full $1.5 million debt secured by Purco's assets has been allocated to the net book value of buildings and equipment on Purco's books.

Figure 12-4
Purco, Inc.

PRO FORMA STATEMENT OF INCOME
(including $1.5 million debt)
For the Year Ended December, 31
(in dollars)

	Actual	Forecast				
	1992	1993	1994	1995	1996	1997
Sales	3,525,000	3,595,500	3,703,365	3,777,432	3,928,530	4,046,385
Cost of sales	1,938,750	1,977,525	2,036,851	2,077,588	2,160,691	2,225,512
Gross profit	1,586,250	1,617,975	1,666,514	1,699,845	1,767,838	1,820,873
% of sales	45%	45%	45%	45%	45%	45%
Selling expenses	410,000	422,300	422,300	422,300	422,300	426,523
Commissions	176,250	179,775	184,775	184,775	188,569	182,087
Administrative expenses	364,000	348,175	348,175	348,175	344,381	346,640
Other expenses	5,000	5,000	5,000	5,000	5,000	5,000
Depreciation	17,500	17,500	17,500	17,500	17,500	17,500
Total expenses	972,750	972,750	972,750	972,750	972,750	972,750
Net income before interest and taxes	613,500	645,225	693,764	727,095	795,088	848,123
% of sales	17%	18%	19%	19%	20%	21%
Interest expense	0	101,250	78,750	56,250	33,750	11,250
Net income before taxes	613,500	543,975	615,014	670,845	761,338	836,873
Taxes	233,130	206,710	233,705	254,921	289,309	318,012
Net income	380,370	337,264	381,309	415,924	472,030	518,862
% of sales	11%	9%	10%	11%	12%	13%

PRO FORMA BALANCE SHEET
(including $1.5 million debt)
As of December 31
(in dollars)

	1992	1993	1994	1995	1996	1997
Cash	98,454	92,669	94,730	106,109	129,017	171,547
Receivables	587,500	599,250	617,227	629,572	654,755	674,398
Inventory	669,036	704,323	740,669	781,160	819,750	859,497
Total current assets	1,354,990	1,396,242	1,452,626	1,516,841	1,603,522	1,705,441
Building	100,000	100,000	100,000	100,000	100,000	100,000
Equipment & vehicles	120,000	120,000	120,000	120,000	120,000	120,000
Total	220,000	220,000	220,000	220,000	220,000	220,000
Less: Accumulated depreciation	(85,000)	(102,500)	(120,000)	(137,500)	(155,000)	(172,500)
Net fixed assets	135,000	117,500	100,000	82,500	65,000	47,500
Other assets	5,000	5,000	5,000	5,000	5,000	5,000
Premium over book value	0	364,202	364,202	364,202	364,202	364,202
Total assets	1,494,990	1,882,944	1,921,828	1,968,543	2,037,724	2,122,143
Accounts payables	200,711	211,297	222,201	234,348	245,925	257,849
Accrued expenses	50,178	52,824	55,550	58,587	61,481	64,462
Total current liabilities	250,888	264,121	277,751	292,935	307,406	322,311
Long-term note	0	1,200,000	900,000	600,000	300,000	0
Total liabilities	250,888	1,464,121	1,177,751	892,935	607,406	322,311
Common stock	100,000	100,000	100,000	100,000	100,000	100,000
Retained earnings— beginning	1,063,731	1,144,101	1,481,366	1,862,674	2,278,598	2,750,628
Profit	380,370	337,264	381,309	415,924	472,030	518,862
Dividends	(300,000)					
Retained earnings— ending	1,144,101	1,481,366	1,862,674	2,278,598	2,750,628	3,269,489
Total equity	1,244,101	418,823	763,517	1,125,258	1,522,689	1,947,095
Total liabilities and equity	1,494,989	1,882,944	1,941,268	2,018,193	2,130,095	2,269,407

PRO FORMA STATEMENT OF CASH FLOW
(including $1.5 million debt)
As of December 31
(in dollars)

	1993	1994	1995	1996	1997
Cash Receipts					
Receivables—beginning	587,500	599,250	617,227	629,572	654,755
Sales	3,595,500	3,703,365	3,777,432	3,928,530	4,046,385
Receivables—ending	(599,250)	(617,227)	(629,572)	(654,755)	(674,398)
Total receipts	3,583,750	3,685,388	3,765,088	3,903,347	4,026,743
Cash Expenditures					
Accounts payable—beginning	200,711	211,297	222,201	234,348	245,925
Purchases	1,680,896	1,731,323	1,765,950	1,836,588	1,891,685
Accounts payable—ending	(211,297)	(222,201)	(234,348)	(245,925)	(257,849)
Material expenditures	1,670,310	1,720,419	1,753,802	1,825,011	1,879,761
Accrued expenses—beginning	50,178	52,824	55,550	58,587	61,481
Labor	331,916	341,873	352,130	362,693	373,574
Selling expense	422,300	434,969	448,018	461,459	475,302
Commissions	179,775	185,168	188,872	196,426	202,319
Administrative expense	374,920	386,168	397,753	409,685	421,976
Other expense	5,000	5,000	5,000	5,000	5,000
Accrued expenses—ending	(52,824)	(55,550)	(58,587)	(61,481)	(64,462)
Total operating expenditures	1,311,264	1,350,452	1,388,735	1,432,369	1,475,191
Taxes	206,710	233,705	254,921	289,309	318,012
Financing costs					
Interest	101,250	78,750	56,250	33,750	11,250
Principal	300,000	300,000	300,000	300,000	300,000
Total	401,250	378,750	356,250	333,750	311,250
Total expenditures	3,589,535	3,683,327	3,753,708	3,880,439	3,984,213
Net Cash Generated	(5,785)	2,060	11,380	22,908	42,529
Cash in bank—beginning	98,454	92,669	94,730	106,109	129,017
Cash in bank—ending	92,669	94,730	106,109	129,017	171,547

The ratio analyses for these two alternatives are shown in Figure 12-5, where Case 1 has Filtco borrowing the full $900,000 against its assets and Case 2 has Filtco borrowing $400,000 and contributing $500,000 of equity capital.

Figure 12-5
Filtco, Inc.

RATIO ANALYSES

	1993	1994	1995	1996	1997
Debt Utilization					
Long-term debt/equity					
Case 1	1.3	0.9	0.6	0.4	0.2
Case 2	1.1	0.8	0.5	0.3	0.2
Total debt/equity					
Case 1	1.4	0.9	0.6	0.4	0.2
Case 2	1.1	0.8	0.6	0.4	0.2
Total debt/total assets					
Case 1	0.5	0.4	0.3	0.2	0.2
Case 2	0.5	0.4	0.3	0.2	0.2
Liquidity					
Current ratio					
Case 1	3.2	3.4	3.6	3.7	3.9
Case 2	3.2	3.4	3.6	3.9	4.2
Quick ratio					
Case 1	1.3	1.3	1.4	1.5	1.5
Case 2	1.3	1.3	1.5	1.6	1.8
Profitability					
Gross profit/sales (%)					
Case 1	39.6	39.5	38.8	38.8	38.8
Case 2	39.6	39.5	38.8	38.8	38.8
Net income/sales (%)					
Case 1	8.6	9.0	8.7	8.7	9.0
Case 2	8.8	9.1	8.8	8.8	9.0
Return on owners' equity (%)					
Case 1	22.7	29.1	24.4	21.6	19.8
Case 2	31.6	27.2	23.3	20.6	19.0
Return on investment (after taxes) (%)					
Case 1	12.9	14.1	14.2	14.7	15.6
Case 2	16.2	16.8	16.3	16.1	16.2
Return on assets (after taxes) (%)					
Case 1	14.0	14.5	14.1	14.0	14.3
Case 2	13.9	14.4	13.9	13.6	13.7
Asset Utilization					
(Note: Receivables and inventory turnover and days' sales are the same in both cases)					
Receivables turnover (times)	7.2	7.3	7.3	7.3	7.3
Receivables days' sales (days)	50.6	50.6	50.5	50.6	50.7
Inventory turnover (times)	1.9	1.8	1.7	1.6	1.5
Inventory days' sales (days)	196.0	212.9	221.1	230.0	244.0
Total asset turnover (times)					
Case 1	1.3	1.3	1.4	1.4	1.5
Case 2	1.3	1.3	1.4	1.4	1.4

Note: Case 1 = Filtco borrowing the full $900,000 against its assets

Case 2 = Filtco borrowing $400,000 and contributing $500,000 of equity capital

These ratios make one point loud and clear: When a cash-rich company (such as Filtco) acquires another cash-rich company (such as Purco), a very high percentage of the purchase price can be leveraged without doing much damage to the combined operation. Although in the first combined year the three debt utilization ratios jumped, they quickly dropped to more than acceptable levels. Liquidity ratios were hardly affected. And the return on investment and return on equity ratios returned to normal in a brief five years.

However, the owner of Filtco considered the company's ability to continue paying dividends during the five-year transition period a more important issue than financial ratios. Although the total dividends paid over five years dropped somewhat (from $2,650,000 in the preacquisition forecast to $2,350,000 in Case 1 and $2,150,000 in Case 2), this lower level was still acceptable. When "what-if" forecasts were prepared, however, the cash balance in the first year, 1993, limited Filtco's equity contribution to $400,000, which, in fact, absorbed all excess cash that would otherwise be used for dividends. Case 2, therefore, represented the optimum combination of debt and equity that Filtco could afford.

ACQUISITION FINANCING

As the Filtco case study demonstrates, the financial strength of both the parent and the target companies determines the premium that can reasonably be paid without damage to the parent company, as well as the amount of leverage debt that can reasonably be absorbed. In many cases, however, neither the parent nor the target enjoy as strong a cash position as Filtco and Purco. Either one or the other, or both, may already have as much debt as it can reasonably service. Assets may be fully pledged: cash reserves may be nominal. The likelihood of interesting a financial institution in lending additional amounts for an acquisition would probably be very remote. Also, very few business acquisitions can be done without borrowing short-term working capital. This usually requires the collateralization of receivables and inventory, removing those assets from available security for long-term acquisition debt.

Although a leveraged buyout may not be in the cards, equity capital can frequently be raised. The fastest, and in many cases the easiest, way is to sell a part interest in your business to a partner. Micro businesses, small service businesses, and professional practices frequently find this the only viable way to raise equity. For such small businesses, partnerships make sense from a management perspective as well. It is never easy to integrate an acquired company into your existing business, and one or more partners could make the job a lot smoother. Also, a corporate office of two or more partners enhances management control over businesses that may be geographically separated. Still, selling a partial interest can be a traumatic experience for independent entrepreneurs, and many shy away from doing so.

One alternative is to set up a limited partnership specifically to raise equity capital. Such a structure restricts management participation by the limited partners while using their equity contributions to finance the acquisition. Five other methods can also be used effectively to raise equity capital under various circumstances:

- Venture capital funds
- Public stock issues

- Exempt registrations
- Blind pools
- Reverse mergers

The rest of this chapter reviews techniques for raising equity capital through the sale of limited partnership units. Chapter 13 deals with the other four methods for raising capital.

LIMITED PARTNERSHIPS

A limited partnership combines certain features of corporations (e.g., limited liability) and standard partnerships (e.g., profit and loss pass-through). It comprises one or more general partners, normally the business owner(s), and one or more limited partners, usually investors. General partners manage the partnership and are liable for its obligations in the same manner as with a standard partnership. Limited partners much like preferred shareholders in a corporation, have involvement in the activities of the business. The term "limited" designates limited legal liability, just as the corporate shield protects shareholders from a corporation's liabilities.

For many years, limited partnerships have been a popular medium for financing business acquisitions. Typically, the acquiring company is set up as a general partner, with individual investors and perhaps a venture capital firm as limited partners.

Since 1986, the IRS "at risk" rules and passive activity loss (PAL) provisions have severely restricted limited partners' deductions of partnership losses on their personal returns. Nevertheless, enough tax benefits still remain to encourage these hybrid partnerships as legitimate business investments, especially when they are formed specifically for acquisitions.

Structuring a Limited Partnership

Limited partnerships may be structured in any number of ways to suit the needs of both the general partner and the investing limited partners. Regardless of the specific agreement, however, when a partnership is initially organized, the allocation of profits and losses must be clearly defined. Although the allocation is usually based on a straight percentage of partnership units owned, it may use any mutually acceptable base. Such an arrangement might be as follows:

- Limited partners are credited with 75 percent of the profits of the partnership and all losses, in proportion to units owned.
- The general partner receives 25 percent of the profits.

Alternatively, all profits could be allocated to limited partners by proportionate shares and all losses charged to the general partner. These allocations could also be reversed. Or arbitrary percentages could be stipulated in the partnership agreement.

In addition to sharing in profits and losses, general partners usually receive salaries, fees, cost reimbursements, and other forms of compensation for administrative and management efforts. These payments are made prior to the determination of partnership profits or losses.

Just as with S corporations or standard partnerships, the timing and amount of cash distributions are completely independent of the allocation of profits and losses. Profits and losses are allocated for tax purposes only so that partners may report these amounts on their individual tax returns. Cash distributions, however, are not taxable (except under unusual circumstances) and can be made at any time and in any proportion called for in the partnership agreement. Cash distributions do affect partners' taxable income, however, upon the liquidation of the partnership. At that time, limited and general partners pay taxes on the amount of liquidation proceeds they receive in excess of the adjusted cost basis of their capital accounts. It's entirely possible that limited partners may be allocated partnership losses for tax purposes and still receive substantial cash distributions in the same year. But when the partnership is liquidated, it's time to pay the piper.

Selling Partnership Units

Selling limited partnership units may be likened to selling stock in a corporation. In closely held corporations, owners might sell minority interests to friends, relatives, employees, suppliers, or even select customers. Sales are made informally, without a broker or underwriter, and frequently without a formal registration. Stock can also be sold through a broker to individual investors. Such private placements normally require that the stock be registered with a state, with the SEC, or both. A full-blown public stock offering must be registered the SEC and sold by underwriters to a wide range of buyers at large.

The sale of limited partnership units follows the same three paths. Units may be sold:

- Informally to a select group of known investors at any mutually agreeable price
- Through formal private placements to unknown wealthy investors, typically for $50,000 to $100,000 per unit
- To the public at large through a formal registration procedure at a much lesser price, say $5,000 per unit

An Informal Sale

The procedures for an informal sale of limited partnership units to a select group of known investors closely follow those for the sale of equity interests in a standard partnership. Although unit prices vary all over the lot, in general, the total amount of capital raised is significantly less than that raised through a formal private placement or public issue. Companies going this route should be able to get all the help they need from their independent accounting firm and from their legal counsel.

Partnership agreement for informal sale

Selling units to known investors does not require formal SEC registration, nor do such investors expect a formal partnership agreement. However, even in the smallest limited partnership (one restricted to family members) a minimal partnership memorandum is essential to add legitimacy to tax deductions and income allocations. Of course, when nonfamily members or key employees are involved, a formal partnership agreement should be executed to avoid future disputes.

Although the format of limited partnership agreements varies with the creativity of the originators, here is one way to get the job done. These major clauses fit into an agreement specifically designed for a group of both family and nonfamily private investors.

Major Sections of a Limited Partnership Agreement:

1. *General partner.* Designate either the operating company itself or the owner and key managers as the general partner(s). If you designate the owner and key managers, they could form a separate S corporation, which then becomes the general partner.

2. *Limited partners.* Specify that all limited partners have nonrecourse liability. Be sure to write the partnership agreement to exclude limited partners from liability for any debts or other obligations incurred by the partnership, and any claims or lawsuits against it.

3. *Allocation of profits and losses.* Allocate all company profits, capital gains, and capital losses to the limited partners and all operating losses to the general partner. Although tax laws keep changing the deductibility of losses on individual returns, this structure stood the test of time.

4. *Management fees.* Develop a policy of charging management fees to the operating business for services rendered by the general partner. Fees allocated to the general partner can then be offset against operating losses for tax purposes.

5. *Additional limited partners.* Provide for the admission of additional limited partners and specify the new allocation of profits, capital gains, and capital losses, based on either contributed capital or other ratios.

6. *Dissolution.* Determine a definite life for the partnership. Also specify that when the dissolution date is reached, a majority vote by the limited partners can reset the dissolution to a later date. Of course, getting-out positions for each member must be specified.

Private Placements

Limited partnership private placements are a favorite vehicle for raising significant sums of equity capital without the cost of going through a registered public stock offering. Large private placements, as well as public issues of partnership units, are frequently used to finance movies, Broadway plays, major

R&D projects, oil and gas ventures, and large real estate developments, in addition to business acquisitions.

The registration process, offering prospectus, and underwriting responsibilities closely resemble the corresponding steps for initial public offerings (Chapter 13). Companies interested in such large offerings should use an investment bank to lead the issue and provide preparatory advice. Nearly all major investment houses handle limited partnership offerings as well as stock issues.

As a first step, the company establishes itself as general partner, thereby leaving existing shareholders in control of both the limited partnership and the operating company. Then partnership units can be sold to individuals, other corporations, or investor groups.

Quite frequently venture capital funds purchase units in small businesses that have potential for significant growth. This still leaves the door open for a future public stock issue, enabling the venture fund to recoup its investment.

Using private placements to raise capital sounds complex, but it really isn't. Although minor expenses such as attorneys' fees to draft the partnership documents, appropriate filing fees, mailing costs, and printing expenses are necessary in the beginning, they are much less than those incurred with a public stock issue, and are usually insignificant compared with the amount of capital that can be raised.

Private placements must be registered in the company's state of residence. Since each state has somewhat different registration requirements, a competent local attorney experienced in this type of transaction should guide the issue through.

Private placement memorandum

Units to be sold interstate must be registered with the SEC. A private placement memorandum similar to an initial public offering (IPO) prospectus must be prepared. Although this memorandum requires the same topical headings as an IPO prospectus (see Chapter 13), it may be considerably more complex.

The topical headings normally include;

- Partnership name and address
- Company (as general partner) name, address, ownership, and capitalization
- Names and titles of investment committee (if any)
- Business objectives of partnership
- Description of offering, including number of units, unit price, total offering price, and dates that deferred payments for units are due (if applicable)
- Full description of company, including mission, markets, product lines, facilities, and management profiles
- Allocation percentages applicable to company operating profits and losses and capital gains and losses
- Allocation methods for distributing cash or other assets, specifying the percentage of each that goes to the general partner and to limited partners, including payments to limited partners to cover personal tax liabilities arising from profit distributions

- Three years' historical financial statements for the company
- Three-year pro forma financial statements for the company
- Three-year pro forma projections for the partnership, showing tax benefits to limited partners
- Compensation of general partner
- Risk factors
- Liquidation date and distribution provisions

General partner compensation

In most private placement limited partnerships, partnership profits are distributed either 100 percent or nearly 100 percent to limited partners. If the partnership actually owns the stock of the company (as opposed to extending loans to the company), then there are only two ways that business owners can receive compensation: by drawing salaries from the operating company and by receiving fees as the general partner.

If fees are involved, and in nine cases out ten they are, the calculation and type of fees must be disclosed in the offering memorandum. Figure 12-6 presents typical fee structures with hypothetical percentages and amounts.

Figure 12-6
Typical General Partner Fee Structures

Initial Offering Stage

1. Reimbursement of organization and other expenses incurred, up to a maximum amount of 7 percent of the gross proceeds of the offering.
2. Reimbursement for professional and other fees incurred in preparing company assets to be sold to the partnership (assuming that is the agreement).

Operational Stage

1. Cash distributions—12 percent of the cash available for distribution until the limited partners have received the return of their investment plus an annual override of 5 percent. Thereafter, 12 percent of the cash available for distribution plus a proportionate share of remaining cash based on the respective partners' capital accounts.
2. Management fee—$200,000 per year adjusted annually for inflation, payable quarterly, commencing January 1, 1993, in consideration of management services provided to the company, plus reimbursement of expenses incurred on behalf of the company, but not general administrative expenses of the general partner.
3. Additional investments—An amount equal to 3 percent of the gross purchase price of investments acquired by the partnership subsequent to the initial investment in the company.
4. Investment dispositions—An amount equal to 2 percent of the gross selling price of prior investments.
5. Bonus—An amount equal to 5 percent of the annual profits of the company in excess of the annual budgeted amount.

Liquidation Stage

1. A proportionate share of all distributions based upon the partners' capital accounts until all such accounts have been reduced to zero. Then such a proportionate share generally accorded to the respective contributions by each partner.

TRANSFERRING PARTNERSHIP CAPITAL TO THE OPERATING COMPANY

Limited partnerships have the same difficulty as standard partnerships when it comes to moving cash proceeds from the sale of partnership units to the operating company. Three different methods can be used:

1. Liquidate the operating corporation and donate its assets to the limited partnership
2. Contribute personal stock holdings in the operating company to the limited partnership and then have the partnership lend the funds back to the corporation
3. Form a new limited partnership, raise the capital, and then have the partnership lend these funds to the operating company

The liquidation method involves a two step transaction. First, transfer all the assets of the corporation to yourself and the other shareholder(s) in exchange for the corporation's common stock certificates, which are retired upon the liquidation of the corporation. Then donate these assets to the limited partnership, increasing the basis of your general partner's capital account in the partnership. This is a tax-free transaction as long as the corporation does not have a negative net worth, in which case taxes are payable on the amount of the deficit.

The second method is even easier. Merely contribute company shares to the limited partnership. This increases your capital account in the same way as the previous method. Again, no taxes are payable. Under this method, the corporation stays intact and everything else remains constant; except that the limited partnership is now the owner of the corporation. When funds are raised by selling limited partnership units, this new shareholder (the limited partnership) merely lends the money to the corporation against an interest-bearing promissory note. No tax liability arises other than interest income to the limited partnership.

The third method retains separate ownership of the corporation and the limited partnership. Funds raised by selling limited partnership units can be loaned to the corporation just as in the second method. The only taxable income is the interest earned on the loans.

Chapter 13

Additional Financing Options

Financing a small-business acquisition can, in many ways, be the most frustrating part of the entire acquisition process. The time and money required to search out target candidates, hire lawyers and auditors, and prepare pro forma financial statements and valuation calculations can all be wasted if, in the end, appropriate financing isn't available. It's one thing to go after an acquisition as a short-cut to establishing a market position; it's something quite different to include a business acquisition as an integral part of a long-term growth strategy. In the latter case, losing a bid after spending six months or more on searching for a target, analyzing financial statements, restructuring a corporate office, and perhaps reassigning key managers to the acquisition task force can materially detract from other long-term strategies. The blow may be severe enough to sidetrack a company's entire strategic plan. For these reasons, it pays to begin the capital-planning process early in the game, preferably in concert with the search and analysis phases.

Furthermore, during the course of developing financing strategies, needs for long-term capital for purposes other than buying a going business or product line may arise. This is particularly common when going after equity capital. More than one small business has turned an acquisition financing search into an opportunity to raise capital for an overseas expansion, an R&D program, or the purchase of state-of-the-art production equipment.

Other than selling equity interests to partners or limited partnerships as described in Chapter 12, small businesses find two capital sources especially suited to acquisition financing (with variations that occur from time to time): private sources, such as venture capital funds, and public stock offerings. Public stock can be further divided into that which will be traded in the open market and therefore must be registered with the Securities and Exchange Commission (SEC) and that which will not be traded in the open market and is therefore exempt from registration.

Furthermore, shares may be offered for sale to the public without disclosing the specific application of the proceeds (called a *blind pool* offering). Blind pools can be conveniently used to create reverse mergers (a privately held company merging into a publicly owned blind pool), thereby creating a much larger capital base. This chapter reviews the requirements for raising equity through each of these means (venture capital funds, initial public offerings, exempt registrations, blind pools, and reverse mergers) and the pros and cons of using each method.

VENTURE CAPITAL FINANCING

Venture capital, also known as *risk capital*, is the primary source of financing for start-up businesses, R&D ventures, and companies bringing out new product lines. It is also an excellent source of capital for certain types of acquisitions. Not only do you avoid the costly exercise of using underwriters or public stock markets by selling equity shares directly to venture investors, you also bring cash into the company much faster than through the convoluted process of issuing public shares. However, not all firms can attract risk capital.

Venture capitalists expect high returns on their money and in most cases they can get them only if a company "goes public" in the foreseeable future—usually within five to seven years. These investors make a fundamental assumption that as a company's financial performance and future growth prospects become known in the marketplace, sufficient investor interest will be generated to make an *initial public offering* (IPO) feasible at a price substantially above their investment. When this happens, the original venture investors cash in, for a substantial gain. In the right situation, venture capitalists may hold their shares for a while after the stock is issued to see whether the market will drive the share price up even further, but only when the spread between the initial offering price and the expected future price is fairly wide.

Venture capital investors usually want to monitor their investments by taking seats on the board of directors. In other cases, fearing the potential liability that goes with board membership, they act as board advisors. Either way, they usually, but not always, insist on a controlling vote. At the same time, most venture investors recognize that if and when a company needs additional financing down the road for expansion or development programs, they must stand ready to provide it. No investor with a major equity stake, will let a company die for lack of financing. This future availability of funds can be an enormous boost in achieving long-term strategic goals.

In addition to financing business acquisitions, companies use venture capital (both equity and debt):

- As *seed capital* for starting up new businesses or business segments—This money is typically used to cover the initial market research, testing equipment, facility rent, basic operating supplies, experimental materials, perhaps the payroll of a project team to get the new venture off the ground, and other expenditures necessary during the set up, development, and testing stages of a new product, process, or business.

- As *working capital* at the end of the development stage when the product or process is almost ready to market—This additional first-stage financing pays for the materials, labor, overhead, and selling expenses required to produce and sell the products in quantities that meet market demand.

Although companies in the process of developing new technologies or products are the main recipients of venture capital, under certain conditions, service businesses with strategies to tap new markets may also attract venture investors. With a risk-averse banking industry, venture capital funds are frequently the only feasible source of financing.

Venture funds regard high returns as their top priority. Appreciation of five to ten times the original investment in less than seven years is typically expected. This means that to qualify, a business acquisition must either enhance the parent company's established high-growth curve or offer high growth potential on its own as a stand-alone investment.

Quite naturally, venture capital investors expect high appreciation gains as well as dividends and/or interest during the holding period. However, except in rare cases, cash flow during the first few years after an acquisition closes won't support large annual payments. Therefore, most of the total returns from investment appreciation, dividends, and possibly interest must come from an IPO. This becomes a decisive factor in the timing and pricing of the offering.

VENTURE CAPITAL INVESTMENT INSTRUMENTS

After the acquisition closes, additional financing may be necessary for working capital or to expand market penetration. Venture capitalists may contribute additional equity or they may solicit new private investors. Most prefer to solicit new investor capital so that risk can be spread over a broader base. A good example occurred when a midsize pharmaceutical company purchased 100 percent of the common shares of Claxfor Pharmaceuticals Corp., a small company that had developed new vaccines for immunizing farm animals.

Mid-World Capital LP financed the initial acquisition, but when Claxfor's new product caught the market's attention, additional production and test equipment was needed to produce sufficient quantities to meet the escalating demand. Mid-World went outside for additional equity contributions. As an incentive, investors were offered board seats plus annual director's fees of $15,000, in exchange for a minimum investment of $50,000 in noncumulative, 9 percent preferred shares with warrants. Four investors took the bait. When the parent company went public three years later, the investors received $170,000 for each original $50,000 investment.

Although additional equity capital may be the right solution for financing further expansion, fresh debt is more likely, simply because it does not dilute ownership interests. The idea is to continue lending sufficient capital to see the company through to an IPO, then settle the obligation with proceeds from a public stock issue. Two types of debt obligations are commonly used:

1. *Term loans* are secured by all hard assets of either the parent company, the subsidiary, or both and, in some cases, personal guarantees of the business owner. Typical interest rates run two to three percentage points above prime.

2. *Mezzanine debt* bridges the gap between the sum of the original equity contributions plus secured term loans and the amount of capital needed to bring the business to a public offering. Mezzanine debt is usually unsecured, although a pledge of common shares may be necessary. Because of the risk, mezzanine interest rates run very high—usually double-digit. Typically, interest is payable monthly or quarterly, with principal payments deferred until a public offering is made.

More often than not, term loans, and in some cases mezzanine debt, carry warrants convertible to common shares either upon default or when the business goes public.

Pure venture capital firms and venture arms of such giant investment banks as Goldman Sachs, Merrill Lynch Capital Markets, and Bear Stearns, which typically act as financing packagers, can be excellent sources of acquisition capital. The venture fund serves as the primary or lead source of capital and brings in other institutions to spread the risk—perhaps a commercial bank for a credit line and a secured lender for term loans collateralized with equipment and machinery. The venture fund itself makes mezzanine loans and equity contributions for the balance of the purchase price.

In exchange for an equity contribution, venture funds normally receive from 15 to 75 percent ownership interest. However, equity interests in excess of 50 percent are required only for very special deals. Most venture investors do not want the responsibility (or liability) that goes with owning a controlling interest in a company.

Many small venture funds, or "boutique" houses, specialize in specific industries or special products and can be invaluable as a source of management or technical assistance as well as capital. For acquisitions whose financing requires special industry knowledge, boutique funds are usually the way to go. Not only do these specialized venture firms possess valuable industry expertise, but because they are smaller houses, they usually give the deal more personal attention. Such hands-on participation often makes the difference between closing a business acquisition and losing it.

In addition to boutique houses, there are three distinctly different types of venture funds that provide acquisition funding for closely held companies:

1. The large ones, often subsidiaries or divisions of investment banks, who handle deals up to $100 million, but prefer those in the $20 to $50 million range

2. The mid-sized venture funds, usually independently owned, that specialize in deals from $10 to $20 million

3. The smaller houses (mainly funded by wealthy individuals), who package deals up to $10 million, but prefer to stay with those ranging from $500,000 to $8 million

It's important to select a venture fund whose size matches the size and type of the acquisition. Going after a large fund for a small deal or a small fund for a large deal only wastes time, money, and effort.

WHEN TO USE VENTURE CAPITAL

Venture capital is certainly the most expensive form of acquisition financing—not in terms of interest rates, but with respect to returns expected by equity shareholders. An annual return of 30 to 45 percent, even if paid out of an eventual public offering, is not a price many companies can afford. In addition, as well as giving up a significant share of the company, business owners must, in most cases, give up significant authority over company policies.

Raising capital through venture funds should never be seriously considered unless all other reasonable means have been exhausted, including limited partnerships and public stock issues. While there can be little question that some companies have benefited greatly from the addition of investor expertise and financial contacts, the cost is more than most can manage. However, venture capital does fill a market need and should at least be considered along with other capital sources.

Although euphoric economic growth during the 1970s and 1980s pushed venture capital funds into ever-greater risk taking in first-stage, rapid growth businesses, by the end of the decade, most funds had begun seriously looking at financing established (but growing) companies. Projections for the balance of the 1990s indicate continued interest in such less-risky projects, which bodes well for small businesses acquiring well-run companies.

Venture Capital Funds for Small Business

Nearly every state has venture capital funds that finance small business growth. They range from one-person operations to divisions of large commercial banks. Venture capital funds are normally grouped into four categories, in addition to Small Business Investment Corporations (SBICs):

1. *Investment banks.* Several reputable investment banks maintain separate divisions or departments that finance small businesses. They are attracted to companies with very rapid growth potential that are managed by entrepreneurs who come highly recommended.

2. *Divisions of large corporations.* Many Fortune 500 corporations have either venture capital divisions or venture capital subsidiaries. This gives them an entree into the technology developed by small businesses, which is an excellent source of new product innovation at a much lower price and with greater coverage than they could achieve if they restricted development projects to internal R&D departments.

3. *Family funds.* Certain very wealthy families (the Rockefellers, the Mellons, the Coors, the Cudahys, and so on) have traditionally funneled some of their wealth into small, high-potential companies with state-of-the-art product development ideas. They are primarily interested in

products and companies in which their investments will have a positive social effect, however.

4. *Private investment funds.* These are limited partnerships and corporations that have the financial backing of insurance companies, pension trusts, and other large blocks of capital. Some are small ($2 million); some are much larger (over $100 million).

Sources of Venture Capital

The best list of well-established national firms such as Hambrecht & Quist (San Francisco), Golder, Thoma & Co. (Chicago), or Sprout Group (affiliated with Donaldson Lufkin & Jenrette, New York) is *Pratt's Guide to Venture Capital Sources.* This comprehensive directory lists the addresses and phone numbers of these and other firms.

The National Venture Capital Association is another good source. Its membership directory may be obtained by contacting the organization at 1655 North Fort Myer Drive, Suite 700, Arlington, VA 22209, (703) 528-4370.

Finally, the *Directory of Venture Capital Clubs* can be helpful in locating private investment clubs formed specifically to invest in first-stage ventures. It is available for $9.95 directly from the International Venture Capital Institute, Inc., P.O. Box 1333, Stamford, CT 06904.

It should be noted, however, that small venture capital firms come and go with dizzying speed. The few big ones are permanent fixtures in the industry; the numerous small ones are not. In addition, the small ones do not have the breadth of management talent that well-established firms do. They are therefore unable to provide valuable free assistance in technical or management matters. Their size also limits a company's access to further financing. If at all possible, it pays to stick with the big firms. They have a reputation to sustain, have extensive contacts in financial markets, and, more often than not, can provide capable management assistance.

Guidelines for Using Venture Capital

Established venture capital firms consider the following guidelines as the primary criteria for providing business acquisition funding:

The Parent Company Should:

1. Have a profitable history and a recent upward trend in sales, profits, and cash flow
2. Have a sound business reason for making the specific acquisition
3. Have a strong management team
4. Be willing to take the company public within five years
5. Demonstrate the ability to integrate the target company with existing marketing, engineering, production, and management activities
6. Be willing to give up an equity share

7. Be willing to accept operating recommendations from the venture capital firm

8. Be unable or unwilling to finance the deal with the company's own equity contribution

The Target Company Should:

1. Be able to demonstrate the ability to generate enough cash flow after the acquisition to make required debt service payments

2. Be growing at least as fast as the parent company

3. Be in an industry that is compatible with that of the parent company

4. Have a strong management team

5. Have a good reputation in the industry, the marketplace, and the community

The Combined Companies Should:

1. Be able to demonstrate cash flow that will return 30 to 40 percent per year to investors

2. Be able to demonstrate that combining the two companies will result in cost savings, additional growth potential, management efficiencies, and other benefits not attainable by each company separately

FORMING A VENTURE CAPITAL INVESTMENT GROUP

Throughout the country, many small venture funds have been formed by doctors, lawyers, public accountants, and other high-income individual investors. In a sense, these funds are merely the high-risk version of investment clubs.

Creative entrepreneurs with good local business contacts can form venture groups to raise capital for their own companies as well as to invest in other businesses. Typically these groups are structured as limited partnerships, as described in Chapter 12. The originator retains decision-making authority as the general partner. Limited partners supply capital in exchange for a share of the profits and the opportunity for capital gains if and when the company goes public.

The following structure (which is a variation on the limited partnership arrangement described in Chapter 12) is one of the simplest formats that can be used. It enables the greatest flexibility for venture capital acquisition financing and provides the most protection for investors.

1. *General partner.* The business owner(s) form an S corporation, which becomes the general partner.

2. *Limited partners.* Limited partners may be people affiliated with financial institutions, lawyers, professional accountants, consultants, physicians, or other professionals or business people. As passive investors, they contribute most of the investment capital, but do not interfere in the management of the operating business. All limited partners must be individually indemnified against liabilities arising from the business.

3. *Allocation of profits and losses.* All profits, capital gains, and capital losses from the business investment will be allocated to the limited partners, and all operating losses will be allocated to the general partner.

4. *Management fees.* The operating company pays the general partner management fees as compensation for time and expertise contributed to the business. These fees can then be offset by the general partner against operating losses for tax purposes.

5. *Additional limited partners.* Additional limited partners may be admitted at a later date. When this happens, a new allocation of profits, capital gains, and capital losses, based on either contributed capital or other yardsticks, is specified.

6. *Dissolution.* The limited partnership must have a definite life; that is, it will be dissolved on a specific date as determined by the partnership agreement. At the dissolution date, a majority vote by all partners can re-set the dissolution this date to a later date. Of course, getting-out positions for each member must be defined in the agreement.

7. *Conversion to equity.* When the operating business goes public, limited partnership units will be exchanged for common shares at a predetermined conversion rate as defined in the agreement. Typically, the general partner and limited partners share proportionately in the exchange, although the agreement may be written to permit either general or limited partners greater or lesser amounts of common shares.

Many other variations are used under various circumstances, but this one is the simplest.

In addition to the basic limited partnership agreement, provision must be made for raising additional capital as the combined business grows—either additional equity contributions or debt. Ideally, further equity investments will be spread equally among all partners. In practice, however, one or more limited partners generally have the responsibility for bringing in new equity as needed. Regardless of the source, as new equity comes in, ownership percentages and profit/loss allocations must be revised.

It's important to choose limited partners who not only have sufficiently deep pockets and/or good contacts with financial institutions to see the venture through, but also bring specialized expertise and personal contacts in financial markets, legal disciplines, and accounting techniques.

APPLYING FOR VENTURE CAPITAL

Preparation is the key to getting venture capital. And the most important preparatory step is the construction of a detailed financing plan that emphasizes *future* performance. Without question, the past performance of both the parent and the target companies is an important piece of the plan, as is the composition of their asset bases. However, venture capital funds look primarily for clear, concise pro forma forecasts that show significant growth opportunities. Pro forma financial statements and cash flow forecast, similar to those prepared in the Filtco case study (Chapter 12) for valuing the target company, together with the consolidated projections that were used to determine affordability, should also be included in the financing plan.

Moreover, since venture capitalists are primarily business-oriented managers, not bankers, the financing plan must include a thorough explanation of the business, including descriptions of product lines, customer base, competition, market size and share, and so on. It should also include a complete profile of the management teams of both companies. Within the business description section, be sure to elaborate on the following marketing-related questions:

- Why are the target's products or services unique?
- What is the market demand for them? (Market size and share)
- Why does the market need and want such products?
- How are the products priced and distributed?
- What competitive products are already in the market?
- Are there any substitute products available?

It is nearly impossible to attract venture capital without the following rock-solid background information.

1. The business owner(s) and key managers are experts in their fields and have outstanding technical and managerial abilities. Reference letters that prove achievements are excellent credentials, as are technical certifications.

2. The parent company will contribute the maximum amount of equity consistent with prudent cash planning. In addition, the business owner(s) should be prepared to offer personal guarantees.

3. Venture investors can realize significant gains in the future through additional ownership interests if and when the combined businesses achieve their projected growth. Equity interests should be offered right up front, including warrants to acquire additional interests under specific circumstances. Pro forma financial statements should extrapolate the timing and proceeds of a public offering.

PUBLIC STOCK OFFERINGS

Public stock offerings are another way to raise large amounts of equity capital. Companies issue common stock either to the public at large (a *public* issue) or to a select group of buyers (a *private placement*). Furthermore, both public issues and private placements may be sold nationally (interstate) or limited to the state of residence (intrastate). Public issues can also be divided into segments, or *tranches*, with one tranche offered in U.S. capital markets and another offered in foreign markets. Regulatory requirements, offering cost, stock appreciation potential, and market acceptance vary with each choice. Although a company's profitability and management capabilities affect the decision as to which route to follow, the main criteria are the amount of capital needed, the percentage of ownership current shareholders are willing to relinquish, and the uses to which the new capital will be applied.

Uses of New Equity Capital

Except in very rare circumstances, it doesn't make sense to offer shares to the public if you intend to turn around in a few years and buy them all back. Although it is certainly possible to take a public company private, this is an expensive proposition and not done indiscriminately. Therefore, the decision to "go public" should be viewed as permanent and made only if the amount of capital needed cannot be raised through alternative means.

Most companies that plan to finance acquisitions through an IPO also have other strategic objectives in mind, such as to:

- Repay current debt obligations
- Make a major expansion involving the purchase of facilities and machinery
- Establish an offshore facility
- Enhance a company's market value in anticipation of selling the entire company
- Increase the value of management-held shares

One or more of these corollary needs might affect the decision to go public more than the desire to fund an acquisition. During the formative process of long-term growth strategies, it is quite common to find that debt and equity arrangements from earlier years no longer meet these growth objectives, and refinancing with new equity capital offers a logical option.

Timing a Public Stock Issue

Although many factors either encourage a company to go public or deter it from doing so, timing the stock offering to sell the greatest number of shares at the highest share price can be the most crucial. Once you get into the acquisition process, events seem to snowball. One thing leads to another, and the next thing you know it's time to have a check ready for the closing. However, public stock offerings cannot be accomplished on the spur of the moment. They take a great deal of preparation and coordination with outside advisors. Furthermore, the market must be willing to accept a stock issue of the size and quality offered. Misjudging preparation time or market conditions will inevitably cause the offering to fail or, at a minimum, limit either the number of shares that can be sold or their price.

Time and again companies begin the trek to market, only to learn after spending thousands of dollars that some uncontrollable circumstance prevents or delays the completion of the job. The main culprits that cause public offerings to fail are:

- A national happening—war, Presidential election, financial market crisis

- Stock market jitters—roller coaster averages trending downward
- A stock market collapse—e.g., October 1987
- A rapidly declining industry—e.g., machine tools and semiconductors in the 1970s
- Out-of-control inflation—rapidly rising prices, interest rates, and unemployment
- A hard recession at the national or regional level

Of course, many other factors may affect the timing of stock offerings, but these indicate the types of circumstances under which it becomes increasingly difficult to bring the offering to market. Investors may be available, but the cost of making the offering will be higher than necessary.

Major Hurdles

Public stock offerings are very expensive and usually cannot be justified for amounts of less than $5 million. To make an IPO cost-effective, a company should be generating annual sales of at least $10 million, although this figure can be lower for very high-growth industries. Issues of $7.5 million or less, defined as *small issues* by the SEC, will be less expensive than larger issues; but even then, a cost range of $250,000 to $500,000 is the rule rather than the exception.

Once the issue has been sold, ongoing administrative costs significantly increase overhead. Costs to produce periodic SEC reports and proxy statements, printing and mailing expenses, and annual fees for accountants, lawyers, registrars, and transfer agents add up in a hurry. New shareholders also look for dividends on their investment, and dividends are not tax-deductible.

Four hurdles other than high cost must be dealt with:

1. Approval must be obtained from the SEC (or from the state securities commission for intrastate issues) before the stock can be sold. Because the timing of the offering can be crucial to its success, the actual offering date should be planned well in advance. More than one issue has flopped because the SEC or a state commission took too long to grant approval and the market window closed before the offering was ready.

2. After the stock is sold, there is no assurance that active trading will follow. This could nullify incentive programs structured to reward management employees with noncash stock options and also make it difficult to use stock for business acquisitions.

3. It doesn't take long to realize that the trading price of a company's shares is directly related to its earnings trend, and this can affect management decisions. Management personnel tend to spend more time worrying about improving earnings per share than about running the company efficiently. Short-term decisions that favorably affect earnings for this quarter or this year may do more harm than good to growth strategies.

4. Probably the most aggravating thing about going public is the loss of the privacy that we, as entrepreneurs, value so highly. SEC regulations require complete disclosure of the most intimate and proprietary company matters; officers' compensation, personal histories of company officers and (in some cases) key managers, incentive programs, forecasts of future earnings, planned new product developments, and strategic operating plans are examples of the most troublesome. Not only must this information be revealed in the offering prospectus, it must be continually updated in quarterly and annual reports—all of which are open to the public.

Does a Public Issue Make Sense?

Given these hurdles, going public may not seem like such a great idea. However, despite high costs and aggravating regulations, public stock offerings remain the best way to raise large amounts of equity capital. But it's important to take the step for the right reasons. Also, as previously mentioned, it pays to prepare for an offering well in advance and then to time the offering with market conditions. The guidelines in Figure 13-1 indicate the variables in reaching the decision to go public.

Figure 13-1
Guidelines for Going Public

Company Structure

1. The company must already be incorporated.
2. If an S corporation election has been made, and the new shareholders will total more than thirty-five, the company must convert to a C corporation.
3. The company must be large enough to have professional management, such as a controller, sales manager, chief engineer, and so on.
4. At least some of the products or services offered by the company should have high growth potential over the next five years.
5. This potential growth must be demonstrable, not the owner's dream.
6. A commanding market share or unique market niche is highly desirable.
7. The company must have three years of progressively improving profitability (two years for a small IPO, under $7.5 million).
8. Projections for the next five years should show continued improvement.
9. The prior three years' financial statements (two years for a small issue) must be audited by a reputable CPA firm.
10. The CPA firm must have issued a clean certificate for each of the years.

The Economic Picture

1. Stock exchange averages should be rising.
2. Per share averages should be running above ten times earnings.
3. General optimism should prevail in the national economy.
4. Regional economic indicators should be at least stable, and preferably rising.
5. Interest rates, national unemployment statistics, and inflation projections should be at modest levels.
6. Industry trade statistics should indicate favorable growth projections for the next three years.
7. U.S. international trade policies should not be detrimental to the company's product lines.

Pros and Cons of Going Public

It goes without saying that every company has its own prerequisites and constraints when contemplating a public offering. What works for one company won't work for another. Nevertheless, certain benefits and risks (some of which have already been discussed) tend to be universal. Without attempting to be inclusive, the following represent opinions from many financial executives of companies large and small that have issued common stock to the public for the first time. The consensus seems to be that the major advantages are as follows:

1. *Financial stability.* A public stock issue may be the only way to raise enough growth capital for business acquisitions or other major expansions. Most companies reach a point where additional growth cannot be financed from their own reserves and debt is too expensive.

2. *Amount of capital needed.* Greater amounts of capital can be raised than with debt financing. In addition to buying a going business, strategic plans may call for the outlay of substantial sums for such activities as implementing major R&D programs, expanding market coverage, or establishing offshore facilities, which require more cash than the company has in reserve. Concurrently, credit constraints or high interest rates may preclude using debt.

3. *Flexible returns.* Equity capital does not require repayment on a predetermined schedule. Although shareholders certainly expect dividends, the timing and amount of these payments are unilaterally determined by the company. This can be extremely important when developing new products or entering new markets, both of which may take several years before turning profitable.

4. *Ownership control.* Initial common stock offerings are better received by the market in small segments, enabling a company's owners to raise substantial equity capital without losing control. Additional offerings that disperse ownership interests among hundreds or even thousands of shareholders can be structured to leave previous owners in effective control with less than a 51 percent ownership interest.

5. *Ready exit.* Disposing of shares in a privately held company when it's time to retire or otherwise get out can be a sticky problem. With an established trading market, insiders (original owners, managers, and other early shareholders) have a ready means of disposing of their shares (subject, of course, to insider trading rules). Also, the market value of shares can be readily established for estate valuations.

6. *Employee incentives.* Stock options are frequently a sought-after incentive for key employees. Not only do options make employees feel they are part of the company and therefore, hopefully, stimulate better performance, they also offer the potential for significantly higher earnings than cash bonuses.

7. *Improved borrowing capacity.* Since additional equity improves a company's debt-to-equity ratio, banks and other financial institutions are more inclined to extend additional credit. Moreover, a substantial reduction in the debt-to-equity ratio leaves the door open for a potential public bond offering.

8. *Improved company image.* Most privately held companies have a difficult time establishing a profile in industries dominated by large public firms. The publicity that goes with a public offering can easily change that, increasing public visibility and thereby stimulating sales and attracting higher-quality personnel.

9. *Increased personal net worth.* Nothing boosts personal net worth faster than establishing a market value for your stock holdings. A good many millionaires have made the jump with an IPO.

Although these benefits may encourage companies to go public, all is not a bed of roses. IPOs also have several disadvantages in addition to the high initial cost. Here are the main ones:

1. *Ongoing expense.* Increased administrative expenses that arise after the stock begins trading can be a significant burden for smaller companies. A variety of reports must be filed regularly—10-Ks, 8-Ks, 10-Qs, and what seems like a constant barrage of news releases. Expenses that privately held companies are never concerned with, such as annual certified audits, added legal fees, printing expenses, and financial public relations promotions accompany public stock ownership. In addition, employees must now devote time to complying with SEC and stock exchange regulations. Additional overhead expenses of $60,000 to $100,000 a year are not uncommon.

2. *Closing out venture capital.* Typically, venture capital firms that finance privately held companies do so with the understanding that at a future date the company will go public. An early IPO closes this door. Although this is not an important consideration for larger companies, it could eliminate a valuable source of capital for funding expensive R&D programs.

3. *Loss of management flexibility.* Once a company has gone public, its management personnel lose flexibility in making decisions and developing strategic plans. Compliance with SEC disclosure regulations can easily undermine valuable competitive secrecy. Furthermore, shareholder approval is normally required for major strategic decisions, such as mergers, additional business acquisitions (or divestitures), new stock issues, and so on.

4. *Liability.* Officers and directors of public companies remain fully liable for any violations of SEC or exchange regulations. This can be extremely burdensome. Devising methods to protect officers and directors

from frivolous lawsuits takes valuable time that could otherwise be used to develop growth policies.

5. *Potential loss of control.* Depending on the percentage of ownership in public hands, the board of directors may lose control of the company. Many adversarial proxy fights have resulted in the dismissal of a company's original owners.

6. *Company skeletons.* Once a company issues public stock, its affairs— past, present, and future—are open to the public. Bankruptcies, criminal records, lawsuits, and other potentially damaging events involving officers and directors must be disclosed in prospectuses and registrations.

7. *Wrong economic timing.* A company might expend a substantial amount of cash getting ready to go public, only to learn that the market isn't ready to accept the offering.

The Offering Prospectus

Once the decision is made to proceed with an IPO, and appropriate professional advisors have been engaged, a rather complicated offering prospectus and registration statement must be prepared. The offering prospectus serves two purposes: It is the primary source of disclosure in the SEC registration statement, and underwriters use it as a selling tool when marketing the issue.

The offering prospectus gives potential investors a clear, concise picture of the company, its management, its financial history, and the intended application of the proceeds from the stock issue. It also includes pro forma financial statements that reflect management's estimate of financial results for five years into the future. SEC regulations specify that the offering prospectus and registration statement must present a conservative picture of the company and must clearly identify the risks to investors of buying the stock. There must be a full disclosure of pending lawsuits, claims, and other contingent liabilities, and a detailed explanation of how the proceeds of the issue will be used. These regulations identify exactly what items must be included in the prospectus and even how financial statistics must be displayed. Figure 13-2 (page 238) describes the major topics to be included.

If the registration is for more than $7.5 million, Form S-1 must be used; for offerings of less than this amount, a simplified registration, Form S-18, may be used. The S-18 is much shorter than the S-1. Moreover, the S-18 requires an audited balance sheet for one year rather than two, and income statements and statements of changes in financial condition for the past two years rather than three. The S-18 also exempts companies from including an elaborate management discussion and analyses of financial condition, as well as the "selected financial data" section.

EXEMPT REGISTRATIONS

After a company decides to go public, it must choose which route to take: a full registration filed on Form S-1, a simplified registration filed under S-18 regulations, or an exempt offering. The decision affects initial and ongoing costs, reporting requirements, and the market value of the stock. It also affects the degree of control exerted by the SEC and financial markets over a company's strategic plans. S-1 registrations carry the most constraints, exempt offerings the least. The choice of offering medium depends on:

- The type of business
- The availability and amount of information already in public hands
- The type of security
- The class of security buyers

Figure 13-2
Topics Included in SEC Registration

1. Name of the registrant, the title and amount of securities being offered, and the date
2. A statement as to whether any securities being registered are from current stockholders
3. A cross-reference of material risks in connection with the purchase of the securities
4. An estimate of the minimum/maximum range of offering price and number of shares
5. The share price to the public, underwriting discounts and commissions, and proceeds to the issuer or other persons
6. Notices about stabilization of the offering price
7. A summary of information contained in the prospectus, the complete address and telephone number of the company's principal executive offices, risk factors (those factors that make the issue speculative or of high risk), and the ratio of earnings to fixed charges
8. Use of proceeds
9. How the offering price was determined
10. Dilution effect on current shareholders
11. The company's dividend policy, including its dividend history, policies currently followed, restrictions on dividend payments (if any), and a statement of whether future earnings are to be reinvested in the company or paid out in dividends
12. A description of the company's debt and equity position (its capitalization) before and after the offering
13. A management discussion and analysis section that provides enough information to allow investors to analyze the company's cash flow position. It must be complete, factual, and conservative
14. A business description section that discloses everything an investor needs to know to make an informed judgment about investing in the shares
15. A complete disclosure of all pertinent information about directors, officers, and key employees
16. A description of how the stock will be distributed
17. The identification of any interest in the registrant by parties acting as counsel or experts
18. A listing of all expenses relating to the issuance and distribution of the securities
19. A list of all required exhibits
20. Company financial statements and the related auditors' opinion certificate

Simplified Registrations

Form S-18 registration may be used by any U.S. or Canadian company not subject to continuous reporting requirements of its respective country, except for investment companies and certain insurance companies. However, the total offering in any twelve-month period cannot exceed $7.5 million.

Instead of the S-18 registration, small companies may choose to file under Regulation A of the Securities Act of 1933. Regulation A offerings are limited to a total of $5 million, and a very complex set of rules applies to the types of companies that qualify. For those who may be interested, here are the major features of Regulation A offerings:

- The company files a *notification,* not a registration statement.
- Notification is filed with a regional SEC office, not Washington.
- An offering circular, not a full prospectus, is required, with the amount of disclosure similar to that required for a S-18 registration.
- Uncertified financial statements may be used.
- Regulation A cannot be used if affiliated persons or the underwriter have been convicted of securities violations or postal fraud.

Private Placement Exempt Offerings

An exempt offering means that a company does not have to file a registration statement, obviously saving a substantial amount of time and money. Exempt offerings fall into one of two categories: private placements or limited offerings. It should be noted that these are exemptions from the Securities Act of 1933—a federal law—and do not necessarily exempt a company from registering under state securities laws. In most cases, however, states that do require formal registration, have more lenient requirements than the SEC.

Private placements are used to raise limited amounts of equity capital in a relatively short period of time at a lower cost; therefore, they are generally more suitable for small-business acquisitions than full S-1 or S-18 offerings. Because private placements are exempt offerings, issuing and ongoing costs are substantially less than with full registrations, although federal antifraud securities regulations still apply.

Several reasons other than cost influence the decision to go with a private placement:

- The economic or market timing for an effective public offering may be way off.
- A company may not have two or three years of steadily increasing earnings (which are usually required to make a successful IPO).
- A company does not have to disclose as much proprietary information.

Who are the investors?

A private placement involves a limited number of investors. In addition to relatives and friends, four types of investors are attracted to private placements from closely held companies:

1. Customers, suppliers, commissioned sales personnel, employees, and other individuals and companies with whom the company does business

2. Professional investors who specialize in getting in on the ground floor of potentially high-flying companies

3. Private investors looking for investments in small companies that can be taken public within a reasonable time frame

4. Venture capital funds expecting a public issue in the future

There are competent securities brokers in all major cities who specialize in private placements and who know where to find investors in each of the last three categories. You might have some ideas for the first.

Types of private placements

In 1982, the SEC adopted Regulation D in an attempt to make the private placement requirements of the Commission and the states more uniform. Most states now allow Regulation D filings; a few do not. Private placement exempt offerings are labeled according to the section of the securities laws to which they apply. They are:

- Rule 504 for offerings of up to $500,000
- Rule 505 for offerings of up to $5 million
- Rule 506 for offerings above $5 million

In addition, Regulation D includes three other rules, 501, 502, and 503, that apply to all three categories. The most important provision of these broad rules limits security sales to "accredited" investors, who by definition fall into the following categories:

- An individual with an annual income of at least $200,000 in each of the two most recent years
- An individual investor with a net worth (including spouse's) of at least $1 million
- An individual purchasing up to $150,000 of the security, as long as the investment does not exceed 20 percent of the investor's net worth
- An insider of the issuing company—directors, executive officers, general partners
- Institutional investors (e.g., banks and insurance companies)
- Plans established by state governments and/or their subdivisions for the benefit of their employees that have assets in excess of $5 million, such as state employee pension funds

- Nonprofit organizations with assets exceeding $5 million
- Private business development companies defined by the Investment Advisors Act of 1940

Moreover, the issuing company must provide proof that each investor meets one of these requirements. Such proof must be in writing and attested to by the investor.

The range of IPO choices can indeed be intimidating, which is precisely why it's important to engage competent professional advisors—lawyers, auditors, underwriters, financial printers, and probably financial public relation experts—early in the process. These experts will guide the choice of registration format and the appropriate timing of the issue.

One word of caution: As discussed in Chapter 6, highly leveraged companies that decide to make an IPO should price the issue with care. Investors in today's markets are becoming increasingly queasy about bailing out less than creditworthy issuers. If the acquisition makes good business sense and both parent and target companies are financially viable, public offerings are a reasonable alternative for raising the required capital. If these circumstances are not present, however, its best to try a different tack—perhaps a blind pool offering or a reverse merger.

BLIND POOLS

A *blind pool* offering is an IPO made by a "shell" company that does not have any operating structure. Although the offering prospectus does not identify the precise use of the offering proceeds, it does, at a minimum, identify the industry in which the proceeds will be invested, such as oil and gas ventures, commercial real estate purchases, or acquisitions of operating companies. In this respect, blind pools are the stock market equivalent of many private placement limited partnerships.

Blind pools are a convenient way for shareholders of privately held companies to raise acquisition capital without relinquishing ownership in the parent company. Many times, however, as an incentive to investors, the prospectus indicates that a significant interest in the target company will be purchased with blind pool funds.

Although some issuers of blind pool IPOs have used the funds improperly (to wit, the "blank check" scandals of the late 1980s), in most cases the proceeds are used to make the acquisition disclosed in the prospectus. If properly constructed, blind pools provide a less costly way to raise fairly large amounts of equity capital. For example, assume that as part of a long-term growth strategy, a potential acquisition candidate has already been targeted. Your company already carries a full debt load, and you do not want to take the company public.

The solution? Form a new company without any assets—for example, New Corporation. Initiate an exempt IPO with a private placement. Write the prospectus to show that the purpose of the IPO is to raise capital for New Corporation, which plans to make the targeted acquisition. Assuming that the company or its underwriter can float the issue, the capital raised can then be used to acquire the targeted company in the name of New Corporation.

Despite the high risk (in fact, because of it), blind pools attract high-yield-oriented investors. It's entirely possible that a private placement could be very interesting to professional practitioners (lawyers, doctors, CPAs) who are not regular investors but who are looking for opportunities that offer high equity appreciation potential. If the proposed objective of the blind pool offers this possibility, shares could easily be oversubscribed.

If this route seems attractive, it is essential to engage an attorney with blind pool experience. Working through a securities house without engaging independent counsel nearly always fails. If it doesn't fail, it will cost two to three times as much as the fees paid to a good lawyer for performing essentially the same work.

REVERSE MERGERS

The purchase of a public shell company can also be an effective way to tap public markets without going through the cost and effort of an IPO. Until formally de-registered in the state of incorporation, nonoperating shell corporations are still usable. Not infrequently, the shell, with no assets other than its name and registration number, can be purchased for a price ranging from $10,000 to $25,000.

The primary buyers of public shells are private companies that want to go public but do not want to incur the expense or suffer the lengthy delay involved in floating a new issue. With a shell corporation in hand, a private company simply merges itself into the public shell, effecting what is called a *reverse merger.*

Assuming that ownership of the public shell is held by many investors (and it usually is), a reverse merger can be an effective first step in raising capital through a subsequent public issue. Although registration procedures similar to those required for an IPO must be followed, the cost should be substantially less. Also, it takes much less time to float a subsequent stock issue. Many of the shell's shareholders will probably buy the new shares with the hope of recouping their initial investment and possibly realizing capital gains once active trading begins.

Companies can also couple a reverse merger with a blind pool IPO, as in the following example:

1. The owners of a private company form a corporation (call it Zorro Corp.) with a nominal amount of capitalization—say $5,000 to $10,000.

2. Zorro then makes a public stock offering, using either the S-18 simplified registration or, more likely, the Rule 504 or Rule 505 exemption, to raise, for example, $1 million. The price of the stock offering should be high enough to leave the original shareholders in control of the company after the issue has been sold.

3. The offering is considered a blind pool because the prospectus discloses that although the company doesn't have any operations at the moment, the purpose of raising the capital is to acquire the operating company.

4. Once the stock has been sold, the public company merges with the private operating company, exchanging stock for stock in such a ratio that the shareholders of the private operating company gain a controlling interest in the merged entity, now a public company. This is a reverse merger because the shareholders of the private company end up controlling the public entity. The owner(s) of the private operating company in effect get the use of the cash generated from the blind pool IPO—which, of course, can then be used to make the previously targeted business acquisition.

5. After the merger, the public stock acquired by the previously closely held company has very little value because, unless Form S-4 is subsequently filed with the SEC, the stock cannot be traded on national markets. The company thereby loses the advantage of being able to use this stock for additional acquisitions, operating bonuses, or other perks associated with publicly traded stock. If the company files an S-4 registration, however, the stock can be resold on the open market. Form S-4 is merely an extension of an S-18 filing that includes additional information about and analyses of the company and its business.

In spite of all the drawbacks and the high initial cost, given the right circumstances, selling stock to the public can be an ideal way to raise equity capital for an acquisition. Obviously, corner groceries or video stores are not large enough to use this means, but any business with sales of more than $5 million should seriously look at the possibility. A public offering is definitely feasible for companies with sales of more than $10 million.

Chapter 14

Wrap-up and Transition

Once a target company has been selected, a purchase price and terms agreed upon, and financing arranged, the final steps in the acquisition process are to draft and negotiate the buy/sell agreement and other closing documents. After that has been accomplished, the official closing can take place, money will change hands, and the transition begins.

This is the last chance for the acquisition team to make certain that no skeletons lurk in the shadows, ready to jeopardize the deal. This final or "wrap-up" due diligence investigation includes the following:

- *An update of the target's financial statements and pro forma forecasts—* This should reveal any significant events that may have occurred since the later of the last financial statements or the original due diligence surveys and analyses.

- *An independent audit of recent financial statements and asset balances—* If the target company has had a full audit within the last nine months, this step can probably be eliminated.

- *An independent appraisal of the target company's real estate, machinery, and equipment—*This step is necessary if the hard assets of the target company are to be used to collateralize acquisition debt, as in a leveraged buyout.

Simultaneously, your attorney should begin drafting the buy/sell agreement so that, if necessary, both parties will have time to negotiate sticky points before the scheduled closing date.

WRAP-UP DUE DILIGENCE

Getting current financial statements and updating pro forma forecasts are not particularly difficult steps, and they don't take much time; however, they must be done in order to be certain that nothing has caused the company to be a less desirable acquisition or required a material change in the negotiated purchase price. Three key issues need to be resolved:

1. Were the estimates for this intervening period reasonably accurate? If sales, profit, or cash flow projections were way off base, there could be

something about the business you don't understand, necessitating further digging and perhaps a postponement of the closing date.

2. Is the target company's management team still intact and functioning the way it appeared to be when the original due diligence investigation was performed? Key employees may have left the company, perhaps new managers were hired, or maybe promotions changed key responsibilities. Minor organization changes may not affect your opinion about the future of the business; on the other hand, major ones could be serious enough for you to call off the closing.

3. Have any major events affected the business or are there any potential trouble spots on the horizon, such as lawsuits, labor strikes, serious damage to the facilities, IRS audit adjustments, and so on? To the extent that any such events might affect the future performance of the company, either a new cash flow projection should be prepared or the closing should be called off.

Although some buyers cut corners by gathering this wrap-up data with a phone call or letter, this tactic usually doesn't pay off. It's too late in the game to be "penny wise and pound foolish." Business dynamics cause constant changes, and the only certainty about forecasting is that what was supposed to happen, didn't happen. Actual results might be better or worse than projected, but certainly not the same. From this point forward, financial commitments can become startlingly large: Money must be expended for legal fees, audit fees, and perhaps facilities appraisals. It makes sense to make one more trip to the target company's facility, gather the data personally, and make sure no major problems have arisen to jeopardize the deal.

Some time can be saved by having the target company send updated financial statements before the final visit so that a checklist of questions to be answered and documents to be obtained can be prepared. From this point forward, time is of the essence, and anything that can be done to shorten the wrap-up investigation will be beneficial. Financing sources won't wait forever. Delays might frighten off customers or suppliers of either the parent or the target company. New competitors may enter the market. And a variety of other events could enter the equation should the closing be delayed for any significant period.

The wrap-up checklist in Figure 14-1 (page 246) is substantially shorter than that used for the original due diligence investigation. Comparing and contrasting financial data for the current period with that for the due diligence period can be the fastest and surest way to spot major discrepancies. Also, unless someone was lying the first time around, a few comparative statistics from the target company's controller and some pointed questions to its legal counsel should provide all the data you need.

Figure 14-1
Wrap-up Due Diligence Checklist

Ask about the following factors since the last financial statements or the original due diligence investigation:

1. Monthly sales by product line
2. Major changes in inventory
3. Monthly operating profits
4. Payments to pension funds or retirement plans
5. Monthly selling expenses and G&A expenses
6. New borrowings against operating lines
7. Employee additions or terminations for each month
8. Monthly orders received and order cancellations (if applicable)
9. Lawsuits filed or settled
10. Federal or state tax audits started, scheduled to start, or completed
11. Changes in union contracts
12. Modifications to bonus or profit-sharing plans
13. New or modified employment or other contracts
14. Major changes in accrued expenses—new accruals and payments
15. Current aging of accounts receivable
16. Current aging of accounts payable
17. Results of physical inventory
18. Changes in insurance coverage or premiums
19. Fixed asset additions or retirements
20. Other changes that may be relevant to full disclosure

At this stage, private discussions with the target company's key employees and professional advisors are crucial; if the seller balks, probe deeper. Deep-seated problems might surface that could prevent a closing. For instance, either the selling shareholder or key employees might have orchestrated a scenario the first time around that they can no longer support. Or the company might be heading for a breakdown in labor relations. Or it may be about to lose a major customer. The seller could have been afraid of losing a viable buyer if these conditions were revealed during earlier due diligence investigations.

Such skeletons must be uncovered now. This is the last chance for the acquiring company to scuttle the deal before committing substantial funds. If nothing arises during the wrap-up investigation, the next step is to arrange for an appraisal of hard assets and an audit review of current account balances.

APPRAISALS

Even if you have already negotiated a purchase price, it's important to have an independent real estate appraisal to determine the market values of land and/or buildings included in the deal. The same holds true for machinery and equipment, provided the amount of such assets is material relative to total assets.

The accounting rule set out by the Financial Accounting Standards Board (FASB) and followed by the SEC is that the premium paid for a going business (that part of the purchase price in excess of the company's book value) must be allocated to the recorded value of hard assets, up to, but not exceeding, their fair market value. Such accounting niceties are important to a privately owned company that buys another privately owned company only if investors and/or lenders require audited financial statements. On the other hand, if acquisition capital is raised through a public stock offering, companies must comply with FASB accounting rules.

In addition to meeting regulatory requirements, hard-asset appraisals are necessary to establish loan values for any debt capital used to finance the acquisition. The loan value of commercial real estate ranges between 60 and 75 percent of fair market value, which is defined as the price the property would bring on the open market. The collateral value of machinery and equipment is calculated differently. In this case, lenders assume that if the company defaults on its loan payments, the collateral will be liquidated as soon as possible (usually at auction prices) to recoup the outstanding loan balance. Appraisals, therefore, must reflect such auction prices.

Here are the definitions of different appraisal values:

- *Replacement value:* The cost of replacing existing equipment, including installation costs. This value is generally used for insurance valuations only. (However, many small business sellers believe that they should get this amount for their business.)

- *Fair market value:* The price that a buyer should be willing to pay a seller, assuming that neither is under duress and that the assets are used in a going business.

- *Orderly liquidation value:* The price that a willing buyer should pay for individual assets during an orderly sale held over a six- to twelve-month period. This value is usually about 60 percent of fair market value.

- *Forced liquidation value:* The price an individual asset should bring at an open auction held at one place at one time and conducted by a qualified auctioneer. This value approximates 70 to 80 percent of the orderly liquidation value.

- *Loan value:* Most commercial lenders consider 80 percent of forced liquidation value as reasonable loan collateral.

When arranging for an appraisal, it's important to designate specifically which values the appraiser will report on. If appraised values are to be used exclusively for allocating purchase price premiums, fair market value will suffice. However, lenders usually demand both fair market value and forced liquidation value. Appraisals specifically aimed at equity investors usually show only fair market value.

Audit Review

Although not always required by lenders or private investors (such as limited partners), an audit review of target company transactions since the last financial statement could, in the long run, save money. Since the last year-end, inventory balances may have changed materially; product line modifications or changes in customer orders may have created obsolete inventory; equipment may have broken down; new uncollectible receivables may have been initiated; insurance claims, lawsuits, or tax audits may have begun; and a variety of other matters could affect the current market value of the company.

An audit review comprises an examination of account balances and major transactions that have occurred since the last year-end, with particular emphasis on the adequacy of internal controls. Auditors also test the realizable value of receivables and inventory and look for consistency between accounting procedures reflected in prior financial statements and those in effect now. The relatively low fees that independent audit firms charge for such a review should be a small price to pay for assurance that original valuation calculations still hold. No one wants to buy a pig in a poke, and that's exactly what can happen without an audit review.

As an example of the type of trouble a buyer can run into, the acquisition team of a midsize manufacturing company decided to reduce cost overruns by forgoing an audit review. It believed that it had done sufficient probing during the due diligence phase and that additional verification was a waste of money. After the acquisition closed, a physical inventory at the new company revealed that the balances shown on the closing statements were grossly overstated. Instead of having sufficient inventory to cover production requirements for the next six months, the parent company had to lay out $250,000 for new parts and components needed to fill current customer orders.

In the opinion of the company's legal counsel, a lawsuit would be difficult to win, since the company had not taken the proper precautions during wrap-up investigations. An audit review would have at least given the company legal grounds for recovery.

Legal Assistance for Preparing Closing Documents

The closing documents used in a business acquisition can be very straightforward (for small deals), consisting of a simple buy/sell agreement, or very extensive (for more complex deals). In the latter case, closing documents could include the buy/sell agreement plus a series of other documents, such as contracts and covenants between buyer and seller, loan agreements, equity agreements, personal guarantees, UCC filings, and lender security agreements. All closing documents must be reviewed and agreed to by all parties prior to the final closing.

Attorneys with extensive experience in business acquisition contracts should be authorized to draft all nonbank closing documents (banks take care of their own) and also to coordinate approval sign-offs from all parties. If your legal counsel does not have such experience, the following should help you select one that does:

1. *A large law firm.* Buying a business is invariably a complex procedure. Closing documents may involve the application of several branches of the law, such as real estate law, pension law, labor law, litigation, tax law, government regulations, and securities law, in addition to business contract law. Most large law firms have partners that specialize in each of these branches. If you need the expertise, it's available without spending time and money researching the answers. Moreover, looking down the road to possible disputes with banks and other lenders, a law firm with noted specialists in creditor relations and banking law can be very beneficial.

2. *References.* Get references from at least three different sources. Other law firms may hesitate to offer critical comments, but public accountants, financial institutions, or consultants that have previously worked with the law firm should be willing to tell you whether their experience was good or bad. Because of the importance of expert legal advice at this stage in the acquisition process, it is seldom wise to rely solely on your contacts or your relationships with a law firm.

3. *Prior experience.* Be certain that the law firm has handled acquisition work for companies of the size of your target candidate and in a similar industry. If not, go elsewhere. A law firm accustomed to handling cases for multinational companies will seldom do a creditable job for a small, privately held company. And those that specialize in financial services industries, for example, will have a hard time structuring a creative buy/sell agreement for a manufacturing company.

4. *Fee structure.* Although most lawyers charge by the hour, try to negotiate a cap for the total job. A contract lawyer's tendency to strive for perfection without regard to the number of billable hours being accumulated can cost far more than the services are worth.

5. *Interview.* Law firms are in business to make a profit, just like any other company. It doesn't make sense to buy a house, a car, or a boat without checking out the various models available. The same holds true for law firms.

In most cases, your legal counsel should be willing to recommend another firm experienced in acquisition work. But recommendations alone are not always the best answer. Nothing beats a personal interview as a way of verifying not only that a law firm has the experience you need, but also that its lawyers are the type of people you can work with. Most capable lawyers welcome a no-fee initial interview. They want to know a client's background before they accept an engagement as much as you want to know their qualifications to handle the work. The checklist in Figure 14-2 (page 250) may help crystallize the type of questions to ask.

Figure 14-2
Checklist for Interviewing a Law Firm

1. Is there a conflict of interest with the seller, participating financial institutions, or outside investors?
2. What are the hourly rates?
3. Will one lawyer be assigned to the case, or will the work be delegated to junior subordinates?
4. What experience do these subordinates have?
5. What are their hourly rates?
6. Will the lawyer in charge be available at home, in the evening, on weekends?
7. What are the professional backgrounds of specialists whose expertise will be utilized?
8. What local financial institutions will give the firm or the case lawyer a good reference?
9. What other acquisition deals has the case lawyer or the firm recently handled?
10. Can these clients be contacted for references?
11. What knowledge does the firm have of the seller's attorneys?

Major Clauses in Buy/Sell Agreements

Closing documents can be grouped into two categories.

1. Those that the buyer brings to the closing, such as:

   - A buy/sell agreement
   - Real estate closing papers, including title search and title insurance
   - Lease assignments
   - Employment contracts with key managers

2. Those that financial institutions or other parties are responsible for, such as:

   - Note terms and conditions agreements
   - Guarantee agreements
   - UCC filings
   - Collateral assignments

Since financial institutions draft their own documents, the following discussions are limited to clauses typically found in buy/sell agreements, under the standard headings of:

- Price, terms, and conditions of sale
- Representations and warranties of seller and buyer
- Conditions precedent to closing for both seller and buyer
- General statements of law

Price, Terms, and Conditions of Sale

The price, terms, and conditions of sale section restates the negotiated agreement for each of these items. Paragraphs identify specifically the assets to be purchased, the seller's responsibility for discharging current bank debt, the total price, and the terms of payment.

Representations and Warranties

The representations and warranties of a buyer are very straightforward. The buyer must warrant that it is a corporation duly registered and in good standing and that the officer of the corporation who signs the purchase agreement is authorized to do so.

On the seller's side, this section is more definitive. The buyer must be certain that contract clauses spell out the remedies that ensue if, at a later date, it is discovered that any officer or controlling shareholder of the target company furnished the buyer misleading or grossly incomplete information during the due diligence investigation or any other phase of the discovery or negotiation process. It's important that buyers have contractual monetary remedies in the event that misrepresentations lead to a breach of contract.

Nine times out of ten, contract language providing for recovery for such a breach causes more heated debate than any other section of the buy/sell agreement. Clearly, selling shareholders object to such a universal warranty. Their argument runs: It is impractical to disclose everything about a complex business during the brief due diligence investigation. In fact, of course, many transactions occur in the normal course of business that key executives or shareholders may never know about.

Business buyers, on the other hand, have a right to all pertinent information so that purchase decisions are based on fact, not fantasy. Such a debate is usually settled by a compromise unsatisfactory to both parties.

In some cases, however, attorneys become so enthralled with negotiating contract language that the whole deal collapses. A case in point occurred while negotiating the final contract language for the purchase of a small printing company. We had successfully negotiated a reasonable price and terms of sale and arranged appropriate financing. We had also agreed to a three-year consulting contract with the selling shareholder.

Our attorney drafted the buy/sell agreement, including standard representation clauses from the seller that all facts had been revealed to us. However, the seller's attorney, who had no experience in business acquisition contracts, was shocked at such a demand, and advised the seller not to execute the contract. To add fuel to the fire, this attorney also argued that the purchase price was too low and that the employment contract was unsatisfactory— even though these matters had already been agreed to by both parties. Thirty days of negotiating were unproductive, and we finally walked away from the deal. A very beneficial package for both buyer and seller was lost because an inexperienced attorney disputed two sentences in the buy/sell agreement.

Conditions Precedent to Closing

"Conditions precedent to closing" is a legal phrase that refers to a listing of all matters to be completed by both buyer and seller prior to the closing. For example, in an asset sale (as opposed to a stock sale), the seller must comply with state bulk sales laws by informing all creditors, in writing, that such a sale of the company's assets will take place. This must be done before title to the assets can be transferred. As another example, when the buyer opts to continue the target company's insurance policies, the seller must deliver the policies prior to closing. Or if leases are involved, the seller must deliver the assignments. Or a listing of all customers or open purchase orders may be required; or an updated version of a union contract or pension plan. This section also discloses any government, creditor, or lender clearances that must be obtained prior to closing.

General Statements of Law

This is usually the final section in the agreement and includes such topics as identification of the state whose laws will govern the contract, arbitration procedures, and the process by which both parties can be notified of events affecting the contract. These matters are usually not open to negotiation and are better left to the lawyers.

TRANSITION MANAGEMENT

The weeks immediately following the acquisition closing date are referred to as the *transition* period. During the transition, any fears that employees, customers, suppliers, bankers, the local news media, community leaders, and perhaps local government officials have that the new owner will dismember or otherwise destroy the company must be assuaged. Simultaneously, word must be passed that no major changes in the company or its relations with outsiders are planned. In a very real sense, damage control actions during the transition set the stage for future cooperation (or obstruction) when you integrate the parent and subsidiary into one cohesive operating business.

Anxiety and antagonism inevitably follow any business acquisition. First the transition and then integration can be extremely costly and disruptive if they are not carefully orchestrated. The challenges begin the first day that representatives of a new owner walk into the facility. Some employees are apprehensive about losing their jobs; others can't wait to bend their new boss's ear for a raise. Customers and vendors that hold contracts with the new subsidiary are likely to push for better prices or terms. Banking relations that were solid under previous ownership probably seem strained. And on and on it goes.

On the other side, overly exuberant managers from the parent company can't wait to visit the site, indoctrinate their counterparts into the idiosyncratic ways of their new boss, and begin the integration process. The first day, week, and month after an acquisition closes can be the most critical time periods of the integration cycle. If the fears of employees, customers, suppliers, and bankers cannot be laid to rest, if those jockeying for political advantage are not gracefully turned away, if the brakes are not applied to eager parent company managers, mistakes will be made. And in the end, the integration process will cost significantly more and take a lot longer than expected.

Probably the biggest danger immediately after the closing date is the common belief that the parent company (or its shareholders) has "deep pockets" and will now begin pouring new capital into the subsidiary. Regardless of the cash reserves that the parent company may or may not have, such a "deep pockets" rumor must be nipped in the bud. If not, it will spread like wildfire throughout the organization and on to customers and suppliers, making it virtually impossible to correct later on. The result? Employees will expect more fringe benefits and wages, suppliers will push for higher prices, and customers will demand lower prices.

The transition plan should assign key managers specific duties to be performed at the new subsidiary's facility along with time periods within which these tasks must be accomplished. Most executives understand the importance of employees' enthusiastic reception of the procedural changes that are necessary in order to integrate their company with the new parent. They also recognize that employees must be motivated to be enthusiastic. But here the shoe binds.

With rare exceptions, the employees of a recently sold business tend to resist a new owner's efforts to change the way they conduct their daily affairs. Hundreds of reasons for opposing new procedures and policies will pour forth. Viewing the new owner as an intruder and adversary, employees automatically believe that change means a loss of jobs. They feel threatened, and small groups ban together to protect one another, to guard the status quo. Such fear and inertia must be laid to rest before any meaningful steps can be taken to integrate the new company's procedures with those of the parent.

First-Day Agenda

The first day after the closing, two contradictory rumors invariably spread throughout the newly acquired company: (1) that new management plans to lay off 25 percent (or some other large percentage) of the work force, including supervisors, and (2) that the owner of the new parent company is very wealthy and plans to expand the operation immediately, with the addition of 100 (or some other large number) new jobs.

When confronting such desultory rumors, it usually helps to map out a plan of attack so that all representatives of the parent company know precisely how to approach new employees and answer questions with positive responses. Figure 14-3 (page 254) lays out a program that has been used successfully in acquisitions of several privately held businesses.

Figure 14-3
Agenda for the First Day

The following points should be covered during separate meetings with supervisors, salaried personnel, and hourly personnel:

1. Present a brief personal profile of each parent company manager. Accent the experience that qualifies each manager to meet the needs of the subsidiary.

2. Provide handouts that describe the business, products, markets, organization structure, and approximate size of the parent company.

3. Hand out copies of the parent's annual report, if available. If it is not available, be prepared with a summary of the company's key financial statistics.

4. Ask each supervisor to provide the following within the next week:
    a. A description of responsibilities and job activities.
    b. A personal profile, including tenure with the company, previous related experience, education, and technical certifications (if any).
    c. A memo outlining opportunities and roadblocks within functional departments.
    d. Departmental organization charts.
    e. A description of activities and qualifications of key departmental employees.

5. Ask all employees to submit, in writing, their criticisms of current policies and procedures and suggestions for improvements.

6. Provide a schedule for a "fireside chat" with each supervisor over the next two days.

7. Ask employees for suggestions for new personnel policies, operating policies, and operating systems and procedures. Emphasize that you need their help to make the business successful.

8. Explain what employees can expect from you, such as:
    a. An "open-door" management policy.
    b. Specific objectives for improving the profitability and growth of the company.
    c. New management incentive programs.
    d. Definitive management performance standards.

9. Disclose in broad terms the type of debt and/or equity financing that was used to purchase the company. If it's a high-leverage deal, tell the employees. Pull out all the stops in explaining that there are no "deep pockets" around to fund additional equipment or higher wages. Don't hold back any secrets about the financing.

10. Conduct an open question and answer period.

These first-day meetings will set the tone for employee-management relations in the weeks and months ahead. First impressions tend to stick, so it's important to win over as many employees as possible during this initial session. The following key points relate to the tenor of these meetings:

1. *Parent company representatives should show humility.* Employees already know that the deal has closed and that they will have new bosses. It doesn't help to emphasize your power over them—that can only alienate people. If you convince employees that you want to learn from them,

that you want them to continue to do the good job they have been doing, and that you recognize that each of them has personal problems that you will listen to and help solve, the odds are very high that you'll be off to a flying start in interpersonal relations.

2. *Everyone will benefit, but everyone must help.* Most people have never been party to a business acquisition. Given the sensational horror stories featured in media coverage of several large buyouts over the past ten years, it is quite natural for employees to expect the worst. If the "deep pockets" rumor cannot be dismissed quickly, employees will also quite naturally assume that the cash flow generated by their company either will be plowed back in the form of higher wages, and benefits and more machinery and equipment, or will be siphoned off by the new owner. At this stage, parent company representatives must use as much savoir faire as they can muster to convince employees of the benefits to be derived from joining the parent company and the necessity for using part of the subsidiary's cash flow to meet acquisition debt service payments. As the two companies grow together, the greater cash flows thus generated will be plowed back; but for the present, acquisition debt must be repaid.

It's important to convince everyone that the parent company will not siphon off cash for its own benefit. If employees believe that cash generated by them is being used to pay dividends to parent company shareholders or bonuses to top managers, active cooperation and support for integrating the two operations will be impossible to achieve.

3. *Employees of the subsidiary company must know what is expected of them.* Explain in clear terms your strategic objectives in buying the business. Then set out in as much detail as possible the type of support you need from these employees to achieve those objectives. Most people are not mind readers and cannot know what you want unless you tell them. Nothing is more frustrating than trying to do what you think the boss wants without knowing precisely what it is.

Develop clear standards of performance for supervisors and the rest of the employees as soon as possible, and let them know the first day that these standards are coming. Explain that their cooperation will bring your cooperation and support in return. Elaborate on growth objectives and the rewards that will be forthcoming if these objectives are achieved.

Planning and Control

The implementation of the reporting system developed during the preacquisition phase and a detailed set of operating plans is practically indispensable to ensuring a smooth transition period, whether it takes one month or six months. But the first and most important activity should be the installation of a tight cash control system.

Ideally, your newly formed corporate office should coordinate a centralized cash management system, as in the Filtco case study. All deposits of customer receipts should be made in centralized bank accounts, controlled by headquarters personnel. And most important, personnel should be reorganized to ensure proper separation of all cash-related activities. For instance, the person making deposits should never write checks. The person responsible for preparing cash reports should not be the same person responsible for collecting receipts, depositing them, or originating check requests.

The reporting of cash receipts and expenditures to the corporate office should include, at a minimum, the following:

- Daily cash reports showing total receipts and expenditures
- Weekly cash reports showing actual expenditures against the current week's forecast and planned expenditures for the following week
- Projected sales, collections, and expenditures, by month, for six months

Once cash is under control, additional internal reports should be implemented. Here are a few ideas for reports that might prove helpful:

- Number of employees by department—weekly
- Customer orders received and order backlog—weekly
- Shipments by product grouping—daily and weekly
- Customer delivery promises kept—monthly
- Customer complaints and returned goods—monthly
- Purchase orders placed and open purchase orders—monthly
- Customer orders and shipments by sales territory or region—monthly
- Gross profit analysis by product line—monthly

In addition, the subsidiary should begin preparing monthly financial statements in the same format as those of the parent company.

The Operating Plan

The next step after installing cash controls and an internal reporting system is to develop an operating plan. Such a plan should include pro forma financial statements in as much detail as possible, together with a cash flow projection. The shorter the plan's time increments, the better the control over the subsidiary's operating performance. A weekly plan for the first two or three months, changing to monthly for the succeeding twelve months, works very well.

Although preacquisition pro forma statements and cash flow projections certainly should be used as guides, they are probably not as accurate as they could be. Now that you have complete access to detailed records and the input of key employees, customers, and suppliers, projections can be refined. This is also the time to restructure the subsidiary's accounting system to provide forecast data and account balances needed for consolidation with the parent company's records.

One of the most important uses for this operating plan, aside from serving as a base for incentive programs and as a control mechanism, is to verify that the cash flows projected during the preacquisition analyses are still reasonably accurate. Too often, the enthusiasm for adding a new business leads acquisition teams to create overly optimistic cash flow forecasts. Now is the time to come face to face with such optimism. If current cash projections do not meet original expectations, there may still be time to take corrective action. It's far better to change direction at this stage than to try to make up cash deficiencies one or two years down the road.

Marketing Strategy

More often than not, the marketing strategies that target companies have in place prior to being acquired do not meet the growth objectives or fit the distribution systems of their new parent companies. Approaches to advertising, sales promotions, and incentive programs are invariably at odds with those of the parent company. Distribution systems may have to be abandoned in favor of the parent company's network. A target company's salaried marketing organization may conflict with the parent company's use of representatives and agents. Or the reverse could be true—an organization peppered with representatives and agents could conflict with the parent company's salaried sales force.

Analyses of expected growth patterns by product line should be given top priority. If the two companies are to integrate their marketing strategies, it's crucial that both be headed in the same direction and use the same industry and economic growth assumptions. During this initial transition, it may be desirable to contact a few major customers to get a feel for the market's acceptance of the company's product lines. Perhaps product development programs need to be implemented, or certain product lines purged, or pricing structures revamped. Clearly, new marketing strategies cannot be implemented overnight. But in these early days, it's important to grasp the essence of the new subsidiary's current marketing program and to decide whether or not you agree with it.

Using business or product line acquisitions as an integral part of a long-term growth strategy is at best a difficult undertaking; at worst it can wreak havoc on a parent company's cash flow, personnel, and even markets for years to come. In many respects, the trickiest part of buying a business is the transition period. So many matters to attend to—so little room for mistakes.

Here's one tip that seems to be universally true. The team of managers that handled the investigation and analyses during the acquisition process can do a better job of managing the transition than new managers. They should know more about the new company than anyone else. And hopefully, they have developed enough insight during the acquisition process to add the personal touch that is so necessary for a successful transition—that is, the intuitive perception of what message to convey, when to convey it, and when to take appropriate action.

Assuming that the transition period can be managed without too much chaos, the final integration of the two companies should move along smoothly. The main objective, of course, should be to significantly add to the profitability and cash flow of the combined operation. If that cannot be achieved within a reasonable time period, you are far better off admitting a mistake and dumping the acquired business rather than continuing to degrade your long-term growth opportunities.

Chapter 15

Foreign Acquisitions

Although "going international" may not be everyone's cup of tea, companies looking for exploding new markets might find an offshore acquisition (particularly in a developing country) just the ticket. Even if entering new markets isn't part of your company's strategic plan, offshore sourcing of raw materials and cheap labor might be desirable—or even necessary—to remain competitive in domestic markets. However, choosing the *right* markets or the *best* sources of materials and labor in overseas locations is definitely more complex than doing so within the United States. Host-country trade and direct investment barriers or incentives; demographic anomalies; infrastructure development (or lack thereof); labor cost, skills, and availability; transportation and communications links, and so on, must be measured against specific market growth prospects and resource needs.

Over the past twenty years the majority of U.S. companies have searched for new markets in Europe, Canada, Australia, and Japan—all highly developed countries, and as affluent as the United States. The search for cheap labor and raw materials has focused on countries in East and Southeast Asia. But now, in the mid-1990s, conditions have changed. By and large, asking prices for companies or major product lines in Western Europe, Canada, Australia, Japan, or the East Asian newly developed countries (South Korea, Taiwan, Hong Kong, and Singapore) have escalated beyond the reach of most small and midsize U.S. firms. Labor and material costs in these nations and in the emerging countries of Southeast Asia (Malaysia, Thailand, and Indonesia) have risen to levels only slightly below those found in developed countries.

The biggest opportunities for tapping burgeoning markets, for sourcing many raw materials, or for attracting cheap labor to build parts, components, and assemblies are in the "developing" or "emerging" nations of Latin America and the Caribbean, and to a lesser extent in the ex-Communist countries of Eastern Europe. Also, it is in these regions that U.S. companies can find the greatest opportunities for buying going businesses (privately held companies, spin-offs from large host-country and foreign corporations, or privatizations from host-country governments) at reasonable prices.

As part of their policies for bringing previously state-controlled economies into the international marketplace, governments in Latin America, the Caribbean,

Eastern Europe, East Germany, and the European republics of the former Soviet Union are pushing massive privatization programs to sell off state-owned businesses, infrastructure projects, and financial institutions. In addition, many smaller private companies, especially in the Caribbean, Central America, and East Germany, are eagerly seeking buyers for minority or controlling ownership interests. Governments and private businesses alike are desperately in need of fresh capital, technical know-how, and management expertise, and in most cases are anxious to sell off majority shares to foreign companies who can bring these assets to the country.

A unique feature of buying businesses in developing or third-world countries is that they do not have to be financed entirely with private capital. The acquisition of many small and midsize businesses, or those with greater risk, can be financed in part by U.S. government and multilateral aid programs. U.S. companies with a genuine interest in pursuing developing-country private business acquisitions should never be deterred because the purchase price appears to be beyond their financial capability.

With very few exceptions, the Overseas Private Investment Corporation (OPIC), the Inter-American Development Bank (IDB), several World Bank organizations, and other U.S. government and multilateral agencies stand ready to finance acquisitions by U.S. companies that can bring much-needed technology and management know-how to developing-nation businesses. In addition, several countries (especially in Latin America and the Caribbean) permit discounted government debt to be swapped for equity in state-owned businesses being privatized, thereby eliminating any need to raise outside capital.

This chapter is devoted to opportunities and strategies for purchasing controlling interests in private operating businesses located exclusively in developing countries, primarily Latin America and the Caribbean. Such acquisitions are referred to as *foreign direct investments*.

Foreign acquisitions are not restricted to manufacturing, distribution, or retail businesses. Investment opportunities are also plentiful in such diverse industries as these:

- Transportation—railroads, shipping lines, taxi services, bus lines, or airlines
- Government concessions—port authorities or toll road operations
- Infrastructure projects—power utilities, water providers, telephone companies, hospitals, or educational facilities
- Financial services—banks, insurance agencies and underwriters, investment services
- Service businesses—fitness centers, rehabilitation clinics, repair shops, advertising agencies, distributorships
- Tourist facilities—travel agencies, hotels, resorts and villas, condominiums

Acquiring a foreign operation is a very specialized growth strategy, one that is probably not applicable to the majority of small businesses, especially those that remain content with the status quo. Although the acquisition process follows lines similar to those for domestic deals (that is, target search, due diligence investigation, business valuation, financing, preparation of closing documents, and transition procedures), strange cultures, languages, labor and contract laws, and taxing methods add complexities not found in the United States. Nevertheless, buying a controlling interest in an offshore business can be one of the fastest ways to enter global trade, and for that reason alone is worthy of strategic consideration.

One caveat is worth noting, however. Neither the acquisition of an overseas operating business nor an investment in foreign infrastructure and other projects should enter a company's growth plans unless it has a firm commitment to stay the course, for at least five years, and generally much longer. It takes at least that long to learn the nuances and conventions of a foreign culture; which of course, is necessary to become a major market force and remain competitive. One thing is for certain: A foreign direct investment cannot be viewed as a short-term strategy.

A foreign direct investment can be made by purchasing a minority or controlling interest from either a private seller or a foreign government. Buying a state-owned business is the most convenient. In Latin America and the Caribbean, and to a much lesser extent in Eastern Europe (including the European republics of the erstwhile Soviet Union), excellent strategic growth opportunities can be realized through government privatization programs.

Acquisitions in Eastern Europe

For companies that already export to Eastern Europe or source materials or components from suppliers in those countries, acquiring a local presence could be strategically beneficial. As additional countries are admitted to the European Community, a presence in Eastern Europe could also serve as an entree to markets that might otherwise be too expensive to consider.

Literally thousands of small and midsize companies either are already on the block or will be shortly in Poland, Hungary, the Czech Republic, Slovakia, and Ukraine. A large number of privatizations have already occurred in East Germany. It should be noted, however, that business acquisitions in any of these countries carry far greater risk than similar investments in Latin America and the Caribbean.

Converting a business run by ineffective bureaucrats, as in Latin America, is far easier and less costly than changing the habits of workers and managers indoctrinated with seventy years of Communist welfare-state traditions. Furthermore, the physical condition of factories and production machinery in Eastern Europe is deplorable, environmental degradation is nearly insurmountable, distribution channels are decrepit, and infrastructures are collapsing.

On the plus side, workers are generally better trained and have greater skills than those in Latin America. Consumer markets are more sophisticated. And at least in East Germany, state divestment procedures are now running relatively smoothly.

The best opportunities for investment in smaller or midsize companies in Poland, Hungary, the Czech Republic, Slovakia, and Ukraine probably won't appear until late 1994 or 1995. Government officials estimate that it will take that long to work out the bugs in experimental voucher systems. By then, however, the privatization machinery should be sufficiently oiled to attract foreign investment.

The East German system is already functioning as well as it ever will under the auspices of the privatization agency *Treuhandanstalt*. However, German investments will be subject to the new European Union regulations covering mergers and acquisitions. A thorough researching of new regulations, which appear on a regular basis, plus their interpretation by a competent local attorney, must be a prerequisite. If an Eastern European acquisition seems like a reasonable strategy, check out planned privatizations throughout Europe in the British publication *Privatisation International*, 91 Grove Park, London SE5 8LE.

LATIN AMERICAN PRIVATIZATION PROGRAMS

The privatization of state-owned businesses has become an integral part of economic reform programs being implemented throughout Latin America and the Caribbean. Privatization programs in Mexico, Chile, Jamaica, and a few other countries have been around for several years and are now winding down. Argentina is about halfway through. Brazil, Venezuela, and Colombia are barely getting started. Other countries remain in various stages of testing administrative procedures for the implementation of their programs.

The types of businesses being privatized run the gamut from factories to retail shops, from banks to telecommunications companies, from office complexes to hotels, from port concessions to toll roads and airlines. Selling prices also vary all over the lot, from very small ($2,000 for a Peruvian communications company) to very large ($214 million in cash and $5 billion in bonds, plus a debt/equity swap equating to $830 million, for 60 percent ownership in an Argentine holding company). Many government-owned businesses throughout the region are for sale for prices in the $100,000 to $300,000 range.

Privatization continues to be a big business for many of the region's governments. During 1991, proceeds from privatization sales topped $9.5 billion in Mexico, $2.2 billion in Brazil, $2 billion in Venezuela, $1 billion in Argentina, and $100 million in all other Latin and Caribbean countries. With Peru, Bolivia, Ecuador, Trinidad and Tobago, and a few Central American countries in the beginning stages of their programs, opportunities should abound at least through 1996 or 1997.

REGIONAL STRATEGIES

Undeniably, good acquisition opportunities are available in Europe, East Asia, and even Africa, and many American companies have opted for facilities in these regions in the past and will continue to do so in the future. At the same time, however, acquisition prices, unsettled political environments, financing bottlenecks, and trade barriers make these areas of questionable value to most small and midsize U.S. companies. By and large, business acquisition opportunities in countries offering far less risk, better financing, and more cooperative government policies can be found in Latin America and the Caribbean.

That is not to say that buying a business in Latin America or the Caribbean is a bed of roses. It is not, as many expansion-minded business owners who have already ventured into this region would attest. A high poverty level still exists. Corruption flourishes in government and business circles. Infrastructures are abysmal in many locations. Inflation eats away at social fabrics. Capital markets remain underdeveloped. And democratically inspired laws covering workers' rights, business contracts, intellectual property protection, taxes, and imports and exports are, in many countries, still in their infancy. Furthermore, the economies of a few Latin American countries still suffer from an overwhelming amount of government debt.

Nevertheless, American companies inevitably find that it is easier, less costly, and more profitable to acquire facilities in these countries than in distant regions across the Atlantic or Pacific ocean. For those companies with a need or desire to open offshore markets or source resources offshore, Latin America and the Caribbean may well be the best alternative. A good starting point for choosing a location is to get a bead on the current status of a country's debt conversion and economic reform programs as a measure of investment risk. It's also helpful to take a look at independent prognostications of a country's credit and financial standing.

Steadily increasing direct investment in Latin American production facilities and financial institutions by American, European, and Japanese firms has created a sound footing upon which local businesses can build. And this, in turn, has converted inflows of portfolio capital into production capital, further fueling regional growth. It seems virtually certain that over the next five to ten years this spiraling activity should make Latin governments more self-sufficient, improve their ability to meet interest and principal payments, and propel these economies headlong into the twenty-first century.

Another improving sign is that both Moody's and Standard & Poor's are granting improved credit ratings to the more progressive Latin American countries, such as Mexico, Venezuela, and Argentina, reflecting renewed optimism that the government debt debacle of the 1980s has been resolved. These ratings apply to country risk (that is, the risk of investing in government debt obligations), not to individual companies. Nevertheless, country-risk ratings indirectly influence the credit risk of local companies to some extent. One of the biggest fears in making business acquisitions in less-developed countries is that local governments will once again nationalize private companies, close the doors to foreigners, or, as Mexico did in 1982, start a calamitous chain reaction by defaulting on its external debt obligations.

As each year passes, however, and Latin American countries become increasingly open to foreign investment and foreign trade, the likelihood of such happenings lessens. Although country risk should certainly be considered, in most cases judgments derived from personal research rather than official rating services seem to be more definitive.

Pseudo-official rankings of the risks of doing business in a specific country can also indicate the outlook for economic revitalization. At a minimum, they point to those countries that should be avoided. One of the better services is an international business forecasting firm located in Syracuse, New York, called Political Risk Services. Over the years, ratings from this service have proven more consistent than others. They are somewhat conservative, however. Figure 15-1 shows a compilation of ratings from Political Risk Services that date from late 1991 to early 1992.

The code A represents the most secure and strongest recommendation for either direct investment or financing export sales; D is at the other end of the spectrum. Given such an independent risk analysis, one must ask the all-important question: Just what type of risk is involved? Out-of-control inflation? Potential nationalization of companies or whole industries? More stringent regulations against foreign investment? Likely overthrow of democratic governments by military dictators?

Economic risk might be worth taking, provided the anticipated returns are high enough. Political risk, however, is seldom worth the gamble; the odds are stacked against foreigners, as many learned during the 1960s, 1970s, and 1980s in Chile, Argentina, and Mexico, and in Haiti and Venezuela during 1992.

VALUING SPECIFIC COMPANIES

Determining a company's profit-making potential can be far more complex and subjective than assessing country risk. Since most small businesses in Latin America would be considered financially distressed companies if they were located in the United States, some of the procedures for evaluating distressed operating and property-based companies described in Chapters 16 and 17 are a good start, but only a start.

One of the difficulties encountered with offshore businesses is that the standards of efficiency, productivity, and asset maintenance are far different from those in the United States. Buying businesses through a privatization program can be especially treacherous. Many governments follow a policy of selling these businesses and properties in an "as is" condition. Since very few, if any, have been run efficiently or profitably by government bureaucrats, an "as is" condition may mean that they are in as bad or worse shape than distressed U.S. businesses.

Furthermore, much of the equipment and machinery in manufacturing companies is obsolete or in need of repair. Factory buildings may not have been maintained. Labor productivity is usually far below American standards. Companies very often have redundant personnel. Managers tend to regard lifetime job security as a right.

Figure 15-1
Forecasts of Risk to International Business

	Turmoil	Financial Transfer	Direct Investment	Export Market
Argentina				
Eighteen months	Moderate	B	B	C-
Five years	Moderate	B-	B+	C-
Bolivia				
Eighteen months	Moderate	B	A	B+
Five years	High	C+	B+	C
Brazil				
Eighteen months	High	C-	C+	C-
Five years	Very high	D+	D+	D+
Chile				
Eighteen months	Moderate	B	A-	B
Five years	Moderate	B	A+	B
Columbia				
Eighteen months	High	A	A-	A-
Five years	High	B-	C+	C
Costa Rica				
Eighteen months	Low	B-	A-	B-
Five years	Low	B-	A+	B-
Dominican Republic				
Eighteen months	Moderate	B-	A-	B-
Five years	Moderate	B-	B+	C+
Ecuador				
Eighteen months	Moderate	C+	B+	C+
Five years	High	C-	C	C-
El Salvador				
Eighteen months	Very high	B-	B-	B
Five years	Very high	D+	C+	C
Guatemala				
Eighteen months	High	A-	B+	B
Five years	Moderate	C+	B+	B-
Honduras				
Eighteen months	High	B-	B+	B+
Five years	Moderate	C	B	C
Mexico				
Eighteen months	Moderate	B	B+	B+
Five years	Moderate	B	C+	B-
Nicaragua				
Eighteen months	High	C	B-	C
Five years	Moderate	C+	B+	B-
Panama				
Eighteen months	High	B+	A-	B
Five years	Low	A-	A-	A-
Peru				
Eighteen months	Very high	C	B+	C+
Five years	Very high	C-	C	C-
Uruguay				
Eighteen months	Low	A	A+	A
Five years	Low	B+	B+	B+
Venezuela				
Eighteen months	Moderate	B	B+	A
Five years	Moderate	B-	C+	C+

Source: Political Risk Services, *LatinFinance*.

Add to these hurdles the normal confusion of strange corporate, labor, and tax laws; peculiar quality standards (although ISO 9000 is gaining popularity); less than efficient transportation and communications modes; failing power systems; and often-corrupt distribution systems, and one must ask, why bother? Because the potential for substantial profit improvements and long-term growth may be excellent—and the price is right.

Granted, several larger businesses and prime properties have sold at premiums rather than discounts, especially in Mexico. However, smaller companies or those in less developed countries can usually be had for substantially less than market value. The question then becomes: How does one determine market value?

Accounting and Financial Disclosure Standards

Since financial accounting standards vary widely from country to country, a hodgepodge of accounting practices makes financial analysis extremely difficult. The immediate write-off of inventory and equipment purchases in one country and the charging of purchased goodwill direct to stockholders' equity in another, for example, make applying standard analysis techniques nearly impossible.

Many times financial statements are prepared in accordance with local tax laws that permit the write-off of equipment and/or inventory as it is purchased (several European countries). In other cases, balance sheet assets carry replacement cost values (Japan and other East Asian nations). Unreported reserves are permitted in Germany. Last-in, first-out (LIFO) inventory valuations are unique to the United States.

Accounting practices in developing nations are even more convoluted. Many of these countries do not have any regulations to control the form or content of financial statements. Others do not require periodic financial statements at all. If financial statements are needed for a special purpose, companies prepare hem on a one-shot basis. Gradually, these conditions are changing, but not fast enough to give one the same degree of confidence in foreign business valuations as in those for U.S. acquisitions.

Although the International Accounting Standards Committee (IASC) is attempting to produce some worldwide conformity through a recommended set of rules to standardize balance sheet and profit and loss statement presentation, so far little progress has been made in implementing its suggestions. One of the main obstacles is that the IASC insists, among other things, that accounting methods used for tax purposes must conform to those used in financial statements—which is contrary to virtually all existing national accounting standards, including those in the United States.

Until worldwide financial reporting standards are adopted, performing a meaningful analysis of a target's financial performance is difficult at best. More often than not, business valuations must be made using incomplete and/or inaccurate internal financial data. As noted in Chapter 12, an increase in the uncertainty about a target company's future cash flow prospects dictates a high capitalization rate for present value calculations. Obviously, if the purchase price is low enough, such future uncertainty might be a good trade-off against new markets and/or resources.

Nonfinancial Analyses

Although each target acquisition in each country requires a slightly different approach to determining its market value, here are the rather broad rules followed by American companies that claim to have paid reasonable prices for viable Latin American and Caribbean businesses and properties.

1. *Industry and competition:* Go after businesses that complement your U.S. business. Foreign risk is high enough without adding unfamiliar products or processes. Search out companies whose products can be exported, preferably products you can use or distribute in U.S. markets. Alternatively, select companies that produce goods or services for local markets that have little competition—a very likely situation for privatized companies, since state-owned businesses generally do not compete in the same markets as private enterprises.

2. *Size:* Stay with smaller businesses. The big ones—companies in telecommunications, transportation, energy, and so on—are usually priced too high and the competition from large multinationals is too intense to make them viable acquisitions. Smaller businesses may take more effort to rejuvenate, but the chances of success are far greater. Ideally, the business should be no larger than your U.S. company, and preferably smaller.

3. *Management:* Select only those businesses that have, at a minimum, one or two trainable key managers who are willing to work for an American owner. Many will not do so, even though they say they will in the beginning. It's important to ferret out those with anti-American feelings. That isn't very difficult; it should be intuitively sensed during a first meeting. Insist on visiting the facility and meeting key managers before offering a bid. Buying a "pig in a poke" in a foreign land can be much worse than doing so at home.

4. *Infrastructure:* If you are not accustomed to doing business in developing nations, it can be a frustrating experience to conduct a company's affairs when the electricity fades in and out or goes out completely, when telephones won't work or a call won't go through, when water supplies dry up, or when transportation systems break down—all common occurrences. Part of the due diligence process should be a survey of other local businesses that are owned or managed by foreigners, preferably Americans. How do they cope with infrastructure failures? What is the frequency of such failures? How does the government respond?

5. *Financing:* Keep your equity investment to a bare minimum. The purchase of nearly all smaller businesses can be financed locally or with the assistance of the OPIC or other U.S. government agencies, especially in

the Caribbean and Central America. Local development banks can be a good second source. Start with the Inter-American Development Bank to get information on local development banks and other sources of assistance. As a general rule, don't use your company's cash reserves for more than 25 percent of the purchase price.

FINANCING ASSISTANCE

Leveraged buyouts (LBOs) may be difficult to arrange in the United States without overcollateralizing debt obligations, but this is definitely not the case in developing countries. The big difference is that American LBOs are financed with bank loans or public debt issues, whereas acquisition financing in developing nations, especially in Latin America and the Caribbean, can be arranged wholly or in part through U.S. government and World Bank aid programs or, in some cases, development banks.

Since the Overseas Private Investment Corporation is one of the U.S. government's most active agencies currently financing U.S. foreign direct investments, this might be a good place to start. However, many other agencies also stand ready to help. The possibilities for raising acquisition capital are so numerous that describing even a reasonable number here would be impossible. The following sections discuss only a sampling of the more promising ones. Further information on financing foreign business acquisitions around the world can be found in my book, *The McGraw-Hill Handbook of Global Trade and Investment Financing*.

Overseas Private Investment Corporation

The Overseas Private Investment Corporation (OPIC) is a self-sustaining government agency whose mission is to promote private-sector economic growth in developing countries. It accomplishes this by assisting small and mid-size U.S. businesses to locate, finance, and insure investments in foreign facilities and projects with:

1. Direct loans or loan guarantees
2. Insurance against political risk, such as currency inconvertibility, expropriation, war, revolution, and civil strife
3. Investment missions stationed throughout the world
4. Investor information service

Eligible projects must "assist in the social and economic development of the host country" and "be consistent with the current economic and political interests of the United States." Clearly, any privatization investment meets the first criterion. And investments in countries considered friendly to the United States (and who isn't friendly these days?) meet the second test.

OPIC assistance programs apply to both American-controlled new foreign investments and the expansion of established overseas businesses. Ordinarily, OPIC will not finance more than about 75 percent of the purchase price, although cases have arisen in which the agency cooperates with other funding sources to provide a higher percentage. The actual percentage OPIC will carry depends on the current status of the country's economic and political development and, of course, the current U.S. policies that support international participation by U.S. companies.

To get OPIC's maximum funding amounts, the target business must, after closing, be owned or controlled by an American company, which must also participate in the management of the acquired business. If ownership or control rests with foreign parties, OPIC will cover only that portion represented by U.S. interests. Furthermore, the U.S. parent company must have a proven record of competence and success in another business the same as or closely related to the one being acquired. In other words, you can't use OPIC funds to diversify into a new industry.

OPIC financing can be applied to three categories of medium- and long-term investments:

1. Projects that are energy-related (water systems, electric utilities, oil and gas drillings, businesses that produce products for local consumption, and the development of alternative energy sources).

2. Projects that offer significant trade benefits to a host country or that contribute toward the development of the host country's infrastructure.

3. Projects in cooperation with small businesses in those countries where the per capita income is greater than $3,800 (the current measure of the country's stage of development).

Direct loans

Only projects sponsored by or involving significant participation of a small business qualify for nonrecourse direct loans, ranging from $200,000 to $4 million. Interest rates are based on current market rates for loans with similar repayment terms and risks. Occasionally OPIC takes equity positions through convertible debt instruments and subsequently sells them to companies or private investors in the host country; however, this is the exception, not the rule.

Loan guarantees

Most loan guarantees apply to purchase prices from $1 million to $25 million, although they can reach $50 million or even higher in some cases. Interest rates on guaranteed loans are similar to those on other U.S. government-guaranteed issues of comparable maturity (from five to twelve years). OPIC charges a fee of from 1.5 to 3 percent of the loan balance, depending on the project's commercial and political risk. Such guarantees cannot be used for business acquisitions that would cause the closing of an existing facility in the United States. Nor will OPIC fund gambling facilities, distilleries, military projects, or projects that pose a serious threat to the environment.

The agency also finances feasibility studies, awards special grants for training foreign managers, and provides guarantees and direct loans for cross-border leasing projects. Other special OPIC programs include surety guarantees for small contractors and a variety of assistance programs for investments in energy exploration projects (such as oil and gas, oil shale, geothermal, mineral, and solar) and peripheral businesses.

Complete details about all OPIC programs can be obtained from:

Overseas Private Investment Corporation
1615 M Street, N.W., Fourth Floor
Washington, DC 20527
202) 457-7010 or (800) 424-6742

Inter-American Investment Corporation

The Inter-American Investment Corporation (IIC) is the merchant banking arm of the Inter-American Development Bank, which is dedicated to helping private enterprise in the Latin American/Caribbean region. The IIC is specifically charged with "assisting foreign companies in the small and mid-size range identify investment projects and potential joint venture partners in Latin American and Caribbean countries" and with "furnishing technical and financial assistance to develop the project."

The IIC also offers nonfinancial assistance in such matters as:

- Technical counseling for the preparation of preinvestment and feasibility studies
- Advisory services aimed at restoring the operating and financial capacity of companies requiring such assistance
- Advice on structuring privatization deals
- The identification of investment projects
- Coordination with financial institutions for additional financing
- The startup of new companies

To qualify for IIC financial aid, the target company or project must meet at least one of the following criteria:

1. Use material and human resources from the host country (or another member country) and create new jobs in the region
2. Create local management skills
3. Encourage exports from the region
4. Transfer technology
5. Promote savings and the use of investment capital
6. Generate and/or save foreign exchange
7. Promote broad ownership structures

For further information about IIC programs, contact:

Inter-American Investment Corporation
1300 New York Avenue, N.W.
Washington, DC 20577
Telephone: (202) 623-3900
Fax: (202) 623-2360

Certain United Nations agencies can also be helpful, not only for financing foreign business acquisitions, but for identifying viable investment opportunities and locating local joint venture partners. The U.N. agencies most active in the Latin American and Caribbean regions are the:

* International Finance Corporation
* Caribbean and Central America Business Advisory Service
* Multilateral Investment Guarantee Agency

International Finance Corporation

The International Finance Corporation (IFC), a division of the World Bank, has a mandate "to assist, in association with private investors [mainly profitable companies from the United States, Europe, and Asia], [those] productive private enterprises that contribute to the development of [World Bank] member countries." Foreign investor assistance includes:

* Identifying the project and structuring ownership interests
* Making equity contributions and providing long-term loans that do not require government guarantees
* Managerial and technical assistance during the due diligence and transition periods

In addition, the IFC helps foreign companies (1) find local partners for joint ventures and (2) negotiate contracts with host government agencies.

To date, the IFC has accepted fee-based advisory assignments in Argentina, Brazil, Chile, Colombia, Haiti, Mexico, Trinidad and Tobago, and Venezuela. These assignments entail assistance in the development of project proposals, advice on the choice of technical partners, and cooperative efforts for the structuring of appropriate financing.

Caribbean and Central America Business Advisory Service

The Caribbean and Central America Business Advisory Service (BAS), a division of the International Finance Corporation, is a special department created to assist companies in making direct investments in going businesses and infrastructure projects in Caribbean and Central American nations. The BAS acts as a bridge between foreign companies and local private businesses and lenders. Normally, a target company's minimum purchase price should be $500,000, although smaller projects in tiny Caribbean island states will be considered.

BAS is not a direct lender or equity investor. It does, however, help potential parent companies structure and appraise investment projects for presentation to prospective lenders and investors. Such assistance might include hiring technical and marketing consultants, advising on alternative sources of financing, and helping companies negotiate with financial institutions. Not infrequently, the addition of BAS to a company's negotiating team assures lenders that the project is economically sound and worthy of funding. And most important, lenders do not generally insist on additional guarantees or external security when financing BAS-backed investments.

Multilateral Investment Guarantee Agency

The primary mission of the World Bank's Multilateral Investment Guarantee Agency (MIGA) is to encourage foreign investment in developing countries by providing:

- Investment guarantees against the risks of currency transfer, expropriation, war and civil disturbance, and breach of contract by the host government
- Advisory services to developing member countries on ways to improve their attractiveness to foreign investment

The agency also assists foreign companies in identifying and qualifying local joint venture partners.

All three U.N. agencies are located at 1818 H Street, N.W., Washington, DC 20433. Detailed information about programs and qualification criteria can be obtained from the:

- International Finance Corporation
  Telephone: (202) 477-1234; Fax: (202) 477-6391
- Business Advisory Service
  Telephone: (202) 473-0900; Fax: (202) 334-8855
- Multilateral Investment Guarantee Agency
  Telephone: (202) 473-6168; Fax: (202) 477-9886

DEBT/EQUITY SWAPS

Debt/equity swaps offer one alternative to raising new capital for financing foreign acquisitions. Such swaps are particularly useful when buying a business through a government's privatization program in which discounted government debt can be exchanged for equity in a local business. Before buying government debt obligations, be sure to verify government's willingness to make a swap and determine whether or not a viable business in that country meets your needs. As a general rule, you should be able to negotiate a swap at a discount of not less than 50 percent of the difference between the debt's market price and par value.

For example, assume that the market price of government bonds was 30 cents on the dollar (or 30 percent of par value). Normally a debt/equity swap must let the government show a gain—for political reasons if nothing else. In this case, the 70-cent spread could be halved, so that the exchange value would be 30 plus

35, or 65 percent of par. The swap transaction gives the government a gain of 35 cents on the dollar, and your company buys the foreign business for a cash outlay of only 30 cents on the dollar. Once the selling price of the privatized business has been negotiated and the amount of government bonds required to meet this price has been determined, the bonds can be purchased on the open market, and the swap concluded.

A slight variation might occur when a business is privately owned rather than state-owned. The swap procedures are the same as in the previous example, except that when the government buys its bonds back at 65 percent of par, you receive payment in local currency, which can then be used to purchase the business.

If this scenario is to work, the local government must play a prominent role in negotiating the purchase price of the target company. Although such intervention would never happen in the United States, it is a way of life in Latin America, where political favors change hands more openly.

GETTING ASSISTANCE

There are so many variations to buying a business in a foreign land that professional assistance is a practical necessity at virtually every step along the way. Many companies have learned the hard way that when they attempt a foreign acquisition on their own, they make enormous cash outlays while they learn the ropes, only to find, that in the end, they paid too much for the company or government barriers make profitable operations impossible. Differences in language, legal systems, tax laws, labor regulations, and bureaucratic protocol make it virtually impossible for a U.S. company to successfully master the acquisition process and the transition period without someone to interpret, educate, and pull strings when necessary.

A good example of what can happen when investors do not solicit competent advice was related in my book *High-Risk, High-Yield Investing*. A privately held, Florida-based electronics assembly company decided to set up a satellite operation in Costa Rica. Minimum research by company personnel indicated a benevolent Costa Rican business climate. This led the company's president and his staff to believe that they could invest in a small, previously state-owned San José radio components assembly business without incurring the expense of a consultant or local advisor. The president closed the deal with Costa Rican bureaucrats and installed an American managing director.

After the first year, the operation was closed. The Floridians cited impossible labor laws, an underhanded local banker, obstinate government officials, and impossible shipping regulations as a few of the reasons for its failure. In retrospect, the company's president commented in the local press that professional assistance in the beginning could have resolved most of these issues before the investment was made.

Extremely competent professionals can be retained from a variety of organizations, all of which are especially well versed in acquisitions of Latin American or Caribbean businesses, either through privatization programs or from private sellers.

For privatization investments, a good place to begin is the International Privatization Group of Price Waterhouse. This group was set up in 1990 under the auspices of the U.S. Agency for International Development. It provides privatization-related technical advisory services and training for foreign investors, host-country government officials, and private-sector consultants.

The organization also conducts applied research and maintains a comprehensive library and information center on privatization. It is located at 1801 K Street, N.W., Washington, DC 20006; Telephone: (202) 296-0800; Fax: (202) 466-4760.

The Ernst & Young organization is also very active in assisting American companies that want to purchase Latin American and Caribbean businesses. The firm has offices in all major cities throughout the Caribbean, Central America, and South America. Ernst & Young's London office is also an excellent place to get assistance for European investments. For local addresses and telephone numbers, check with the firm's Washington office at 1225 Connecticut Ave., N.W., Washington, DC 20036; Telephone: (202) 862-6000; Fax: (202) 862-6399.

Four New York banks employ capable professionals in advisory services departments (really consulting services, but banks don't like to advertise that). They are:

- Bankers Trust Company, 200 Park Avenue, New York 10017
  Telephone: (212) 850-4578; Fax: (212) 826-2817
- Citibank, N.A., 399 Park Avenue, New York 10043
  Telephone: (212) 559-2396; Fax: (212) 308-0566
- European InterAmerican Finance Corp., 400 Madison Ave.,
  New York 10017
  Telephone: (212) 751-2200; Fax (212) 319-7833
- The Chase Manhattan Bank, N.A., 1 Chase Manhattan Plaza 14,
  New York 10081
  Telephone: (212) 552-6743; Fax: (2121) 269-3221

The New York offices of Lazard Freres & Co., Salomon Brothers, and Singer & Friedlander Limited also provide consultation services for larger offshore acquisitions.

Once one of these organizations has been contacted, one thing leads to another, and before long you should be able to locate appropriate financial, legal, and consulting professionals that can provide the type of assistance you need.

Chapter 16

Acquisitions of Distressed Companies

A truly creative growth strategy that can be implemented at low cost and minimal risk, and without large commitments of new debt or equity capital, has thrust itself upon the American business scene over the past few years: the purchase of a controlling interest in privately held, financially distressed operating companies and property-based businesses. At first glance, the wisdom of acquiring a business that cannot meet its debt obligations, has no cash reserves, and is probably in a weak competitive position looks suspect. And rightly so. For many of these small businesses, the end is right around the corner. If they are not already awaiting the liquidator's heavy hand, they are close to it. Although such businesses can usually be purchased with very little or no down payment merely by assuming part or all of their outstanding debt obligations, the difficulty of turning them around into high-growth operations is insurmountable. In the end, attempts to integrate a downtrodden company into a prosperous, growth-oriented parent usually destroy them both.

On the other hand, many small businesses are in financial difficulty because greedy owners have milked the company dry or because external events over which the company has little or no control have impaired its ability to produce and/or sell its products. Prolonged labor strikes, natural disasters, or the loss of a major customer or source of supply, for instance, can decimate a small business, even though it has excellent personnel, product lines, and market position. Given a broader customer base, new access to credit, or more professional management, many of these companies can add significantly to the long-term growth of a parent, especially a parent boxed in by new competition, market shifts, or costly government edicts (such as environmental clean-up orders or infrastructure changes).

A case in point occurred when the state of Pennsylvania opted to build a new superhighway bypassing the intersection of two heavily traveled roads in suburban Philadelphia. A highly profitable Holiday Inn franchise located near the intersection suffered an immediate drop in room occupancy. Undaunted, the hotel owner worked out a new long-term strategy, shifting market emphasis away from transient highway travelers to busloads of shoppers from New York, Harrisburg, and Baltimore who flocked to a new nearby discount center every day of the week. However, it needed a much-expanded food and beverage operation to capture this untapped market.

The hotelier purchased a near-bankrupt seafood restaurant and bar by assuming its outstanding debt (with no cash down), and peppered the bus tour guide's handout pamphlet with a barrage of advertising. In less than six months, out-of-town discount shoppers not only made the restaurant and bar a paying proposition, but increased hotel room occupancy to an average of 82 percent.

Not all distressed businesses can be turned around that easily. But the right combination of facilities, products, and markets can make a distressed business as good a buy as a profitable company or even better. And one thing is clear: There are plenty of distressed businesses on the market.

The wave of bankruptcies, near-bankruptcies, defaults, and liquidations that hit the American business community during the 1989–1992 recession (twice as many companies filed for bankruptcy protection in 1991 as in 1981) is by now well documented. Although the first wave of restructurings, recapitalizations, and reorganizations ended during 1992, a second wave hit in 1993. It seems inevitable that the rest of the 1990s will continue to witness a large number of small (and large) businesses bite the dust, giving this decade the dubious distinction of having had the most business failures of any ten-year period in American business history.

Although such external factors as foreign competition, technological advances, and burdensome (and costly) government regulations have certainly caused a good number of companies to fold, it appears that the greatest blame must be laid at the feet of imprudent bank lending practices, government giveaways, and overexuberant investors. Such practices created far more expensive capital than could be efficiently employed, resulting in the production of far more goods and services than consumers needed or wanted, at higher prices than they were willing and able to pay. It also encouraged the construction of far more office buildings, factories, hotels, residences, and shopping centers than tenants could use, at higher rents than they could afford. In other words, easy credit and unwarranted financial market optimism were and are major factors encouraging companies to incur debt that they could not and cannot, with normal growth patterns, repay.

As long as the economy continued its historic rapid expansion, there was some hope that companies could find a way out. Now, however, the United States has entered an extended period of low inflation, low interest rates, slow economic growth, and skeptical capital markets. Companies are faced with bonds coming due, bank loans that must be repaid, and appreciated venture capital that has to be returned. Many businesses that rode the high leveraging wave of the 1980s have entered a prolonged period of slow or even declining growth with little hope of meeting these obligations. Defaults on junk bonds are common. Loans go unpaid. And bankruptcy courts overflow.

Such a doomsday scenario faces those caught in the default vise. However, prudently managed companies that kept clear of such strategies now stand to reap significant rewards. For the rest of this decade, there should be a great many unusual opportunities to acquire financially distressed businesses and properties at very low purchase prices.

This chapter looks at evaluation techniques, investment strategies, and sources of information for acquiring a controlling interest in distressed operating companies, either privately held businesses or spin offs from public companies. Chapter 17 covers strategic growth opportunities in buying distressed property-based businesses.

To develop meaningful strategies for purchasing distressed companies, one must first identify those factors that point to a potential recovery for the company. Although buying a company and liquidating its assets may bring high returns, these gains are short-term and do little to enhance the long-term growth potential of the acquiring company.

EVALUATING OPTIONS

No individual industry or company size determines whether a business will experience financial distress. Companies engaged in manufacturing, retail, distribution, services, and research suffer the same unmanageable debt loads. Both micro businesses and multinational corporations face exorbitant cash drains to repay imprudent borrowings. However, most of the good acquisition opportunities seem to be businesses in the $7 million to $50 million sales range. Below this level, personnel organizations tend to be too shallow and markets too narrow to effect a reasonably rapid turnaround; above this cap, companies tend to be too unwieldy to integrate efficiently (unless your company is significantly larger).

When evaluating a financially troubled acquisition target, it's crucial to do enough research to determine:

- The current position of the company's markets and products
- The fundamental reason(s) for its financial difficulty
- The caliber of its management personnel

Once such reseach is completed an analysis of the company's financial statements should reveal those steps necessary to (1) stop the bleeding by bringing expenditures in line with revenues, (2) generate extra cash (perhaps by selling off noncritical business assets), and (3) redefine markets, products, and sales strategies.

Market and Product Analysis

Buying a controlling interest in a distressed operating business makes sense only if (1) its products, markets, personnel, or facility can be efficiently incorporated into the parent company's growth plan and the cost of doing so is less than that of acquiring such assets individually, or (2) as a stand-alone business, it sells products in growing markets that complement those of the parent. If neither of these conditions exists, potential gains can be realized only by reducing operating costs. And in most cases, costs can be cut only so far (generally not far enough to effect a turnaround) before the business itself is damaged beyond repair.

Therefore, the first step is to determine the target's market size, its competition, and its growth potential. Although the opinion of the current owners and key managers should be sought, be aware that such opinions are nearly always overly optimistic. "All we need is another $50,000 (or $20,000, or $100,000, or another number) to get our new product line to market (or to hire more salespeople, or to expand advertising, etc.) and we could double sales!" seems to be a common prescription for a company's deficiencies.

Pouring good money after bad doesn't work. And if you can't independently verify that markets and products are worth having, it's better to look elsewhere for expansion opportunities.

Reasons for Financial Problems

If the cost of righting those deficiencies that have caused the target to be in financial trouble is relatively minor and the time it takes to do so relatively short, further analyses are probably justified. Otherwise, it's usually best to walk away from the deal. In most privately owned businesses, the blame for financial failure can be ascribed to one, or at most two, reasons. Here are the most common ones, in order of frequency:

- Excessive owner's salary and expenses—"milking the company" is far and away the most common reason that privately owned businesses fail
- Too many employees, employees performing the wrong tasks, and/or incompetent employees in key slots
- Ineffective marketing strategies or incompetent sales personnel
- Too rapid expansion and inadequate financial planning
- Increased competition from much larger companies with more resources
- Product obsolescence
- Shrinking markets
- Obsolete equipment or facilities
- Labor problems
- Constricting regulations from the EPA, OSHA, or other government agencies
- IRS or state tax deficiencies

Other factors come into play occasionally, but those (especially the first four) are the main reasons why private companies run out of money. It goes without saying that once you have identified the real reason for the company's financial difficulty, if you don't have the immediate means to take corrective action, buying the business would be foolish.

Management Analysis

Assuming that the market indicates a good potential for growth and the fundamental problems can be corrected, the next step is to evaluate management capability. While in many, if not most, cases companies get into financial difficulty because of bad management practices, this is definitely not universally true. The larger the company, the higher the probability that at least some managers are competent. Even very small businesses may have one or more employees worth keeping.

The number of qualified supervisors and the level of their competence is far more important in distressed acquisition candidates than in profitable ones. Although most key managers will probably have to be replaced with parent company personnel, at least one or two employees who can be relied upon for background information on customers, suppliers, production processes, and many other matters are necessary to ensure the integration of the target business without major disruptions in the parent's operations such as occurred in the following case.

The long-term growth strategy of a profitable, well-managed (and well-known) book publisher called for diversification into several highly specialized niche markets. The company's first acquisition was a small, financially troubled house that specialized in sailing and power boat "how-to" books. The previous owner had borrowed to the hilt, milked the company dry, and stifled the initiative of all supervisory employees. The new owner quickly saw the integration of the two businesses turn into a nightmare: Customers clamored for old contracts to be fulfilled, unexpected book returns siphoned off valuable cash, key authors demanded settlements of prior claims, and printing houses balked at new orders.

Not one employee of the new subsidiary could help because no one knew what verbal commitments and agreements the previous owner had made. Before the newly acquired business had been fully integrated with the buyer, more than $3 million had been spent—ten times the amount of the debt assumed by the buyer as the purchase price!

Without a core of capable, technically proficient functional managers who, at a minimum, can supply a historical perspective on unexpected roadblocks, the risk of buying a distressed business is practically unmanageable. Furthermore, hiring an entirely new management team or, worse, retraining existing personnel takes valuable time, money, and effort away from the primary goal of working with customers, suppliers, and lenders. A distressed business brings with it enough hazards without adding management risk.

Assuming that markets, products, and management personnel pass muster and that the problems causing financial difficulty seem solvable, the next step should be an analysis of financial statements. It's a waste of time, however, to start with financial statements unless you are satisfied about markets, the correctability of primary deficiencies, and management competence.

Financial Analysis

The process of calculating the future benefits from a distressed private business differs from that of analyzing healthy companies, mainly because of these reasons:

- The forces that caused financial distress in the first place have already tainted historical financial statements, making them worthless for evaluating future growth potential.

- Financial statements tend to be unaudited, misstated, and fraught with omissions and inaccuracies. Most of the omissions and inaccuracies result from the absence of internal controls, but at times they can be a direct result of management's attempt to coverup an event or condition.

- Financial statements are frequently prepared on the same basis as federal tax returns, using other than generally accepted accounting principles.

Nevertheless, a careful analysis of the target's financial condition is crucial at this stage, even if raw bookkeeping data must be used. The most important financial data to uncover and/or have prepared are the following:

- Cash flow forecasts by month for the ensuing twelve months based on the current operating policies and organization. The forecast must be in sufficient detail to (1) separate major from minor revenue-generating products or services and (2) identify major categories of expenditures (e.g., payroll, taxes, purchases, debt service, etc.)
- Analysis of customer order backlog, if applicable
- Aged accounts receivable listing with explanations for large overdue amounts and/or those from major customers
- Aged accounts payable listing of all amounts due suppliers, taxing authorities, service providers, and so on
- Analysis of all lease obligations, showing dates and amounts due
- Copies of all loan agreements and current status of interest and principal payments
- Listing of all open claims, lawsuits, and other contingent liabilities

Obviously, if you decide to move ahead with the acquisition, an abundance of other financial data will be required (as in any due diligence investigation), including an independent appraisal of hard assets—if necessary. The above listing is a good start, however, and should provide enough information to construct a preliminary cash flow forecast leading to an initial go/no-go decision. Further research will then be necessary to prepare complete pro forma financial statements and detailed cash flow projections.

STRATEGIES FOR BUYING DISTRESSED OPERATING BUSINESSES

Excluding intentional liquidations, only two conditions make distressed operating businesses attractive buys: (1) the opportunity to purchase a controlling interest for very little or no capital outlay, and (2) the opportunity to resurrect the company and make it profitable, either as a stand-alone business or as part of the parent company. If you can't achieve both, it's probably a bad investment.

The opportunity to buy a controlling interest for little or no capital arises because, for one reason or another, all financially distressed companies are in trouble with lenders. To save the company and thereby generate additional loan business, most lenders are willing to write off a portion of the existing loan and restructure the balance on more favorable, extended terms. A lender's unwillingness to do both should be sufficient cause to back off.

Of the three types of distressed operating businesses (those that are financially strapped and approaching bankruptcy, those that are already in bankruptcy but have a good chance to reorganize, and those that must be liquidated), the last can be dismissed as a long-term growth strategy. The best chance for long-term returns normally comes from those businesses that are approaching but not yet in bankruptcy. However, the best purchase price can usually be negotiated for companies that have the potential to be reorganized out of bankruptcy.

Businesses Approaching Bankruptcy

Strategically, potential benefits to be derived from financially strapped businesses that have not yet entered bankruptcy should be viewed over at least a five-year period, and perhaps longer. It takes this long to correct operating deficiencies and begin a normal growth pattern, both of which must be done before any sizable returns can be achieved. As previously discussed, it's important to analyze the reasons for financial problems and the most likely solutions before making the acquisition. There isn't time to experiment after the deal closes. Then the initial thrust should be to bring appropriate expertise and perhaps new capital to the business so that cash drains can be halted in a relatively short time.

Although many variations come into play, prebankruptcy tactics involve two primary negotiations:

1. Negotiations with secured creditors—normally banks or other financial institutions—to write off a significant part of the total outstanding loans, generally 40 to 60 percent, and to restructure the balance into extended-payment term loans. In return, of course, secured lenders want assurances that the company is still viable, that the restructured loan will be repaid on schedule, and that additional loans will be required once the company has been turned around.

2. Negotiations with the business owner or owners to purchase at least 51 percent of the outstanding voting stock. Buying less than a controlling interest in a distressed company makes no sense, for a variety of reasons. Furthermore, the seller should deposit most, if not all, of the purchase price in company bank accounts as a working capital loan.

In addition, the parent company must be careful to isolate itself from all liabilities pertaining to prior debts of the target company. This usually involves iron-clad "hold harmless" and indemnification clauses in the stock purchase agreement. It may also be desirable to place liens on personal assets of the selling shareholders (at least those assets that have not been specifically pledged to bank creditors), such as personal residences, minority shareholding interests, or personal art collections and antiques.

After the deal closes, the transition period should be dedicated to getting the new subsidiary on a sound financial footing as soon as possible. This may involve negotiating extended terms with suppliers, taxing authorities, and other unsecured creditors. It may involve a wholesale realignment of personnel, laying off employees that are not essential for the short term. It could involve negotiating early payment terms for outstanding receivables or selling noncritical assets—storage space, vehicles, furniture, excess equipment, perhaps whole product lines or divisions—to raise cash.

Whatever it takes, the immediate objective must be to reduce the risk of bankruptcy and hasten the new subsidiary's return to profitability. Once the turnaround has been accomplished, integration with parent company systems and procedures can begin. Normal growth strategies, including new product development and refinancing, can then be considered.

The long-term objective should be to bring the business (or its product lines, if they are integrated with the parent company's products) into the black with as dominant a market position as possible. Refinancing should begin as soon as possible. Finally, the entire subsidiary operation should be structured so that it can be disposed of in five to seven years if markets, technology, or material sourcing make the business noncompetitive. It's important to plan for such a getting-out position right at the beginning.

Businesses in Chapter 11

Buying a business that is already in Chapter 11 bankruptcy takes a bit more finesse and a lot more effort. This is not the time or place to get into a lengthy discussion of bankruptcy law or the many variations available to bankrupt companies. Suffice is it to say that any sale of a controlling interest in a company in Chapter 11 must be approved by the bankruptcy court, the secured creditors, and, in most cases, a committee representing unsecured creditors.

To get court approval, the buyer must present evidence of its ability to bring the company out of bankruptcy, and this involves the preparation of a proposed reorganization plan. When the court, the secured creditors, and the unsecured creditors' committee approve the sale, they also normally approve the reorganization plan. It can then be submitted to a vote by all unsecured creditors. If the majority of unsecured creditors approve the plan, the court permits the company to emerge from Chapter 11.

Before going through this rather convoluted procedure, it makes sense to work out a refinancing deal with secured creditors. Normally, but not always, only one secured creditor, called a *debtor-in-possession*, has agreed to finance the bankrupt company after the court grants it a first claim on all company assets (referred to as a *super-priority lien*).

The process of negotiating a refinancing arrangement is not entirely different from that of negotiating with lenders before a target company enters bankruptcy. You should still shoot for a discount on the loan, extended terms for repaying the balance, and an additional credit line for working capital.

A buyer/seller coalition has a lot more leverage with creditors after the company has filed for bankruptcy than before, mainly because of the always-present threat of liquidation. In other words, if the creditors refuse to grant permission to sell the business at the price and terms previously negotiated with a buyer, they know that the selling shareholders can always choose to liquidate the company's assets and close the doors. They also know that in nearly all cases, creditors receive substantially less from liquidation proceeds than they would if the company remained in operation. This is especially true when machinery, equipment, or inventory secure outstanding loans; it is less true with receivables and real estate as collateral.

One word of caution: Because of the peculiarities of bankruptcy law, insiders (majority owners and/or officers of a bankrupt corporation are considered insiders) constantly run the risk of a lawsuit to recover preferential payments (discussed in Chapter 9). One of the things negotiated with secured creditors should be a hold harmless agreement that indemnifies the acquiring parent company, its officers, and its shareholders against such claims. Once the purchase has been approved by all parties and a reorganization plan has been put in place, a buy/sell agreement can be executed. After the closing, the turnaround procedures previously discussed can be implemented.

Prepackaged Bankruptcy

While on the subject of bankruptcy, it might prove helpful to take a look at a quirk in the law that allows companies to negotiate a deal with unsecured creditors *before* filing for Chapter 11. Such a *prepackaged bankruptcy* can be very advantageous in that it permits a company to avoid months and maybe years of drawn-out negotiations with secured and unsecured creditors. Legal and court fees will be less. Customers that might leave for a competitor during an extended bankruptcy proceeding are more likely to remain. Even creditors benefit. Although they receive less than the full amount owed, such deficiencies can easily be made up through new sales to the company once it gets up and running again.

It is unlikely that all creditors will agree to take a hit without a fight; however, a provision in the bankruptcy code authorizes a "cram-down" procedure. This means that a reorganization plan can be put in place provided 50 percent of each group of creditors that hold two-thirds of the debt agree to go along. And, of course, it's easier to reach agreement with 50 percent of the creditors than with all of them.

When the company files a Chapter 11 bankruptcy, it immediately presents the court with the reorganization plan, signed off on by the appropriate creditors. In a matter of weeks, not months or years, the company can be back in business with a cleaner balance sheet than before.

The prepackaged route won't work for companies that have already filed under Chapter 11; however, if you find a good investment and it looks like a filing might occur before the deal closes, proposals to major creditors for a prepackaged arrangement might be just the step needed to make the deal viable.

LOCATING DISTRESSED BUSINESS OPPORTUNITIES

If the purchase of distressed companies seems to make sense as a long-term growth strategy, the most likely source of potential deals is commercial banks that hold problem loans (and virtually all banks have them). To give these loans special attention, many banks transfer them to a separate department called a *workout* or *problem loan* department. Some banks have fully staffed workout departments that manage a portfolio of problem accounts, whereas others relegate the task to one or two people. Although identifying these departments can at times be difficult (banks don't like to advertise that any loans are in trouble), a few phone calls generally uncover the right person.

Although banks must be careful to avoid conflict of interest accusations, most welcome acquisition-minded companies that are willing to inject fresh capital into one of these problem customers. The same holds true for asset-based lenders, or finance companies. These higher-risk lenders frequently end up as debtors-in-possession for Chapter 11 companies and are just as willing as banks to have financially sound companies take problem loans off their hands—even if they have to discount the paper.

If you strike out with banks, try management consultants who specialize in financially distressed companies. They can be found in virtually all major cities and some smaller ones. Although it's hard to identify these specialists (crisis management consultants don't like to advertise any more than bank workout departments do), a few discreet calls to banks and bankruptcy lawyers usually open doors.

Bankruptcy lawyers are another good source. Most pretend to be discreet, but when presented with a potential investor with money, they usually open up. Public accounting firms should be a good source; however, for confidentiality reasons, most hesitate to give out leads about their clients. Any of the large securities houses are good contacts for locating troubled branches, divisions, or subsidiaries of public companies that are on the block.

If all else fails, a small advertisement in the *Wall Street Journal* that reads, "Profitable company wants to buy financially distressed companies" will bring an avalanche of replies.

A MAJOR OBSTACLE

In addition to the previously discussed precautions, companies that seek a controlling interest in distressed operating businesses should be on guard against an often-overlooked obstacle: the potential liability for the target company's unpaid employee withholding taxes. The liability for unpaid taxes can easily be missed during a due diligence investigation, thereby creating a potentially serious problem after the closing.

The tax code clearly defines a list of parties who are potentially liable for the payment of employee taxes. In addition to the company and its officers and directors, "any lender, surety, or other person [person includes individuals, corporations, partnerships, or any other business entity] who is not the employer but pays employee wages on behalf of the company, or who supplies funds to or for the account of an employer for the purpose of paying wages" may be held personally liable to the U.S. government for employee withholding taxes and delinquent interest.

Court cases have assigned liability to such diverse third parties as the president/principal stockholder of the purchaser of a troubled company, banks that control a bankrupt debtor's receipts through a lock box, minority shareholders, creditors who loaned companies money both prior to and after entering bankruptcy, and a variety of others.

To make matters worse, the IRS may begin proceedings anytime within ten years of the assessment of the employer's tax. Since three years is normally the statute of limitations on employers' tax payments, conceivably the IRS has thirteen years to file claims against third parties. For those interested in exploring precedent-setting cases in this area, check out *Clouse* v. *United States*, ED Mich., 87-2 USTC.9595; *United States* v. *North Side Deposit Bank*, WD, PA, 83-2 USTC.9503; and *Caterino* v. *United States*, CA-1, 86-1 USTC.9452.

Although in many cases the amount of unpaid employee withholding taxes is not very large compared to other debts, the sums can be significant in larger companies or in companies that have been failing for some time. In any case, parent companies should protect themselves against such liabilities with iron-clad indemnification contracts. Such indemnification should come from both the target company and its officers and directors personally. Indemnification should also be obtained from the company's secured creditors—banks or otherwise. If you cannot get enforceable indemnification contracts, it is probably best to withdraw from the deal, regardless of how good it may look.

Chapter 17

Acquisitions of Distressed Property-Based Businesses

Whereas ease of entry and product differentiation permit many manufacturing, distribution, retail, and service businesses to base growth strategies on relatively short-term criteria (such as market preferences, technological improvements, and competitive pressures), the same cannot be said of companies that generate income from real property assets. Except in those instances where location or legislative barriers (such as zoning laws) give them a corner on the market, property-based businesses sell basically generic products and services, with little differentiation among competitors. Such businesses must, by definition, look to much longer-term strategies to further growth.

A wide variety of businesses can be categorized as property-based businesses, including but certainly not limited to hotels, resorts, B&B inns, shopping centers, apartment complexes, sports stadiums, golf courses, physical fitness studios, movie theaters, and certain types of educational facilities. In nearly all cases, property-based businesses can be characterized as being easily leveraged, illiquid investments, adaptable to financing and ownership by privately held companies and investment groups, and susceptible to long-term asset appreciation.

In the 1989–1992 recession, many highly leveraged property-based businesses fell on hard times. Easy credit during the 1980s contributed to a construction surge that resulted in an enormous oversupply of residential homes, apartment and condominium complexes, shopping centers, office buildings, factories, hotels, vacation homes and villas, and resorts. As an increasing number of properties stood vacant, defaults on long-term mortgages escalated.

The S&L disaster followed by tightening capital ratios in the commercial banking industry caused lenders to restrict new loans and to demand repayment of overdue mortgages, further exacerbating the financial difficulties of already staggering businesses. The result has been a flood of mortgage foreclosures and a buyer's market that provides unusual opportunities to acquire property-based companies as part of expansion or diversification growth strategies.

The starting point, as for acquiring financially distressed operating business (see Chapter 16), is to focus on strategies that will yield the highest returns with the most manageable risk.

INVESTMENT STRATEGIES

Purchasing a controlling interest in distressed property-based businesses can be accomplished through two means: (1) by buying defaulted debt obligations and subsequently taking control of the business, or (2) by buying majority equity interests directly from private owners. Debt obligations consist of commercial mortgages, long-term leases, revenue bonds, and term loans (secured or undersecured).

As a rule of thumb, the strategic advantage of investing either in nonperforming obligations themselves or in the underlying businesses should be based on two factors: (1) the liquidation value of the assets securing the debt, and (2) the extent to which the acquired business can be integrated into the parent company. When the liquidation value of secured assets is high relative to outstanding debt obligations, it may pay to buy discounted debt, restructure payment terms, and collect interest income until the business can be turned around. Similarly, if the target's location, product offerings, service capabilities, or other characteristics make immediate integration with a parent company's management policies or marketing organization unlikely, cash flow benefits may be better realized by holding debt obligations than by taking over management of the business.

On the other hand, if the market value of the underlying collateral is not significantly greater than the outstanding debt balances or if enough synergisms exist with the parent company to make immediate integration feasible, it would probably be strategically advantageous to buy the business rather than its debt obligations.

Buying Defaulted Debt

Companies considering going the first route—that is, buying defaulted debt at a discount for the purpose of collecting interest income—should be aware that this strategy tends to be riskier than buying operating businesses and can easily backfire. There is always the possibility that the debtor will continue to default even after the loans have been restructured. Then the only solution is to foreclose. And more often than not, foreclosure leads to liquidation. Although liquidating a foreclosure can produce significant short-term profits, it is also a nasty business, contributing little to a company's long-term growth. On the other hand, short-term profits cannot be ignored. Excess cash resulting from liquidation gains could be a welcome resource for long-term expansion.

An example of reaping substantial gains on a liquidation involved North River Associates Management Enterprises, Inc. This real estate management company saw an opportunity to turn a quick profit by purchasing defaulted revenue bonds and a construction loan. The debt was secured by twenty-five acres of land under development for fourteen residential homes and a community center. Before filing bankruptcy, the developer had completed six unsold homes, roadways, and the foundation for the community center.

The project had been funded by a $16 million development bond issue from the municipality. The bonds were secured by a letter of credit issued on behalf of the developer by a midsize S&L. In addition, the developer had arranged a

$750,000 construction loan from the same S&L to cover initial working capital needs. When the completed homes did not sell, the developer defaulted on $125,000 of the construction loan drawdown and $450,000 of revenue bonds issued as a first release. The house of cards crumbled.

The underwriter closed on the L/C, and the S&L was left holding the revenue bonds. In turn, the S&L was taken over by the Resolution Trust Corporation (RTC). At an RTC auction, North River Associates purchased the construction loan for $40,000 and the outstanding bonds for $155,000. The management company then liquidated the six finished homes for $1,200,000 and the developed land for another $500,000. Although the debt obligations were never collected from the developer, North River pocketed a cool $1.5 million gain.

Buying Businesses that Have Defaulted

In many sections of the country, severely depressed markets for hotels, shopping centers, and office buildings offer some interesting strategic possibilities for companies that have the personnel to manage such businesses. Commercial banks and finance companies, as well as several federal agencies, such as the RTC and the Federal Deposit Insurance Corporation (FDIC), have foreclosed on many of these properties and are actively trying to sell them as going businesses. Hotels seem to offer especially good opportunities to acquire potentially profitable businesses at very low prices.

As a case in point, a small restaurant chain (Starward Home Cooking, Inc.) owned four restaurants in and around Norfolk, Virginia. The owners developed a diversification strategy of acquiring small hotels and resorts in North Carolina, within which they would franchise their restaurants. They learned of two independent hotels that the FDIC was trying to dispose of. Starward purchased the two hotels for a trifling $4,000 per room (compared with a current area construction cost of $80,000 per room). Part of the deal involved the assumption of old mortgages, which the FDIC discounted 65 percent, plus a new ten-year bank loan. Of the total purchase price, Starward paid 5 percent down and restructured the FDIC mortgage and the bank loan into one thirty-year mortgage.

Although not all foreclosed properties can be acquired with such high leverage, a good many can. In addition to properties in the hospitality industry, more than a few foreclosed shopping centers, apartment complexes, office buildings, ranches, and farms can be picked up for ten to forty cents on the dollar of market value. Even if strategic objectives do not call for managing such businesses, an acquisition at this price could produce excess cash in the short term (as in a liquidation) to invest in a more synergistic business later on.

High-Depreciation Strategy

One of the unique features of buying distressed property-based businesses is that depreciable assets represent a very high percentage of the purchase price. High depreciation tax deductions frequently permit a company to generate cash profits while also reporting tax losses. Under certain conditions, purchases may be structured to utilize the target company's operating tax loss carryforward against the parent's taxable income. Although current tax laws generally prohibit such an offset, it is still possible to achieve, provided very specific conditions are met.

If you can't benefit from the target's tax loss carryforward, you may still save substantial taxes with current depreciation write-offs. One way is to set up the newly acquired business as a limited partnership or S corporation and keep it entirely separate from your operating business. Depreciation-caused operating losses can then be passed directly to the personal tax returns of partners or shareholders.

Such a strategy works especially well when acquiring hotels and resorts. It also works for investments in leased property, assuming that tenants are reputable businesses or individuals. Buying low-income property, where tenants may not meet current lease payments, is generally too risky. Also, these properties are hard to sell or liquidate, and maintenance costs run high.

As long as cash flow from the business covers out-of-pocket expenses and debt service, three or four years of operating losses created by high depreciation write-offs can significantly reduce personal tax liabilities. Assuming that the purchase price was sufficiently below liquidation value and the market doesn't deteriorate further, a healthy gain should materialize on a subsequent resale.

LOCATING FORECLOSURE OPPORTUNITIES

Although banks, finance companies, and venture capital firms are excellent sources of both defaulted debt and foreclosed properties, the U.S. government is by far the most active seller. Several agencies that back mortgage loans have in recent times deemed it advisable to foreclose.

The General Services Administration (GSA) maintains the largest inventory of government-owned businesses, real estate, and other assets for sale, including a wide variety of assets seized in drug and other criminal-activity raids. (Pleasure boat auctions are held in Miami several times a year.) The GSA also manages a minor number of foreclosure sales on behalf of smaller agencies.

The U.S. Department of Housing and Urban Development (HUD) is responsible for selling foreclosed property taken over by the Federal Housing Administration and its various lending bodies. The Veterans Administration handles sales of foreclosed property taken over from defaulted VA loans. And the FDIC has a rapidly growing inventory of real estate and business properties inherited from failed commercial banks.

EVALUATING DEBT OBLIGATIONS

Some loans are excellent strategic investments; others are hopeless. On the plus side, many loans are classified as nonperforming or slow-paying—not necessarily defaulted. Interest rates are normally much higher than on quality loans; double-digit rates are not unusual. For buyers who can work with debtors to structure new payout terms or even new collateral, nonperforming loans can be a good long-term investment.

On the other hand, many loans carry excessive downside risk. Bob McCrillis, an asset-based specialist with the RTC's Northeast regional office, has warned that in some instances these loans may be literally worthless. Some debtors are so far in the hole that no restructuring short of total debt forgiveness can salvage them.

The evaluation of any loan starts with a credit check. But don't expect much help here. Businesses that are severely behind on their debt service payments, are by definition reported as "poor credit risks." Loans to good credit risks wouldn't be nonperforming.

Instead of relying on credit checks, it pays to do your own research. Either of two approaches, or both, may be used. The first requires a realistic appraisal of the liquidation value of the assets securing the loan.

Clearly, the purchase price of a nonperforming loan must be less—and substantially less—than the liquidation value of the assets securing it. Even if the business is capable of making payments on a restructured loan, without a realistic threat of foreclosure and liquidation, the debtor will have no more incentive to pay off the balance than when a bank held the paper. On the other hand, it has been proven time and again that nothing increases the incentive to meet debt payments more than the knowledge that a major creditor can and will close down the business and realize a greater return by liquidating assets than by keeping the company open.

Liquidation values are easier to establish for property-based businesses than for those whose hard assets are primarily machinery, equipment, and vehicles. A large number of qualified commercial real estate appraisers are listed in the phone book for any large or midsize city. Appraisers of non-real estate hard assets also proliferate throughout the country, although liquidation estimates for the assets are usually less reliable than those for real estate.

EVALUATING PROPERTY-BASED BUSINESSES FOR ACQUISITION

The second evaluation procedure involves estimating whether the business can be salvaged as a going concern. Can it be righted fast enough to prevent full default and subsequent bankruptcy? Although most foreclosed property-based businesses—apartment complexes, shopping centers, commercial and industrial buildings, and hotels and resorts—are still in operation, meaningful evaluations must recognize the intrinsic value and distinct economic curves of real property. This means that although the same procedures for evaluating the potential benefits of buying financially distressed operating businesses (described in Chapter 16) should apply to most property-based businesses, additional steps must be taken to determine the company's realistic income potential and the property's liquidation value.

For example, in the case of hotels and resorts, as described in my book *The Small Business Valuation Book*, an analysis of historical revenue generation (that is, occupancy and room rates) should yield a reasonable approximation of expected revenues in the near future. It's difficult for owners or managers to fudge revenue statistics; operating expenses, on the other hand, are as suspect here as they are in distressed manufacturing or retail businesses.

An analysis of historical revenue generation is also a good measure of future revenues for shopping centers, apartment complexes, and commercial and industrial property. Outstanding leases authenticate such historical revenues and provide a good fix on what the future will hold. Operating expenses tend to be discretionary and under management control.

The condition of adjoining neighborhoods, growth or decline in the local economy, nearby competition, and local government tax and licensing laws frequently have as much effect on future growth as direct sales efforts. Also, real property businesses have a finite capacity for growth—it is limited by the number of rooms, storefronts, apartments, or offices in the structure. If future revenues from leases or competitive room rates at projected occupancy percentages won't produce satisfactory returns, the decision to pass becomes obvious—except, of course, where market values indicate a good liquidation gain.

In addition to revenue generation, the investment potential of a business is strongly influenced by the market value of the property. Typically, the appraised value of real property is based on competitive market prices for similar structures, not on the much lower auction liquidation value used for assets of manufacturing companies. Appraised values are also used as the basis for determining the mortgage loan value of a property. Therefore, independent appraisals play a major role in determining purchase price.

The most reliable, cheapest, and fastest way to get an appraisal is from a reputable national consulting firm (e.g., Parnell, Kerr, Forster & Co.) or a national commercial property appraisal firm (there are many good ones in virtually all major cities).

BANK FORECLOSURES

Although government agencies are far and away the largest sellers of foreclosed properties, practically all large banks also have an inventory of foreclosed commercial and industrial property-based businesses. Most bank foreclosures are against the real estate itself rather than an operating business; but some of the bigger banks—Citibank, Chase, BankAmerica, and so on—and national finance companies like GE Capital and Heller Financial also inventory foreclosed property-based businesses. Hotels and resorts make up the largest segment of this inventory; leased property (e.g., apartments, shopping centers, factories, warehouses, and so on) ranks second.

Banks don't like to manage businesses, for a variety of reasons, including potential conflict of interest and regulatory constraints. Consequently, once a bank forecloses, it usually hires a management company to run the business (as with hotels and resorts) or to manage collections and maintenance (as with leased property). By so doing, the bank can market the property as a going business, presumably worth more than the real estate alone, and cannot be accused of breaching federal or state regulations.

This gives potential buyers an excellent opportunity to obtain operating statistics directly from a management company that understands the business, rather than from a bank, which probably doesn't. Buyers also have the option of retaining the management company after the acquisition. Not infrequently, especially with hotels and other more or less specialized businesses, a professional management company can do a better job of turning the business around than a buyer from outside the industry could do.

Once a property has been selected, effective tactics for negotiating with banks vary all over the lot. Although to a large extent local conditions determine the contractual terms necessary to minimize risk and maximize returns, as a general rule, four conditions must be satisfactorily negotiated or the deal doesn't make sense:

1. Undisclosed liabilities or contingent lawsuits must remain the responsibility of the bank. No bank willingly agrees to such contractual language; however, a slight price concession usually carries the day.

2. The purchase price must be far enough below liquidation value to provide a reasonable cushion in the event that the property cannot be made profitable.

3. When current debt is assumed, it must be discounted at least 40 percent and restructured to a ten- to fifteen-year payout, with interest rates discounted from LIBOR (LIBOR will probably stay below prime over the fifteen-year period). Preferably, new terms should also permit the deferral of principal payments for the first year or two.

4. If banks holding the debt obligations will not finance the deal, the purchase should be contingent upon arranging satisfactory financing elsewhere.

Since overcapacity in most of the country will probable keep the prices of property-based businesses depressed for several years to come, you should be able to negotiate a purchase price that is between 10 and 20 percent of market value. However, that in itself may not yield sufficient returns to offset the risk. The deciding factor may very well be the amount of tax savings that can be generated by high depreciation write-offs, as previously described.

Bear in mind, however, that the ability of partners in limited partnerships or shareholders in S corporations to write off operating losses against other income depends entirely on current tax regulations. Expected new tax laws, a continuous stream of IRS regulations, and Tax Court rulings may very well invalidate such a strategy, so it pays to stay current with competent tax advisors.

TAX MATTERS

The following discussion of certain tax matters is intended as a brief overview of certain key elements of the tax code and should not be interpreted as definitive tax advice. That can come only from tax advisors who stay abreast of current developments. It does pay, however, to have at least a brief understanding of the general principles related to two tax code provisions that affect the deductibility of business operating losses by individuals. These two provisions are "at-risk" rules and passive activity loss (PAL) regulations.

At-risk and PAL provisions were enacted in 1986 specifically to prevent individuals from taking tax deductions for losses from a business in which they do not actively participate (except as an offset against passive income) and/or are not at risk, in terms of either losing actual invested money (equity or loans) or being responsible for the payment of business debts. These rules apply to individual investors as well as to limited partners and shareholders of S corporations. In other words, they apply to any situation in which business operating losses are reported on personal tax returns.

At-Risk Provisions

At-risk provisions limit the deduction of a person's proportionate share of business losses to the amount of money the person has at risk in the business and could actually lose. In other words, such losses are limited to the sum of a partner's or shareholder's adjusted capital basis, plus any amounts borrowed by the business for which the individual has personal liability or has pledged personal assets.

Persons actively engaged in managing a business usually don't have any problem complying with at-risk rules. They seldom are free from liability for company debts anyway. But even without such liability, shareholder loans to the company are added to equity investments to arrive at the adjusted tax basis. If it appears that the business will have a loss in any one year, and your adjusted basis isn't sufficient to take the deduction, merely loan the company money—with interest, of course—to cover the discrepancy.

Passive Activity Loss Rules

Beginning with the Tax Reform Act of 1986, passive investors have been prohibited from deducting losses from partnerships, limited partnerships, or S corporations from other earned income. The tax code now clearly differentiates between an active participant in a business and a passive investor. Assuming that at-risk rules are met, an active investor (partner or S corporation shareholder) may deduct business losses from other earned income. Passive investors may not. Losses sustained by passive investors are referred to as *passive activity losses*, or PALs.

The rules governing PALs fall into three broad categories: rules defining activity as passive or active, material participation rules, and recharacterization rules. Generally, a passive activity is either a rental activity or a trade or business activity in which the taxpayer does not actively participate.

Material participation rules define the criteria for qualifying as an active investor. For example, one of several included definitions specifies that spending 100 hours a year actively doing something in the business qualifies a person as an active participant. That amounts to two hours a week and can be met by attending board of directors' meetings, answering a telephone, writing letters, making bank deposits, or general consultation, among any number of other activities. It should be noted, however, that the IRS is tightening this definition.

Recharacterization rules are even more vague. Here are two examples that demonstrate how confusing recharacterization can be:

1. *Significant participation rule.* Net income from a significant participation activity is treated as nonpassive income even though a loss from such activity would be a passive loss.

2. *Self-enhanced rental property rule.* Net rental income, including any gain from the disposition of rental property, is nonpassive if (a) the gain on disposition occurs during the taxable year, (b) the use of the property in the rental activity commences less than twelve months prior to the date of disposition, and (c) the taxpayer materially or significantly participates in an activity that involves the performance of services for the purpose of enhancing the value of such property.

None of these PAL rules are sacrosanct, however. Frequent changes result from Tax Court precedents, special IRS rulings, and language clarifications. These examples merely show the level of complexity involved in tax planning.

The calculation of PAL offsets, appropriate planning to avoid PALs, and further explanation of additional special rules affecting the handling and definitions of PALs are far too complex to be included here. Just knowing that passive activity loss rules exist, however, should help you get the right answers from tax advisors.

LIQUIDATION

Strategically, it's usually a good idea to have a getting out plan in hand when buying any distressed business. Markets may turn bad, target company personnel may be unreliable, new competition may arise, and many other factors could conceivably cause the business to return to its financially distressed condition. The only sensible way to deal with such a condition is to cut your losses, and get out as soon as possible. This usually means liquidating the company's assets to pay off as much current debt as possible. The difficulty most of us have, however, is knowing when to throw in the towel.

Three conditions point to a liquidation decision:

- When net cash flow (revenues less cash operating expenditures, including debt service) turns negative
- When market conditions turn sour, as in losing a hotel's franchise or a shopping center's major tenant
- When tax laws result in greater returns form liquidating than from continuing to operate the business

Strategically, businesses purchased for their liquidation value should be viewed as short-term, quick-cash-out investments. Occasionally, the business can be turned around so rapidly and profits increased so much that it pays to continue for an extended period or even to sell it as a going business. Some companies also find it strategically desirable to intentionally buy distressed businesses for the short term—in other words, buy them cheap, milk them dry, and get out.

Liquidating a business is a traumatic event for everyone—owners, employees, customers, and suppliers. It seems somehow un-American to close down a business, regardless of how much money it loses. Certainly banks feel this way. Very few have the stomach for a liquidation, even when it costs them an arm and a leg to keep a foreclosure going. Obviously employees and suppliers get hurt. Nevertheless, a person needs to be hard-nosed to buy distressed properties to begin with; becoming softhearted about liquidating only results in losses.

It's always best to liquidate gradually, perhaps over a year or two, provided the company's cash flow is sufficient to avoid out-of-pocket losses. Prices will be higher with an orderly liquidation. Employees, customers, and suppliers will be hurt less. And in the long run, an orderly liquidation results in fewer potential liabilities arising from tax, government, or employee claims. In addition, the property can be fixed up, a wider range of buyers can be found, and if the liquidation extends over a year-end, taxes will probably be less.

When it's necessary to liquidate immediately, the best and quickest results are obtained by turning the job over to a well-known, reputable auctioneer. Even though most auction companies claim to be national in scope, in practice, they specialize regionally. The best way to locate a qualified auctioneer, other than through a local chamber of commerce, is by asking a large finance company or leasing firm. These folks use auctioneers very often and know which ones can be trusted to get the highest prices.

Finally, it's always a good idea to get competent tax advice before putting a property up for auction. It's too easy to get stuck with exorbitant tax bills when a minimum amount of tax planning could eliminate or defer all or part of the liability.

Index

About the Author

Lawrence E. Tuller has owned and operated 13 companies. He is a graduate of Harvard University and the Wharton School and holds a CPA certificate. He is the author of *The Complete Book of Raising Capital, Tap the Hidden Wealth in Your Business, Financing the Small Business*, and *Buying In: A Complete Guide to Acquiring a Business or Professional Practice*.